A History and Critique of Methodological Naturalism

A History and Critique of Methodological Naturalism

The Philosophical Case for God's Design of Nature

Joseph B. Onyango Okello

Orlando, Florida
2015

WIPF & STOCK · Eugene, Oregon

A HISTORY AND CRITIQUE OF METHODOLOGICAL NATURALISM
The Philosophical Case for God's Design of Nature

Copyright © 2016 Joseph B. Onyango Okello. All rights reserved. Except for brief quotations in critical publications or reviews, no part of this book may be reproduced in any manner without prior written permission from the publisher. Write: Permissions, Wipf and Stock Publishers, 199 W. 8th Ave., Suite 3, Eugene, OR 97401.

Wipf & Stock
An Imprint of Wipf and Stock Publishers
199 W. 8th Ave., Suite 3
Eugene, OR 97401

www.wipfandstock.com

PAPERBACK ISBN: 978-1-4982-8374-8
HARDCOVER ISBN: 978-1-4982-8376-2
EBOOK ISBN: 978-1-4982-8375-5

Manufactured in the U.S.A.

To Sophie, my wonderful wife,
who lovingly and patiently encouraged me
to complete this project.

Contents

Acknowledgments | ix

1 Introduction | 1

2 Supernaturalism in the Ancient and Medieval Periods | 14

3 Supernaturalism and Epistemology in the Early Modern Era | 48

4 Deism and Supernaturalism | 88

5 Hume's Argument Against Miracles | 116

6 Evolution of Methodological Naturalism | 159

7 Conclusion | 205

Bibliography | 213

Index | 221

Acknowledgments

THE FOLLOWING DISSERTATION, WHILE an individual work, benefited from the insights and direction of several people. First, my dissertation chair, David Bradshaw, exemplifies high quality scholarship to which I aspire. In addition, Dr. Bradshaw provided timely and instructive comments and evaluation at every stage of the dissertation process, allowing me to complete this project on schedule. Next, I wish to thank Dr. Sanford Goldberg, Dr. Harmon Holcomb, Dr. Hubert Martin, and Dr. Robert Rabel. Each individual provided insights that guided and challenged my thinking, substantially improving the finished product.

In addition to the technical and instrumental assistance above, I received equally important assistance from family and friends. My wife, Sophie Okello, provided ongoing support throughout the dissertation process. My mother, Rose L. Owako, instilled in me, from an early age, the desire and skills to obtain the PhD. Finally, I wish to thank Dr. Jerry Walls and Dr. Mike Peterson, who both believed I could handle doctoral-level work even when I felt incapable of doing so. Their encouragements and insights gave me a desire for critical thinking, thereby creating opportunities for future work.

— 1 —
Introduction

MANY RELIGIONS OF THE world, most notably Christianity, widely maintain belief in miracles. It is a belief that also had its place in ancient and medieval philosophy and theology. However, methodological naturalism has tried to refute, quite vigorously, the notion that a Supernatural Being has interacted with nature in a manner deemed miraculous.

What is methodological naturalism? It would appear that under this broad term there are at least two predominant strands of thought. One argues that science, by definition, excludes non-naturalistic forms of explanation. Proponents of this view sometimes allow that a given phenomenon might be susceptible to non-naturalistic explanation; they merely insist that such an explanation ought not to be considered scientific. I shall call this view definitional methodological naturalism.

We may take John Macquarrie, Ernan McMullin and Michael Ruse as representatives of this view. Macquarrie insists that the "scientific conviction" is that events occurring in the natural world can be explained in terms of other events within the natural world. According to Macquarrie, the scientific enterprise assumes that all events in our world can be explained by appealing to the occurrences of other events belonging to just this world. Suppose, then, we find ourselves unable fully to explain the occurrence of a given countenanced event, science remains committed to the belief that additional research will expose more factors relevant to the inquiry. Those factors, however, will remain just as natural (as opposed to supernatural) as the factors cognitively accessible to us already.[1]

As presented here, definitional methodological naturalism would seem to presuppose that any unexplained residue in an event must always

---

1. See Macquarrie, *Principles of Christian Theology*, 247–48.

in principle be subject to further naturalistic inquiry. Although Macquarrie does not explicitly draw this conclusion, it would seem that on this view there can be no room for non-naturalistic explanations supplementing or complementing those of science; such explanations would always appear to be mere dodges evading the need for further naturalistic inquiry.

By contrast, Ernan McMullin proposes a more modest form of definitional methodological naturalism. He thinks that methodological naturalism accepts the application of epistemological methods different from that of methodological naturalism. He merely insists that for any method to qualify as scientific, it must proceed according to the assumptions of methodological naturalism. According to McMullin, rather than control the scientific investigation of nature, methodological naturalism merely specifies the kind of enterprise that might be deemed properly scientific. Suppose the epistemologist wishes to locate a different approach to nature among the many approaches in existence today. An epistemologist committed to methodological naturalism will find no reason to object, specifically because, as a scientist, the epistemologist committed to methodological naturalism must adopt this kind of openness. However, McMullin adds that the methodological naturalist finds no value in the claim that a specific sort of event in nature might be explained by tracing the origin of is course to a supernatural being.[2]

McMullin and Macquarrie agree in ruling out epistemological systems that invoke supernatural entities to account for natural events; for such invocations, they argue, are unscientific. As Alvin Plantinga observes, claims of this sort have achieved the status of philosophical orthodoxy.[3] Michael Ruse epitomizes this orthodoxy by insisting that methodological naturalism, or part of it, is true by definition. According to Ruse, if Scientific Creationism remained entirely successful in justifying its contention to being scientific, it would still fail to offer a scientific account of the cause of the universe. What it could succeed in proving is the contention that scientific explanation of origins remains unavailable. Consider, for example, how creationists hold that the universe had a miraculous origin. The problem with this view, as Ruse sees it, stems from the consideration that miracles remain profoundly unscientific, specifically because science, by definition,

---

2. McMullin, "Plantinga's Defense," 57.
3. Plantinga, "Should Methodological Naturalism," 114.

deals only with natural and repeatable phenomena governed by the law of nature.⁴

Ruse is more explicit than Macquarrie or McMullin in making clear exactly why non-naturalistic explanations do not count as science. Science by definition "deals only with the natural, the repeatable, that which is governed by law." Like McMullin he seems to allow for the possibility in principle of non-natural explanations, although he adopts toward them a more dismissive tone.

William Alston and Alvin Plantinga have provided a powerful critique of definitional methodological naturalism. In an unpublished article, Alston argues as follows: it is just not true that engaging in the practice of modern science requires assuming a closed natural order. The only thing a scientist is committed to assuming, by virtue of engaging in the scientific enterprise, is that there is a good chance that the particular phenomena he is investigating depends on natural causal conditions to a significant degree.⁵ Alston observes that the assumption of medical research, for example, is that by discovering natural causes of pathological conditions, we can put ourselves in a better position to forecast, prevent, and cure diseases. Believing that not every detail of every disease and of every recovery is due to natural causes, believing that some are due to particular divine interventions, scarcely precludes one from engaging in medical research. As a matter of fact, every medical researcher and every medical practitioner comes across cases that he finds inexplicable. In Alston's view, there is no reason to hold that either research or practice is undercut if some of these are due to particular divine intervention. So long as it is *generally* the case that the onset, development and cure of disease follows certain natural regularities, that will give the scientist all he needs; a few exceptions do not matter.⁶

The methodological naturalist could give the following objection to Alston: modern science could give us a reason to believe that all that happens in the natural order happens in accordance with the laws of nature. Such a reason would show that a particular divine intervention would be a violation of such laws.⁷ It is not clear, however, what or how such a reason would look like. This lack of clarity could be taken as a response to the methodological naturalist's objection.

4. Ruse, *Darwinism Defended*, 322.
5. See Wolterstorf, *Divine Discourse*, 124.
6. Ibid., 124–25.
7. Ibid., 125.

At any rate, Alston gives the following rejoinder. First, many of the law statements scientists embrace are idealizations to which actual occurrences only approximate. Second, many of the laws discovered by twentieth-century science are probabilistic rather than deterministic in character. Such laws would not be violated by an influence that results in the occurrence of what they imply to be improbable. Third, even for those deterministic natural causal laws which fit the actual phenomena with great precision, if we suppose divine intervention would be a violation, it is because we are thinking of physical laws as specifying unqualifiedly sufficient conditions for an outcome. The most we are ever justified in accepting is a law that specifies what will be the outcome of certain conditions in the absence of any relevant factors other than those specified in the law. The strongest laws we have reason to accept lay down sufficient conditions only within a "closed system," that is, a system closed to influences other than those specified in the law. None of our laws takes account of all conceivable influences.[8]

But since the laws we have reason to accept make provision for interference by outside forces unanticipated by the law, it can hardly be claimed that such a law will be violated if a divine outside force intervenes. Hence it can hardly be claimed that such laws imply that God does not intervene. Thus even if physical laws take a deterministic form, the above considerations show that they by no means rule out the possibility of direct divine intervention in the affairs of the physical world.[9]

What about Ruse's claim that science by definition deals only with what is natural, repeatable, and governed by law? Plantinga objects to this contention first by noting that enormous energy has been expended, for at least several decades, on the "demarcation problem," the problem of giving necessary and sufficient conditions for distinguishing science from other human activities. Plantinga notes that this effort has apparently failed. If there were a definition of the sort Ruse appeals to, then presumably there would be available a set of necessary and sufficient conditions for something to be considered science. But Ruse does not consider the many and successful arguments for the conclusion that there is no such set of necessary and sufficient conditions, let alone such a definition of the term science.[10]

---

8. Ibid.
9. Ibid., 125–26.
10. Plantinga, "Should Methodological Naturalism," 114.

For example, naturalists like John Dupre have noted that there is no consensus about there being one master conception of scientific nature. Even if we try to unite all the varieties of scientific methods, Dupre contends that we will not succeed for at least one reason: the idea of a single scientific method is problematic; for it is hard to believe that there is anything in common between, say, a field taxonomist, a biochemist, a neurophysiologist, and a sociologist. The variety of scientific practice makes any unified form of scientific method unlikely.[11]

Second, Ruse proposes three properties that he says are by definition characteristic of any bit of science: It deals with events that are repeatable, merely natural and governed by natural law. But the big bang is a unique and, presumably, unrepeatable event—at any rate it might turn out to be unrepeatable. If so, we would be obliged to conclude that contemporary cosmological inquiries into the nature of the big bang and into the early development of the universe are not part of science![12]

Finally Plantinga observes that it is hard to see how anything like a reasonably serious dispute about what is and is not science could be settled just by appealing to a definition. The question of whether a hypothesis that makes reference to God could be part of science remains a question that cannot be answered just by citing a definition.[13] This fact remains because the issue of God's existence will have to be settled first before one attempts to answer the question. But this very issue has been the subject of much philosophical dispute. To give a negative answer to the question by simply citing a definition, as Ruse does, erroneously assumes that the dispute has been settled.

In light of these weaknesses of definitional methodological naturalism, the methodological naturalist may prefer to opt instead for a stronger view, which I will call substantive methodological naturalism. Instead of arguing from any purported definition of science, this view argues instead that, given the success in practice of naturalistic methods, it would be irrational to accept a non-naturalistic explanation. As this statement suggests, substantive methodological naturalism is not only a claim about what ought to count as science; it is a claim about how we ought to proceed in any rational investigation. Its scope therefore includes history just as much as science.

11. Dupre, "Miracle," 43.
12. Plantinga, "Should Methodological Naturalism," 115.
13. Ibid., 115–16.

Again John Macquarrie can be cited as exemplifying this view. Macquarrie regards the practice of modern science as so successful in achieving its aims and so important for our lives that it would be silly and irresponsible to undermine it by appealing to the supernatural. For Macquarrie, the success of modern science makes the traditional notion of miracle irreconcilable with the modern scientific worldview. According to Macquarrie, the view that finds miracles as interruptions of nature by supernatural entities is a mythological view and, for that reason, remains a misfit within a scientific consciousness. Such a view entails a traditional understanding of a miracle quite at odds with current conceptions of both science and history.[14]

Langdon Gilkey, another prominent contemporary theologian, also adopts this way of thinking. According to Gilkey, contemporary theology neither anticipates nor postulates supernatural events within a natural and historical framework of epistemology. Enlightenment science and philosophy introduced an understanding of causation into the Western world—an understanding adopted by modern theologians and thinkers. Such thinkers inescapably execute their philosophical frameworks in the contemporary scientific world. This modern view of causation and submission to the authority of methodological naturalism in interpreting natural events profoundly influences the theologian's hermeneutics, especially when the theologian tries to determine the authenticity of biblical stories and the meaning they try to convey. This fact warrants the theologian to reject the historicity of a wide array of biblical narratives that speak of miracles. This rejection finds additional basis on the view that Bible characters lived in the same causal nexus of space as the contemporary interpreter of Scripture—one in which neither miracles nor divine voices were countenanced.[15]

Macquarrie and Gilkey go beyond an appeal to the definition of science to restrict historical interpretation as well. Indeed, their main emphasis is on the application of methodological naturalism, so construed, to biblical interpretation.

The most sustained attempt to argue for substantive methodological naturalism has been made by the historians Ernst Troeltsch[16] and Van Harvey.[17] They believe that taking supernatural agency seriously involves

14. Macquarrie, *Principles*, 247–48.
15. Gilkey, "Cosmology," 31.
16. Troeltsch, "Historiography," 716–23.
17. Evans, *Historical Christ*, 184–85.

a "precritical" view of history. Troeltsch and Harvey are quite clear that the problem with traditional Christian approaches to the gospel narrative does not arise from particular historical findings, but from the method to which the modern historian is committed. Thus the issues to be faced do not concern the evidence for or against some particular miracle; rather they concern the general principles historians should follow.[18]

According to Troeltsch, there are three principles of critical historical investigation that cause problems for the traditional believer. First, is the principle of criticism. Essentially, this is a claim that historical judgments are always provisional, corrigible, and approximative. Such judgments are always more or less probable, based on the evidence available for them. Second, there is the principle of analogy. This principle is a kind of assumption of uniformity, in that it is assumed that our present experiences are not radically different from the experiences of humans in the past. The same kinds of causal laws and natural processes operative today were operative in the past. Third, there is the principle of correlation. This is essentially an assumption about causality, which holds that one must always understand a historical event in the context of its natural antecedents and consequences. Historical events must be understood in terms of their natural historical contexts.[19]

Harvey then takes over Troeltsch's three principles and reinterprets them in order to eliminate certain objections. He places them in the context of more contemporary discussions of evidence and epistemology. Harvey's own account of the morality of knowledge involves four principles. The first principle is the autonomy of the historian understood in terms of the Enlightenment ideal as articulated by Kant, namely, one that dares him or her to use reason. The only authority that exists for the critical historian is the authority that the historian confers on his or her sources. According to Harvey, if the historian permits his authorities to stand uncriticized, he abdicates his role as a critical historian. He is no longer a seeker of knowledge but a mediator of past belief. He is not a thinker; he is, more accurately, a transmitter of tradition.[20]

What is Harvey's justification for this first principle? He appeals to the historically conditioned nature of witnesses and authorities. According to Harvey, what a witness thinks he sees is in large part filtered through the

---

18. Ibid.
19. Troeltsch, "Historiography," 718.
20. Harvey, *Historian*, 42.

prism of his own individual mode of perception and conception. This, in turn, is heavily influenced by the modes of thought of the culture of which he is a part. For Harvey, human beings are historical creatures, and their judgments reflect the "world" that they bring with them and to which they appeal in support of those judgments.[21]

Harvey's second principle is the responsibility of the historian to employ arguments and cite evidence that can be rationally assessed. The third aspect is the need of the historian to exercise sound and balanced judgment. Harvey says that the historian is committed to publicly assessable evidence for claims made and that "sound judgment" must be employed in assessing that evidence.[22] The fourth principle is the need to use "critically interpreted experience" as the background against which sound judgments are made about the past. Harvey understands this principle to imply that historians must apply their first three criteria in a way that is informed by the new way of looking at the world created by the sciences.[23] This means that on the basis of our present experience of the natural world as governed by scientific laws, we rule out all causes other than natural causes.[24]

C. Stephen Evans has provided a powerful critique of the views of Harvey and Troeltsch. As Evans observes, Harvey's first principle makes the ironic assumption that the critical historian is immune from filtering what he sees through the prism of his own individual mode of perception—a perception that is, in turn, heavily influenced by the modes of thought of the culture of which he is a part. Harvey does not see that the critical historian he puts forward as an ideal may similarly be a product of historical circumstances. Thus Harvey is uncritical of the assumptions of this "enlightened" thinker.[25]

Evans argues that we cannot follow Harvey in thinking that the autonomous historian is one who necessarily takes a superior and suspicious attitude towards all historical sources, especially if we follow C. A. J. Coady in his view of testimony. Coady holds that testimony is like observation and perhaps memory, an independent source of epistemic warrant or justification. It would therefore be a mistake to say that we should instead

---

21. Ibid., 41–42.
22. Ibid., 38.
23. Ibid., 68.
24. Ibid., 196.
25. Evans, *Historical Christ*, 189.

accept testimony only if we have evidence that testimony is reliable.[26] In Coady's view, such a reductionist thesis about the evidential value of testimony is very difficult to defend; for unless testimony as such carries some epistemic weight, some presumption in its favor, we cannot possibly have any evidence that testimony is reliable. This is because any such evidential case for testimony must be communal in character; one could not possibly show the reliability of testimony in general simply by examining one's own experience. Rather, one must examine the testimony of humans generally, and critically examine that testimony. But one can only learn about other people's testimony, and examine its reliability, by taking the word of a lot of other people.[27] To be sure, testimonial claims constitute *prima-facie* evidence just as is the case for observation and memory. They can be and often are overridden. However, we cannot reasonably regard testimony *per se* as inherently dubious, though of course we could well have reasons for doubting certain kinds of testimony. For these reasons, Harvey's concept of "autonomy of the historian" is quite overblown.[28]

Harvey's second and third principles are also problematic. Recall Harvey's contention that the historian is committed to publicly accessible evidence for the claims made and that "sound judgment" must be employed in assessing that evidence. These principles look perfectly formal, and also perfectly platitudinous. This is because it seems unlikely that such formal machinery can exclude inferences to supernatural explanations. Take the following claim as an example: Miracles can only be explained by the work of God. Therefore, any event involving miracles must be due to divine agency. Harvey's second and third principles provide no reason why this kind of warrant should be excluded. If I accept it and if my data involve an event that I have good reason to believe is an exception to a law of nature, such as a resurrection of a person from the dead, then I would have rational warrant for believing that God was part of the cause of the event.[29]

To exclude such a case, Harvey might perhaps want to understand the "publicly assessable" provision in his principle as requiring warrant that is acceptable to all historians, including secular historians. A warrant principle such as the one above would then be excluded as not "public" since it is not accepted by those committed to the assumptions that are embedded

---

26. Coady, *Testimony*, 79–100.
27. Ibid.
28. Ibid., 190–91.
29. Evans, *Historical Christ*, 193–94.

A HISTORY AND CRITIQUE OF METHODOLOGICAL NATURALISM

in modern-day thinking, assumptions that are in practice naturalistic. In such a case, the principles of Harvey cease to be purely formal and platitudinous. But it is not clear that the principles are now obligatory for all reasonable historians; for in this case the religious believer might wonder why the unbeliever should have the authority to decide which warrants are proper and which are not. Why should not Christian historians and others open to supernatural explanations employ the forms of warrant that seem reasonable to them? Sensible rational people commonly give explanations that attribute an event to the actions of persons acting for reasons. If God exists, and if God is personal, then there is no obvious reason why such explanations should be rejected in advance, particularly if we know something about God and God's character such that one might understand some of the reasons God might have for performing certain kinds of actions.[30]

Harvey's fourth principle rules out certain historical explanations as impossible. He says, for example, that miracles may be logically possible. But to be a serious candidate as a historical explanation something must be a "relevant possibility, a likely candidate to account for certain data." But an alleged miracle "contradicts our present knowledge in a specific scientific field." Hence it is always in tension with well-established warrants.[31] We have already dealt with the alleged conflict between supernatural explanations and modern science in our critique of definitional methodological naturalism. For the present, it is sufficient to note that these claims made by Harvey are philosophical in character, and all of them, like most philosophical claims, seem eminently disputable. It is not clear why a historian who does not share Harvey's philosophical biases would be disqualified as a "critical historian."[32]

What about Troeltsch's principles of analogy and correlation? The principle of analogy is supposed to work as follows: Since we do not observe miracles occurring today, we cannot reasonably believe that they occurred in the past either. But this inference is dubious. The hypothetical proposition "If miracles do not occur today, they could not have occurred in the past" may well be false. For example, if one believed that the incarnation of Jesus was a historical event that made possible the redemption of humanity

---

30. Ibid., 194–95.
31. Ibid., 196.
32. Ibid., 196–97.

and the whole created order, one might reasonably believe that miracles might accompany that event even if they do not occur today.[33]

Furthermore, even if the inference were sound, the antecedent proposition is questionable. However fashionable such a belief may be among secular intellectuals and among religious people intimidated by secular thought forms, it is not shared by millions of people, including many highly educated people.[34]

While Troeltsch's principle of analogy is dubious, his principle of correlation seems ambiguous. If we mean by this principle simply that events must be understood in relation to the actual causal forces and effects that surround them, then it seems plausible enough. However, the religious believer will claim that it is possible that God, who is actively at work in all of creation, is one of those causal powers. Unless Troeltsch knows *a priori* that naturalism is true and there is no God or that God never exercises causal power in the natural world except in accordance with natural laws, then he has no reason to exclude the possibility that the activity of God can be located in the causal network in terms of which an event must be understood.[35]

The objections to methodological naturalism outlined above have an important place in contemporary epistemology. They have succeeded in showing that the methodological naturalist is not justified to rule out the supernaturalist's appeal to supernatural agency as a way of explaining certain natural phenomena.

I conclude that neither definitional methodological naturalism nor substantive methodological naturalism has been adequately defended by its contemporary proponents. Both are deeply problematic and ultimately seem to rest more on arbitrary stipulation than on rational argument. This ought to make us wonder why they have come to be so widely accepted. Surely there must be other factors at work than the arguments given by methodological naturalists themselves.

The answer, of course, is that methodological naturalism is indeed far more deeply rooted than the arguments given by its proponents would suggest. Macquarrie, Ruse, and the others can be seen as attempting to articulate (perhaps rather poorly) a long-standing consensus within Western thought, one that goes back to the Scientific Revolution and the

33. Ibid., 198.
34. Ibid.
35. Ibid., 199.

Enlightenment. Ever since the seventeenth century, the tendency of both science and history has unquestionably been toward a greater and greater reliance upon naturalistic explanations. There are many reasons which have prompted this pervasive change of outlook. No critique of methodological naturalism can be complete without coming to grips with the reasons which have, in actual historical fact, led to the dominance of the naturalistic worldview.

I intend to show that nothing inherently problematic exists about the supernaturalist's appeal to supernatural agency. I will begin by showing that many philosophers of the ancient and medieval periods, as well as those of the early modern era, believed that some aspects of nature could not be explained except by appealing to supernatural agency. I will then trace how such supernaturalism was gradually replaced by methodological naturalism. For this purpose I will focus particularly on two pivotal figures: Hume and Darwin. This historical review will show that the reasoning which led to the widespread rejection of supernaturalism in Western thought was fundamentally unsound. Since the reasons given by contemporary defenders of methodological naturalism are also unsound, as we have already seen, my conclusion will be that methodological naturalism itself is ungrounded.

The second chapter is devoted to showing how ancient and medieval scholars subscribed to supernaturalism by examining the testimony from nature and perceived marks of design in it. We will see that this allowed them to rationally envision an intelligent designer as the cause of those marks.

The third chapter is devoted to showing that despite their disagreements about epistemological method, prominent scientists of the early modern era demonstrated striking agreement in their supernatural commitments. Supernaturalism was part of their scientific and epistemological enterprise. I will show that this was true of three groups who otherwise differed sharply, the New Pyrrhonists, the Cartesians and the evidentialists.

The fourth chapter is devoted to the anti-supernaturalistic views of the deists. My contention here is that the anti-supernaturalism of the more prominent seventeenth-century deists is ineffective as a critique of supernaturalism. This is because, first, their rational belief in God from the testimony of nature was at odds with their anti-supernaturalistic critique of revealed religion. Second, the critique of miracles offered by the deists is unsuccessful. This chapter will also enable us to see how the deists' controversy with the evidentialists provided an eye-opening background for David Hume's argument against miracles.

The fifth chapter is devoted to outlining different responses to Hume's argument from Hume's time to the twenty-first century. Hume is important both because of his historical influence and because his argument against miracles is widely regarded today as a standard refutation of supernaturalism. The chapter shows how some responses to Hume drew attention to a number of flawed assumptions that Hume made. Others tried to defend Hume, contending that his argument was forceful. The contention of this chapter is that Hume's rescuers have failed to defend him adequately.

The sixth chapter shows how the God-affirming world-view was gradually dropped from the scientific enterprise altogether. It begins by surveying the methodological naturalism of pre-Darwinian thinkers. Some of these, like Laplace, saw no need for incorporating the supernatural in their explanation of the universe. The majority of scientists before Darwin, however, accepted that some aspects of nature could only be explained supernaturally. When Darwinism fully matured into Neo-Darwinism through the synthesis of evolution with genetics, the biological sciences finally followed astronomy in doing away with the supernatural. The contention of this chapter is that this "doing away" with the supernatural was not based on any solid decisive scientific reasons.

The upshot of this consideration is that methodological naturalism has little epistemic warrant. Thus the possibility cannot be excluded that some events can best be explained by appealing to the actions of supernatural entities. Although I will not attempt to show that this is in fact the best explanation in any specific case, our historical review of supernaturalism will bring to light a wide range of plausible contenders.

— 2 —
Supernaturalism in the Ancient and Medieval Periods

I WILL SHOW, IN this chapter, that the ancient and medieval philosophers and theologians perceived certain features of our world as intelligently designed—a perception which enabled them to have a common definition of nature that provided grounds for belief in the possibility and actuality of miracles. This consideration will, in turn, show that belief in a supernatural, powerful and intelligent designer, who interacts with our world in a way termed miraculous, was seen as a rationally acceptable way of viewing our world.

Here is how I intend to proceed. The first section will be devoted to showing how the scholars, alluded to above, examined the testimony from nature and perceived marks of design in it, which allowed them to rationally "envision" an intelligent designer as the cause of those marks. In the second section I will argue that if nature is intelligently designed, then a common definition of nature can be located among ancient and medieval scholars, despite the attendant non-uniformity of definitions of nature evident in their explications. Once this common definition is located, we can formulate a subsequent working definition of miracles. In the third section I will show that having arrived at crucially similar conclusions about the nature of the designer (e.g., Mind, Intelligence, Wisdom, Power, Creativity), the scholars in question provided grounds for believing that just this intelligent designer intervened in nature in a manner properly termed miraculous. In light of these considerations, it will be evident that miracles should not be construed as random purposeless events occurring in isolation; they occur within specific contexts.

Design Perception as Support for Supernaturalism

To begin with, we need to ask: how did the above-mentioned ancients perceive that the natural empirically verifiable order was designed by a being that exists beyond and apart from it? As noted earlier, the testimony from nature led them to acquire this belief. Arthur Stanley Pease notes, to this effect, that all diligent readers of ancient literature will encounter evidences of belief in the doctrine of the deliberate adaptation of life to some definite end or purpose, as opposed to the effects of blind chance on the one hand, and on the other, to those of merely automatic survival of the fittest and elimination of the unfit.[1]

In order to get a glimpse of Pease's contention, we will trace the views of different philosophers from the pre-Socratic period to those of the neo-Platonists. We will then examine the views of the ancient and medieval Christian theologians. What will become clear is the fact that despite differences in their understanding of the nature (and perhaps the number) of the designer in question, they all seem to agree that the universe we live in was created by a supernatural designer. Such a contention, as will appear from their writings, was seen as a rationally acceptable way of thinking about our universe.

Following Pease let me begin with Anaxagoras. In *Pericles*, Plutarch contends that Anaxagoras was the first to enthrone Mind in the universe as the source of its orderly arrangement.[2] Anaxagoras thought of Mind as an entity that rules all things, existing alone and by itself. He saw Mind as an entity possessing the greatest power as well as judgment about everything. This enabled him to attribute creative power to Mind since it set all existing things in order by an activity he called "rotation."[3]

The dichotomy between Mind, on the one hand, and the things it created by rotation on the other, reflected the sort of medieval dualism that would later draw distinctions between mind and matter. However, Frederick Copleston draws our attention to the possibility that Anaxagoras probably did not envision this sort of dualism, given that he spoke of Mind in material terms—that is, as being the "thinnest of all things."[4] Bertrand

---

1. Pease, "Caeli," 163.
2. Plutarch, *Pericles*, 4.4.
3. See Simplicius, *Commentary on Aristotle*, 155.14–25.
4. Copleston, *History of Philosophy*, 70.

Russell makes an even bolder claim, namely, that Anaxagoras was probably an atheist,[5] though he does not clarify this claim.

But, Copleston argues, given that philosophy labors under the difficulty of expressing non-sensuous thought in language designed to express ideas in sensuous terms, it is equally possible to think of Anaxagoras as introducing a spiritual-cum-intellectual principle, despite the fact that he fails to understand fully the essential difference between that principle and the matter which it forms or sets in motion.[6]

It was essential, I think, for Anaxagoras to postulate Mind in this way. He seems to be driven by the concern that mental qualities could not be brought about by physical means. But Plato takes the notion of Mind further than Anaxagoras. In an apparent agreement with him, Plato finds it rational to think of the universe as ordered by Mind—a marvelous intelligence and wisdom—rather than by nonrational entities. Here, Plato argues for this sort of intelligence by first postulating four classes of things: the finite, the infinite, the composition of the two and the cause of the composition. According to Plato, we cannot imagine that whereas the first three classes of things exist, the last one, that is, the cause, should not have designed the noblest and fairest of things. For Plato, the cause is a presiding one, of great power, which orders and arranges years, seasons and months. This cause may properly be called Wisdom and Mind.[7]

More clearly in the *Timaeus*, Plato held that the whole sphere of the universe was moving, initially, in an irregular and disorderly fashion. But the creator brought order out of this disorder, since order was in every way better than disorder. Also, on the whole, no unintelligent creature was fairer than the intelligent. And intelligence could not be present in anything devoid of soul.[8]

Later, in the *Memorabilia*, Xenophon recollects Socrates' contention that the gods have ordered the world for the sake of human beings. Here, Socrates and Aristodemus agree that between the creators of the senseless and motionless phantoms and the creators of living, intelligent and active beings, the latter ones ought to be admired. They also agree that he who created human beings from the beginning had some useful end in view

---

5. Russell, *History*, 82.
6. Copleston, *History of Philosophy*, 70.
7. Plato, *Philebus* 30c–d.
8. Plato, *Timaeus* 30a–b.

when he endowed humans with his several senses. They further agree that sensation in humans reflects the handiwork of a wise and loving creator.[9]

Moving on to Aristotle, we discover that his position is somewhat similar to that of the authors we have hitherto considered. For instance, in his book, *Metaphysics*, Aristotle draws attention to Anaxagoras' view that reason was the source of order and arrangement. While ranking the views of Anaxagoras' contemporaries somewhat lower, Aristotle found, in Anaxagoras, a sober individual.[10] Moreover, alluding to the notion of design, Aristotle notes, in the *De Caelo*, that God and nature create nothing that has not its use.[11] According to Aristotle, Nature, similarly to Mind, always does whatever it does for the sake of something.[12] Nature never makes anything without a purpose.[13] This fact remains, Aristotle says, because all things that exist by nature are means to an end, or will be concomitants of means to an end.[14]

Moreover, just as human creations are the products of arts, so living objects are manifestly the products of an analogous cause or principle. For Aristotle order and definiteness are much more plainly manifest in the celestial bodies than in our own frame. For this reason, he finds it inadmissible to hold on the one hand that every animal exists and was generated by nature, while on the other maintaining that the heavens were constructed to be what they are by chance and spontaneity. This position is inadmissible for Aristotle, specifically because he did not find a discernible hint of disorder in the heavenly bodies.[15] "Absence of haphazard" on the one hand, and "conduciveness of everything to an end" on the other, are to be found in nature's works in the highest degree.[16]

Pease notes that by arguing in this way, Aristotle arrives at a fuller conclusion than Plato's in his *Timaeus*.[17] However, D. M. Balme points out that Aristotle does not invoke a supernatural agency in his treatment of design. According to Balme, Aristotle treats the relation between the cosmos

---

9. Xenophon, *Memorabilia*, IV.2–14.
10. Aristotle, *Metaphysics*, I.3.984b15.
11. Aristotle, *De Caelo*, I.4.271a 34.
12. Aristotle, *De Anima*, II.4.415b 15.
13. Ibid., III.9.432b. 21.
14. Ibid., III.12.434a 30–32.
15. Aristotle, *De Partibus Animalium*, I.1.641b.10–28.
16. Ibid., I.5.645a 23–26.
17. Pease, "Ceali," 171.

and the Unmoved Mover quite differently. Balme holds that Aristotle does not present Nature as a quasi-conscious entity capable of purpose. Aristotle's personification of nature is no more than a rhetorical abbreviation for "each natural substance."[18]

Whereas Balme's view seems to be true of Aristotle's esoteric texts like the *Physics* and the *Metaphysics*, it is not true of his exoteric texts. Pease points out that in an eloquent passage translated from Aristotle's early and popular (exoteric) but now lost dialogue *De Philosophia*, Aristotle strikingly sets forth the effect which would be produced upon intelligent but hitherto uninformed minds by a sudden realization of the beauty and order of the starry heavens.[19] And in his treatment of dreams in *De Divinatione* Aristotle postulates that nature is divinely planned though nature itself is not divine.[20] Thus if we take a fuller picture of Aristotle's claims, we could conclude, contrary to Balme, that Aristotle seems to be invoking supernatural agency in his treatment of design.

When we turn to the Stoics, we discover that they exploited the argument from design to the full, and found evidences of divine craftsmanship everywhere in nature.[21] For instance, according to Cicero, Zeno argued that just as the several departments of nature are sprung from their own seeds, and thrive within the limits prescribed by them, so also the nature of the universe as a whole has its own chosen movements, directing its actions in accordance with these movements. This is similar to the way we act when stirred by our spirits and feelings. For Zeno, such is the mind of the universe; and for this reason, it can be termed "Prudence" or "Providence."[22]

Cleanthes, a disciple of Zeno, gives four reasons he believed that the gods exist. The first involves our foreknowledge of future events. Cleanthes seems to imply that such foreknowledge is impossible unless the gods reveal it to us. The second involves the abundant blessings derived from the climate, the fertility of our lands, and so on. The third involves terror experienced through natural catastrophes and supernatural phenomena. Again, Cleanthes seems to imply that only the gods can cause terror of such magnitude. The fourth, Cleanthes argues, involves the fact that when we consider the uniform movement, undeviating rotation of the heavens,

---

18. Balme, "Aristotle," 259.
19. Pease, "Ceali," 173.
20. Aristotle, *De Divinatione*, 2.463b.13–15.
21. Furley, "Zeno," 607.
22. Cicero, *Nature of the Gods*, II.58.

SUPERNATURALISM IN THE ANCIENT AND MEDIEVAL PERIODS

individuality, usefulness, beauty and order of the sun and moon and stars, we discover that they provide sufficient proof that they are not the outcome of chance, but of Mind. Thus, supposing a person enters a house or athletics center or market, and observes the systemic ordered arrangement of everything there, he could not conclude that it was accidental. He would realize that there was someone in charge exacting obedience.[23]

Following a similar line of argument, Chrysippus argued that if there is anything in the universe which man's mind and reason, and his human thrust and capacity, cannot achieve, that which creates it is inevitably superior to man. But man cannot create the heavenly bodies, and all those objects whose orderly progression is never-ending. Therefore, that by which they are created is superior to man, and what better name can be ascribed to this than God? Moreover, if gods do not exist, there can surely be nothing in creation better than man; for he alone possesses reason, which no other faculty excels. But that a man should exist believing that nothing in the universe is superior to him would be insanely arrogant.[24]

Having dealt with the Greek philosophers let me now turn to ancient and medieval Christian theology and philosophy. Notice that despite differences in explicatory nuances such as specific claims to divine revelation and the number of deities, biblical writers and later Christian theologians and philosophers echoed similar sentiments in their perception and subsequent treatment of design. One of the earliest statements from the book of Psalms reads as follows:

> The heavens declare the glory of God; the skies proclaim the work of his hands. Day after day they pour forth speech; night after night they display knowledge. There is no speech or language where their voice is not heard. Their voice goes out into all the earth, their words to the end of the world.[25] (NIV)

According to the psalmist, the cosmic order points us to God's creative power. Evidence of this power is accessible to us "day after day" and "night after night." Evidence of this power is universal to the extent that it is accessible to all rational creatures. In light of the realization that God has revealed himself through nature in this way, the psalmist, almost immediately, begins to focus on God's laws as follows:

23. Ibid., 13–15.
24. Ibid., 16.
25. Ps 19:1–4.

> The law of the Lord is perfect, reviving the soul. The statutes of the Lord are trustworthy, making wise the simple. The precepts of the Lord are right, giving joy to the heart. The commands of the Lord are radiant, giving light to the eyes. The fear of the Lord is pure, enduring forever. The ordinances of the Lord are sure, and altogether righteous. They are more precious than gold, than much pure gold; they're sweeter than honey, than honey from the comb. By them is your servant warned; in keeping them there is great reward.[26] (NIV)

It appears here the psalmist is trying to show that obedience to God's laws predisposes and enables one to see God in nature. I will say more of this below. Meanwhile, as if picking up on this very line of thought, St. Paul also writes:

> The wrath of God is being revealed from heaven against all the godlessness and wickedness of men who suppress the truth by their wickedness, since what may be known about God is plain to them, because God has made it plain to them. For since the creation of the world, God's invisible qualities—his eternal power and divine nature—have been clearly seen, being understood from what has been made, so that men are without excuse.[27] (NIV)

A brief look at St. Paul's words leads us to make several deductions about the biblical vantage point. First, God has made his existence plain to all people. Second, God has done this through the created order. Third, we find an ethical implication to this vantage point—the requirement of obedience to God's laws.

Notice the similarities between the psalmist and St. Paul. Both agree not only that specific features of nature point to a designer of great power and eternal qualities, but also that his existence and his creative power implies that his creatures should see the need to pledge their allegiance to him. And the more they pledge their allegiance to God in this way, the more they are predisposed to perceive his workings in nature.

One might very well draw analogies between this manner of divine perception and Plato's allegory of the cave. The psalmist and St. Paul seem to argue, much as does Plato, that the more one is ethical, the more one is enabled to gain correct knowledge of the world.

---

26. Ps 19:7–11.

27. Rom 1:18–20.

SUPERNATURALISM IN THE ANCIENT AND MEDIEVAL PERIODS

This biblical vantage point was endorsed by the early church fathers like Ambrose and Novatian. Ambrose held that we can find it easy to understand, that in a moment of his power, God created our beautiful world out of nothing.[28] In his *Treatise concerning the Trinity*, Novatian also focuses on the creative aspect of God. According to Novatian, God remains invisible to the naked eye. For this reason, we arrive at belief in his existence by considering the greatness and majesty of his creation. The human mind learns about hidden things from those concretely existing. Therefore, from the greatness of God's work, which the mind perceives, it considers the greatness of God himself, the Architect of those works[29]

Thomas Aquinas also provided philosophical arguments that developed from the views considered above. For example, Aquinas' fifth way begins by acknowledging that certain things that lack knowledge act for the sake of an end. According to Aquinas, this fact holds because those things always or more frequently act in the same way in order to achieve the best outcomes. Therefore, they reach their goal by striving rather than by chance. However, things that lack knowledge do not strive for goals unless a being with knowledge and intelligence directs them. Therefore, an intelligent being exists who orders all the things of nature to their ends. This being, for Aquinas, is God.[30]

To be sure, one could object that Aquinas seems to jump very quickly into the conclusion that this being is God. However, I think we can fairly say that Aquinas "feels" justified to arrive at this conclusion on the basis of his previous arguments for God's existence. In other words, his fifth way ought to be seen together with the other four ways, and not apart from them.

At any rate, we must note that, on the whole, what emerges from our consideration of the different versions of the perceptions of design hitherto explored is the belief that the universe was fashioned by a designer. Among the major forerunners of Western philosophy, this belief was a rationally acceptable way of thinking about our world. By contemplating nature and its attendant complexity, the ancient and medieval philosophers and theologians apprehended natural features which, in their view, could best be explained by recourse to a power above and beyond nature. By perceiving different marks of design in this way, they all agreed that this

---

28 Ambrose, *Six Days of Creation*, I.5

29. Novatian, *Treatise concerning the Trinity*, 3.

30. Aquinas, *Summa Theologica*, I, Q2., art. 3.

contriving power was seen as intelligent and wise, and exists as a metaphysical necessity.

What should we make of our findings from the ancients? Consider Anaxagoras. Anaxagoras seems essentially correct when he insists that nonmind could not beget mind. To hold that the rational can be produced by the nonrational borders very closely, in my opinion, to an intellectual error; for if true, it leaves us wondering whether we can even trust our cognitive faculties to interpret our external world correctly—much less, to deliver reliable information. This observation is only a brief one, which properly belongs to the delicate branch of philosophy of mind. Since C. S. Lewis and (more recently) Alvin Plantinga have dealt with this objection at length, I will not attempt a recapitulation here. Also owing to space limitations, I will focus more on the positive reasons for thinking that the ancients were correct in their view.

Let me begin by noting that if we reflect on the view of the ancient and medieval philosophers, we discover how their perception of design is best captured, I think, by a Reidian perception of design more recently articulated by Del Ratzsch. Ratzsch has argued that basic design recognition is perceptual rather than inferential.[31] To see the point of his argument, consider that in certain situations our sense experiences bring about particular cognitive states that do not follow inferentially from the content of those sense experiences. According to Ratzsch, we simply find ourselves convinced and powerless to resist the belief that the cognitively apprehended thing exists together with its apprehended properties.[32]

Something analogous to this manner of apprehending objects in the external world captures the cognitive dynamics involved in apprehending design. It appears, I think Ratzsch would say, that the ancient and medieval philosophers perceived in these objects qualities that they would often voluntarily and non-inferentially recognize as marks of design.[33] From these marks, they came to believe in a power of design in the mind of the ultimate cause of these marks.

According to Ratzsch, the ancient and medieval philosophers found objects to have design because they bear marks of design, whose relevant qualities were such that only Mind could have brought them about. These qualities include contrivance, order, organization, intent, purpose,

---

31. Ratzsch, "Perceiving," 131.
32. Ibid., 126.
33. Ibid., 128.

usefulness, adaptation, aptness or fitness of means to ends, regularity, beauty and so forth.[34] And for some of these marks the ancient and medieval philosophers could plausibly state of them that genuine intent requires an intender, thereby inferring an intender, with certainty, from intent.[35] If inductive design inferences are needed, such as those given by Plato, the Stoics and Aquinas, they must rest on foundational cases of a sense of design perceptually recognized but through a non-inferential process.[36]

I think Ratzsch is correct here. I do not have to prove that I am, say, using a pen and a pad to put my thoughts together at this moment, or that I am sitting on a chair, crouched toward my desk in a particular university library. Grasping these activities is a process best interpreted as "perception" rather than as inference. What one needs to do is to walk to the relevant location in order to actually see me execute these tasks. But in itself, this conclusion is neither provable nor unprovable,[37] specifically because both provability and unprovability belong to the realm of inferences.

By the same token, when confronted by marks of design, we should understand those marks as directly perceivable signs of a designer, rather than as implying a designer. As noted even by biologists, we all speak of things in nature as designed. In other words, design seems to confront us at every turn of our epistemological pursuits. Ironically, on this very issue Francis Crick, the co-discoverer of the structure of DNA, who, according to Ratzsch,[38] is also no friend of religion, warned that biologists constantly remind themselves how the objects of their scientific investigation are objects that evolved over time. They are not objects that were designed.[39] Also, the historian Timothy Lenoir commented that even for professional biologists[40] modern biology consistently resists teleological thinking. Ironically, biologists remain hard-pressed, in nearly all areas of their research, to use language that rejects the notion of purposiveness to living forms.[41]

Having made these considerations let me make two observations here. First, we find that, despite their agreement that some form of supernatural

---

34. Ibid., 128.
35. Ibid., 129.
36. Ibid., 131.
37. Ibid., 126.
38. Ibid., 135.
39. Crick, *What Mad Pursuit*, 138.
40. Ratzsch, "Perceiving," 135.
41. Lenoir, *Strategy of Life*, ix.

agent created nature, some differences still remained among them. The Stoics, as we shall see, argued that nature was God. The Judeo-Christian conception maintained, and still maintains, that God exists apart and beyond nature. Second, belief in the existence of a designer was met by specific objections. Seneca's friend Lucilius, for instance, objected that the existence of evil counted as evidence against the existence of God.[42] As we shall see in chapter 5, naturalists in the modern period, such as Charles Darwin, raised similar objections.

To conclude this section, I contend that instead of resisting teleological thinking, the ancient and medieval theologians we have examined so far embraced it, accepting it as a rational and correct way of thinking about our world. They had good reasons for doing so. But following Ratzsch, it is best to think of the ancient and medieval philosophers as first and foremost perceiving marks of design in nature rather than inferring design. But having looked at the world as designed, what part of it should we construe as "natural"? What part of it should we think of as "supernatural"? What role do miracles play in this kind of world? In the following sections, I try to formulate answers to these questions.

Miracles and Nature

Having seen that belief in the existence of God was seen as an acceptable way of thinking among the more prominent philosophers and theologians of the ancient and medieval period, the next step is to consider how the miraculous aspect fitted into their epistemology of nature. Some theologians, as we shall see in the third section of this chapter, often contended that although miracles were not contrary to the workings of nature, they were supernatural, or above nature so to speak. However, other theologians held that miracles were actually "contrary to nature." But what exactly did they mean by "nature" or by the phrase "contrary to nature"?

My contention here is that a common definition of nature can be located among the different definitions offered by the ancient and medieval philosophers. In the previous section we saw that, according to these philosophers, belief in a powerful and intelligent designer was a rationally acceptable way of viewing our world. This view will in turn enable us to find a common definition of nature (that is, *phusis*) that will be crucial for our definition of miracle. When Judeo-Christian theologians such as

42. Pease, "Ceali," 184.

Augustine used the expression "contrary to nature" in relation to miracles, this common definition of nature is what they envisioned. Understanding this meaning of nature will then enable us to delineate, in a general way, how the theologians understood the miraculous. In the third section of this chapter, we will give a more specific delineation.

In order to shed light on my contention here, we need to trace briefly the history of the concept of nature. Aristotle was the first to define systematically the word "nature" (*phusis*). Besides a general description of nature in the *Physics*, his more comprehensive analysis is found in the *Metaphysics*, where he gives seven definitions. First, *phusis* is the genesis of growing things. Second, it is that immanent part of a growing thing, from which its growth first proceeds. Robert Grant thinks this growing thing is probably the seed.[43] Third, it is the source from which the primary movement in each natural object is present in it in virtue of its own essence. Fourth it is the primary material out of which any natural object consists or out of which it is made, which is relatively unshaped and cannot be changed from its own potency. Fifth it is the essence or form of natural objects. Sixth it is the essence or form in general. Seventh, which is the primary meaning, *phusis* is the essence of things which have a principle of movement in themselves qua themselves.[44]

Aristotle can speak of some things as coming into being "by nature," some "by art," and some "spontaneously."[45] By nature humans beget humans; by art a man builds a house; spontaneously certain animals reproduce without seed,[46] or "by chance" an unskilled person may accidentally cause a cure by imitating the physician's art. What comes into being by nature always comes into being for a purpose.[47] Also, in his treatment of dreams, Aristotle argues, as we have already seen, that nature is divinely planned though not itself divine.[48]

Whether or not monstrosities in nature can exist remains a question whose answer should be derived from a comparison with art. For example, in art the grammarian can make a mistake in writing, and the doctor can dispense the wrong dose. Analogously, therefore, such errors can occur in

---

43. Grant, *Miracle and Natural Law*, 6.
44. Aristotle, *Metaphysics*, IV.4, 1014b16–1015a19.
45. Ibid., VII.7, 1032a 12.
46. Ibid., 1033a31–1034b7.
47. Aristotle, *De Caelo* I.4, 271a34.
48. Aristotle, *De Divinatione Per Somnum*, 2.463b 13–15.

the operations of nature. Some principle has been corrupted. We cannot say that such a result is due to chance; it is due to spontaneity.[49]

As Grant observes, the monstrosity Aristotle discusses is admittedly "contrary to nature," contrary not to the whole of nature but to nature as it is generally.[50] Thus, in a certain sense, Aristotle says it is "according to nature," for when we consider nature as it always and necessarily is, nothing takes place contrary to it. Things according to nature are always orderly specifically because nature is the source of order for all things. Such things are never disorderly.[51] According to Aristotle, monstrosities belong to the class of things contrary to nature. However, their contrariety is not to nature in its entirety but only in the generality of cases. To the extent that nature always remains what it is necessarily, nothing runs contrary to it. However, unnatural occurrences remain among things which occur as they do in general cases, and even here, they may occur otherwise.[52] Even in those instances, what seems contrary to nature never happens in a merely random fashion. Therefore, it may appear less of a monstrosity because, in a way, though contrary to nature, it remains in accordance to nature.[53]

On the one hand, it may be premature here to insist that Aristotle argues for the occurrence of miracles by allowing that monstrosities occur in nature. There seems to be little evidence for such a concession from Aristotle. This is because in the context in which he discusses such monstrosities, he alludes more to what we would call "mistakes" in nature. If we take the case we already discussed, as an example, a doctor prescribing the wrong dose would count as a monstrosity in the art of medicine. Similarly, Aristotle would argue that there are mistakes (that is, monstrosities) in nature. But as we shall see later, Aristotle is open to the possibility that the miracle of prophecy indeed happens. In such a case, God is taken to have interacted with that part of φύσις called a "human being."

Among the Stoics the term "nature" is used very loosely. It is the whole of existence, it is God, it is Zeus, it is the rational principle of the universe; it is the first cause; it is providence; it is a spirit or a fire.[54] Zeno defined it as an

---

49. Aristotle, *Physics*, II.6 197b 32.
50. Grant, *Miracle and Natural Law*, 4.
51. Aristotle, *Physics*, I.252 a11.
52. Aristotle, *De Generatione Animalium*, 770b 10–15.
53. Ibid., 770b 15–19.
54. Zeno, *Stoicorum Veterum Fragmenta* II.1076.

artificent fire leading the way for coming into being.[55] Diogenes Laertius, who says that the Stoics speak of nature sometimes as embracing the universe and sometimes as producing things on earth, provides a more complete definition. Here, in a manner that later influenced Augustine's view on miracles, the Stoics define nature as "a self-moved condition which follows inseminated rational principles and produces and preserves its products in definite periods of time, and produces effects which correspond to their causes." As the producer of a succession of causes it can thus be identified with fate and necessity.[56] Nothing takes place except according to nature and its rational principle.[57]

In the early Roman Empire we find nothing new in terms of philosophical treatments of nature. Rhetoricians and philosophers repeat the phrases, especially the Stoic phrases, of earlier periods.[58] The difficulty with the Greek and Roman idea of nature, Grant argues, is that it included many variant meanings within one word such that philosophers preferred *arguing* about these meanings over *looking* at "nature" itself. The Hippocratic writers and Aristotle provide only partial exceptions to this general rule. Most writers preferred meditation on the order of the universe to critical examination of the order they assumed to exist. In Greco-Roman thought the ideas of sympathy and antipathy were far more popular than the biological treatises of Aristotle or the Peripatetics. They were more popular, and in late antiquity the scientific study of nature was practically dead.[59]

In later Christian writings we find nothing new.[60] But from our considerations of the historical understanding of nature, we are at once confronted by a significant problem. From the pre-Socratic period to the medieval period we find no uniform definition of nature. Plato, as we have seen, used the phrase "contrary to nature" in reference to ethics. Aristotle gave us seven different definitions. The Stoics equated God with nature. And the medieval theologians left it undefined, for the most part. And when they used it in reference to miracles, they generally did not clarify the meaning of the phrase "contrary to nature."

55. Ibid., I.171.
56. Ibid., II.1076.
57. Ibid., II.937.
58. Grant, *Miracle and Natural Law*, 14.
59. Ibid., 15.
60. Ibid., 17.

I suggest, therefore, that before we even begin to classify miracles as events contrary to nature, we must explain how *phusis* is used in this context of the miraculous. Once this is understood, then perhaps the question of the miraculous, and its definition, will not be as vague. It would seem to me that the vagueness of the term among the ancient and medieval philosophers and theologians sprang, not from the fact that there were multiple definitions, but quite possibly from the fact that there was a uniform understanding of *phusis*, as used in relation to miracles, that needed no specific definition. This hypothesis seems to account for the apparent lack of definition of the term.

If we look at the different conceptions of nature above, I suggest that a common understanding of *phusis* would involve that whole set of empirically detectable material or physical entities comprising the universe, along with their characteristic features. Recall that the ancient and medieval philosophers postulated that belief in a designer was a rational way of viewing our world, or for that matter, what we have identified in this section as *phusis*. They agreed that *phusis* pointed to a designer. Aristotle, for example, held that *phusis* is divinely planned. More specifically, they perceived marks of design in *phusis*, from which they came to believe in an intelligent power of design—which, they believed, was the ultimate cause of these marks. Thus, the philosophers in question recognized and spoke of at least two kinds of power in their perception of design: the power of nature, endowed by God, and the power of God proper. The Christian medieval theologians added a third dimension, namely, the power of super-nature—including, for example, immaterial rational entities like angels—which they believed was another aspect of God's creation. In order for any miracle to happen, God's proper power must work or be evident in nature in a way that could not be attributed to nature alone. To be sure they held that God's power must of necessity be greater than the power he gave his creation in order for miracles to happen.

God's power would be evident in nature in one or all of these three ways: First, his power must be such that it is capable of overriding the power of nature. As T. G. Patterheads notes, the event must be intrinsically of a kind that could never happen naturally.[61] Causing the sun to stand still by a simple command and parting the waters of a sea in some mysterious way are fitting examples of just such a power. If these were to happen, it would

---

61. Patterheads, "Miracles," 668.

perhaps be correct to think of these sorts of miracles as going contrary to nature.

Second, God's power must be apprehended as accomplishing a task, not contrary to nature, but *apart* from nature, in a way impossible for nature to accomplish by itself. For example, his power must be capable of raising the dead or turning water into wine. The observation here is that nature is simply not equipped with powers to accomplish such tasks. In this way God's power would be seen as working beyond or above nature's ability to do or accomplish the same.

Third, God's power must be seen to work *with* and alongside nature to accomplish what nature could not accomplish by itself. Patterheads argues here that a strong sign that God has worked along with nature is the fact that, say, once a prayer is offered, the sick person experiences instantaneous healing of his or her advanced organic disease.[62] The biblical story of a raven feeding the prophet Elijah seems to fall into this category as well, since the story depicts God working with nature (the raven) to feed a human being. Whereas there seems to be nothing contrary to nature in this event, it seems extremely unlikely (perhaps bordering on impossibility) that the natural order can bring about an event of this sort on its own.

These three understandings provide us with the frameworks to formulate an initial but working definition of a miracle as follows: An event is miraculous if in that event God's power overrides the power of nature, or accomplishes a task apart from nature, or works with and alongside nature to accomplish what nature could not accomplish by itself. Although Patterheads leaves the concept of a miracle undefined, I think he will allow that an event must meet any one of these three requirements to be classified as a miracle. Notice, however, that this is only a working definition. As we shall see from the Church fathers, whereas any one of these three requirements is crucial for the definition of a miracle, the aspect of context has to be taken into consideration as well.

The upshot of this consideration is that once we get clear on what the Christian theologians meant by the term "nature" and the phrase "contrary to nature" formulating an initial working definition of miracle is a relatively easy task. Is it correct, then, to argue that God has interacted with nature in a way deemed miraculous; and if so, how? This is a question I intend to answer at the end of this chapter. In the next section, however, we will see

62. Ibid.

that prominent ancient and medieval philosophers believed that miracles do in fact happen.

Ancient View of Miracles

We have seen that perceiving the existence of a designer was seen as a rational explanation for the existence of nature. However, it is not entirely clear, hitherto, from the ancient and medieval theologians, whether God has occasionally and miraculously interacted with nature. What needs to be established is whether God, understood in the way explored in the first section, is seen as the sort of being capable of subsequently interacting with *phusis* in a manner deemed miraculous. As we have already seen, the ancient and medieval philosophers believed that *phusis* derived its power from Mind, or for that matter, God. But would it be reasonable to take this contention further, namely, that ancient and medieval theologians believed that God interacted with *phusis* miraculously? The evidence suggests an affirmative answer.

To see this, let me begin with Socrates. In the *Apology* Socrates argued that his philosophic mission was a divine calling. More accurately, he saw his mission of teaching concepts such as justice and morality as a prophetic mission with a divine mandate. He considered his method of cross-examination a duty imposed upon him by God, signified to him by oracles, visions and in all manners he believed God's will was ever made known to humans.[63] After he was declared guilty of teaching false doctrine, and subsequently sentenced to death, Socrates issued what he believed was a prophetic utterance. Therein, he addressed the Athenians who condemned him, noting how, for example, humans find themselves gifted with prophetic power as they approach their final earthly minutes. In his prophecy, he warned the Athenians how immediately following his death, they would find themselves under punishment far heavier than the one they inflicted on him.[64]

Later, when Crito visits Socrates in jail, Socrates speaks of a vision he received in which a messenger reported to Socrates that his death would take place two days later. Thus, we find in Socrates a firm belief in the miracle of prophecy, a responsibility he believes God gave him. For Socrates, then, it is not simply that God can interact with *phusis* in a miraculous way.

63. Plato, *Apology*, 33. C.
64. Ibid., 39. C.

God has interacted with him in this way, and he believed he was a witness to this. As noted, Socrates had a conviction that his philosophic mission was a divine calling. The conviction was so firm that he was ready to die for it than abandon it altogether. According to him, to abandon the mission would be a sign of disobedience to God.[65] This is part of the moral context, of which a fuller view will be given in our treatment of Origen. As it stands, however, it remains, from a Christian perspective, somewhat inadequate.

Let me now turn to Aristotle's view on prophecy. Aristotle refers to prophecy as divination in dreams. According to Aristotle, it is not incredible that divination should occur in dreams, since such an occurrence has a show of reason.[66] But on an extremely skeptical note he argues that if we abstract from the causality of God, none of the other causes commonly assigned to prophetic dreams, appears probable.[67] The dreams in question must be regarded as causes, or as tokens, or else as coincidences, or as some or all of these.[68]

Moreover, Aristotle cautions that we should suspect, perhaps even reject, any dreams supposedly sent by God to commonplace persons rather than to what he considers the wisest of humans and the best of humans."[69] Indeed, Aristotle argues that a special proof that a given dream has not been sent by God is that it occurs to persons of inferior type. This fact, in Aristotle's view, implies that God did not send this dream to them. Rather, the person's physical temperament was garrulous and excitable, causing him to perceive sights of all sorts of descriptions.[70] It seems, then, that Aristotle is open to the possibility that a prophetic dream is genuine provided it can be shown that such a dream comes from God. One way to show this, according to Aristotle, is that the prophetic dream should be given to the wisest and best rather than to ordinary people. Notice, though, that what we get from Aristotle is the claim that prophetic miracles are possible. However, the skeptical tone with which Aristotle explicates his view on dreams leaves the reader wondering whether he really believed that prophetic miracles actually happen.

---

65. Ibid., 37. E.
66. Aristotle, *De Divinatione Per Somnum*, 462 b 16–17.
67. Ibid.
68. Ibid.
69. Ibid.
70. Ibid.

But we can fairly say that the Aristotelian view of prophetic miracles would quite likely treat Socrates' prophecy as authentic. This is because Socrates was regarded as one of the wisest and best by some of his intellectual peers. According to Aristotle, dreams and visions are from God, and thus genuine, when they come through the wisest and best. Thus Aristotle's requirement is satisfied in Socrates, provided Socrates also satisfies Aristotle's understanding of what he takes to be the "wisest and best."

Among the Stoics, we also find allowance for the possibility of the miracle of divination. For example, in presenting his four arguments for the divine existence, Cleanthes contended that we can know of this existence through foreknowledge of future events, as well as unnatural prodigies, both human and bestial.[71] And in his argument for God's existence, Balbus takes great pains, in the presence of Cicero, Cotta and Velleius, to recount miracle stories believed to have happened in his day.[72]

David J. Furley observes that the Stoics used the term "sympathy" to explain such prodigies, and these included astrology and divination. According to Furley, the notion of sympathy is given a rationale, and receives more emphasis among the Stoics, than in any previous philosophical system.[73] Notice also that in their explication of miracles, the Stoics do not use the expression "contrary to nature," quite possibly because they might have held that since nature is God, and vice versa, it would be irrational for them to imagine God contradicting himself.

From the Greek Philosophers, we move to the Christian theologians. Here, I begin with Athenagoras. According to Athenagoras, whether or not God can interact with nature in a miraculous way is a question that can be answered in the affirmative.[74] He argues that since God is capable of creating bodies, it follows that he has sufficient power to raise dead bodies.[75]

In his *Discourse on the Resurrection*, Methodius advances a similar argument. He observes that if God brings human beings into existence out of nothing, how much then will God be able to bring back a dead human being?[76]

---

71. Cicero, *Nature of the Gods*, 2.13–14.
72. Ibid., 2.6–7.
73. Furley, "Zeno of Citium," 606.
74. Athenagoras, *On the Resurrection of the Dead*, II.
75. Ibid.
76. Methodius, *Discourse on the Resurrection*, XIV.

SUPERNATURALISM IN THE ANCIENT AND MEDIEVAL PERIODS

Quite rightly, I think, Athenagoras and Methodius hold that once we admit God's existence and his creative power, belief in the possibility of miracles falls cogently into place. In short, belief in the existence of God was the primary conviction in maintaining an open but cautious mind to the claim that a genuine miracle had occurred. What we must now investigate and establish is the third claim I posited at the beginning of this chapter, namely that the ancient and medieval authors believed that miracles of the sort reported by Judeo-Christian theology did in fact happen. They believed this not only on the basis of what they understood as rational belief in the existence of an intelligent designer, but also on the basis of contextual frameworks in which, it was maintained, authentic miracles occurred.

I will begin this investigation with the early church fathers. Here we will examine the views of Quadratus, Justin Martyr, Irenaeus, Tertullian and Origen. I will then outline the views of the later church fathers, specifically, the views of Lactantius, and Hilary of Poitier. In the next section we will examine the views of Augustine and Aquinas.

Let me begin with Quadratus, the early second-century apologist. Grant depicts him as the oldest witness to the argument from miracles. Grant observes that almost all of Quadratus' writings are no longer extant, except for a portion of his writings that appears in Eusebius' works.[77] Here, Quadratus argues that those who had been either healed or raised from the dead lived during Jesus' time, and even beyond. In fact, according to Quadratus, some of them lived during Quadratus' time.[78] Quadratus seems to imply, from this observation, that the witnesses of the miracles of Jesus were available during his time, and could be consulted as proof that the events in question occurred as reported, if necessary.

From Quadratus we move to Justin Martyr. In his *Dialogue with Trypho* Justin Martyr responds to the claim, apparently from the Jews and the Greeks, that the miracles of Jesus were really magic tricks. Justin Martyr responds to this attack by drawing his critics' attention to the fact that the coming of Christ and the works accompanying his earthly sojourn were long ago predicted by the prophets.[79] Thus, prophecy in Justin's view attested to the non-magical but miraculous nature of Jesus' deeds.[80]

---

77. Grant, *Miracle and Natural Law*, 188.
78. Eusebius, *Church History of Eusebius*, IV.3.2.
79. Justin, *Dialogue with Trypho*, 69.
80. Ibid.

Like Justin Martyr, Tertullian argued that miracles by themselves could never have provided satisfactory testimony to Jesus' divinity.[81] To be sure, Tertullian reasons, Jesus himself subsequently discounted this claim when he affirmed that many would come, and would work signs and perform great wonders—wonders that could even lead God's elect astray. Here, Jesus made it clear, according to Tertullian, that credit of signs and wonders is precarious, as these are quite easy even for false Christs to perform. Therefore, Jesus could not possibly have been content to accept for himself approval, understanding and recognition from sources such as miracles alone.[82]

Thus, from Justin Martyr and Tertullian, we find that even though the church fathers accepted the claim that miracles do happen, they were hesitant to accept testimonies of all miracles at face value without additional considerations; for they held that some events masquerade as miracles, and were quite capable of being mistaken for such. Magic, for example, belongs to the category of such events. Magic is essentially a human-initiated event, whose intention is to deceive. For this reason, the church fathers would not see it as originating from God, given their view of God as a being who does not employ deceptive techniques in his dealings with us. Thus if an act is done by magic, for instance, it could not be a genuine miracle, though it might appear miraculous to the undiscerning. Moreover, if the miracles of Jesus were really magic, then the implication was that he used deceptive means to accomplish his purposes. This would fall in sharp conflict with the moral motif of his message.

Origen elucidates this concept well. For instance, according to him, Celsus argued that Jesus wrought his miracles through magic.[83] According to Origen, Celsus believed Jesus was able to perform his miracles by magic. When Jesus foresaw how other individuals would eventually acquire magical skills to perform similar miracles and subsequently claim that such miracles were of divine origin, Jesus expelled them from his society. By driving them out, Jesus became a bad man. However, if he was not a bad man for driving them out, neither were the others bad when they acted in the same way he did.[84]

---

81. Tertullian, *Tertullian against Marcion*, 173.
82. Ibid.
83. Origen, *Origen against Celsus*, I.6.
84. Ibid.

SUPERNATURALISM IN THE ANCIENT AND MEDIEVAL PERIODS

According to Origen, Celsus argued that Jesus fabricated the story of his virgin birth.[85] As Origen observes, Celsus contended that Jesus came from a Jewish village and from a poor country woman who earned her living by spinning. But the woman was driven out by her husband because she committed adultery. The husband was a carpenter by trade. The woman then secretly gave birth to Jesus. And being poor, Jesus hired himself out as a workman in Egypt, trying his hand at certain magical powers on which the Egyptians pride themselves. Jesus then returned full of conceit because of these powers, and on account of them gave himself the title "God."[86]

Origen replies to this charge in several ways. First, if Jesus was indeed an Egypt-trained magician who gave himself the title God, one wonders why a magician would take the trouble to teach a doctrine which persuades every man to do every action as before God who judges each man for all his works. And one wonders why he would instill this conviction in his disciples whom he intended to use as the ministers of his teaching.[87]

Second, given that the apostles were fisher-folk and tax collectors with no primary education, and who with great courage not only spoke to Jews about faith in Jesus but also preached him among the other nations with success, should we not try to find out the source of their persuasive power?[88] For without miracles and wonders, the apostles of Jesus would not have persuaded those who heard the new doctrines and new teachings to leave their traditional religions and to accept the apostles' teaching at the risk of their lives.[89]

Third, Origen observes that no sorcerer uses his tricks to call the spectators to moral reformation.[90] Moreover, no sorcerer educates, by the fear of God, people who were astounded by what they saw. Also, the sorcerer does not attempt to persuade onlookers to live as men who will be judged by God. Sorcerers do none of these things, since they have neither the ability nor even the will to do so. To be sure sorcerers do not even want to have anything to do with reforming men, seeing that they themselves are filled with the most shameful and infamous sins.[91]

85. Ibid., I.28.
86. Ibid.
87. Ibid., I.38.
88. Ibid.
89. Ibid., I.46.
90. Ibid., I.68.
91. Ibid.

These three considerations led Origen to conclude that the life of Jesus was of such a character that no one could reasonably compare him with the sorcerers. An important thing to note here is that Origen gives a moral test by which we can see that a miracle is authentic—that is, that the miracle is from God. The moral test includes a call to moral reformation brought about by the miracle-working agent's call to moral purity—a call confirmed by the relevant miracle. In addition, instead of attributing the miraculous event to himself or herself, the miracle-working agent draws his audience to God as the power behind the miracle. But this is also on the supposition that the moral character of the miracle worker is consistent with this kind of submission and devotion to God. Admittedly, however, Scripture does point us to miraculous events brought about by persons seen as immoral, such as King Saul's prophetic utterances. Notice also that the moral test is not a necessary condition for all miracles, since Scripture points to some miracles (such as Jesus' walking on water) for which the moral test hardly applies.

However, whether the miracle working agent is moral or not, having seen the power of the miracle, the agent will surely be aware of the moral inconsistency and perhaps, the dangers, of attributing such powers to himself or herself rather than to God. On the one hand, unless one is God, it would be morally inconsistent to call people to moral reformation through the use of miraculous powers, while at the same time, with an air of pride, attribute the source of these powers to oneself. On the other hand, if God truly is the source of the miracle, it seems dangerous to deny God what truly belongs to him.

We have already seen from Origen's considerations why it would be erroneous to equate Jesus' miracles with magic. Lactantius adds another dimension to this argument. He observes that magic can go only so far. There are some things that the miracles of Jesus accomplished that magic cannot accomplish. For instance, it does not seem to be the case that one can raise the dead by magic, or walk on water by magic.[92]

Let me now turn to Hilary of Poitiers. In *The Trinity*, Hilary argues that it is beyond our understanding how miracles happen. But the fact that they happen is indisputable, given the evidence.[93] He states that God's powers are such that even when their nature remains humanly ungraspable, our

---

92. Lactantius, *Divine Institutes*, IV.XV.
93. Hilary, *Trinity*, II.8–9.

faith raises no objections about them specifically because of the evidence of what God has accomplished.[94]

Hilary then draws our attention to the miracle of changing water into wine. Here, Hilary notes that our power of reasoning will not be able to ascertain how this nature was changed so that the insipidity of water disappeared and the taste of wine originated.[95] According to Hilary, this was not a mixture but a creation. Moreover, it was a creation which did not begin from itself, but emerged from one thing into another. And that which was weaker was not the result of the pouring out of something stronger; rather, that which *was* came to an end, and that which *was not* came into being.[96] Hilary concludes that the manner in which this came about baffles the sight and understanding; but the power of God is realized in what was done.[97]

A major point of Hilary's argument is the relationship between the cause of the miracle, and the miracle itself. That the miracle happened, for Hilary, there is no question. The fact that God caused the miracle, again, for Hilary, remains unquestionable. What remains mysterious is what appears to be a lack of continuity between the cause of the miracle, and the miracle itself. Nevertheless, that the miracle happened indicates that the continuity—that is, the causal relationship—is there. But the human mind is simply not equipped to understand this causal relationship. This is because the sense of continuity, though it certainly exists, *seems to be lacking*, from our point of view. This apparent lack of continuity, according to Hilary, is essentially incomprehensible and mysterious.

From Hilary, we move to John Chrysostom. Chrysostom gives a very brief argument for miracles. According to him, miracles were done for the sake of the unbeliever, and specifically to bring the unbeliever to faith in God.[98] In addition to this, miracles were done for the sake of manifesting God's power, especially when believers were taken captive by nonbelieving captors who attributed their victory to the might of their own gods.[99] Chrysostom also presents himself as an eyewitness to specific miraculous works. For example, he bears witness to many wonderful works shown forth

---

94. Ibid.
95. Ibid.
96. Ibid.
97. Ibid., 69.
98. Chrysostom, *Gospel of St. Matthew*, I.17.
99. Ibid.

at a time when they had just come to faith.[100] He notes, however, that when true religion had taken root among the nonbelievers, miracles ceased.[101] Interestingly, the view that miracles ceased with the establishment of religion is endorsed by quite a number of church fathers, including Augustine, whose view we shall examine at length in the next section.

However, at this point let me discuss the relevance of context as evidence for miracles. Let's take the moral as well as the prophetic test as elements of context, since both can quite conceivably work together. Suppose, for the sake of argument, a person p claims to be God's prophet, and predicts the future occurrence of a certain event e which, given the normal workings of natural law, would be impossible. Suppose that p is a morally upright person, known by members of his community as honest, full of integrity, not garrulous in the Aristotelian sense, but wise in the Socratic sense. If e eventually occurs, it would be safe to conclude that e most likely originated from God rather than from another source. Such a conclusion is based, first, on our knowledge of p's moral track record—namely, that p is an honest person and would have no reason to tell a lie—and subsequently on p's testimony that God communicated to p. And the more p's subsequent predictions are fulfilled with impeccable consistency, the more we get fuller assurances that the predicted events were caused by God, in much the same way we concluded about the initial event e.

Of course, if e fails to occur at the time it was expected to occur, then we would conclude that p was mistaken in believing that God spoke to him. We would then be justified in questioning the reliability of p and perhaps p's moral integrity as well. Admittedly, though, if p was honestly mistaken he may not be morally at fault.

Suppose, however, that p is initially not a morally upright person, but somehow proceeds to prophecy, quite unexpectedly, that God will bring about the occurrence of e at some future time. If e occurs as predicted, we would not quickly jump to the conclusion that e was caused by God. Given p's moral track record, we would be inclined to think that e's subsequent occurrence was purely coincidental despite p's prediction of e. However, if after the occurrence of e we see a significant change in p's behavior, attended by future prophecies from p that find constant impeccable fulfillment, it would be wise on our part to rethink our judgment about p's initial prediction despite the fact that he did not come across to us as morally upright.

100. Ibid.
101. Ibid.

This treatment of context, I believe, is an outline of the view endorsed by the church fathers thus far considered. I now turn to the views of two representative medieval philosophers—Augustine and Aquinas.

Medieval View of Miracles

According to Augustine, a miracle is anything seemingly difficult or unusual—beyond the hope or cognitive power of individuals inquiring after them.[102] According to Augustine, miracles impress us and are out of the ordinary because they have a hidden and unexplainable cause. And when causes are hidden in this way, the effect is of an unusual occurrence because it is either unique or rare. Thus, it is a cause of wonder to us.[103]

Three things can be said about this definition. First, it classifies anything unusual or surprising as a miracle. As we shall see below, acts of magic will thus qualify as miracles. Second, Augustine's definition makes no mention of context. However, we shall see his view below that miracles, in some cases, are a demonstration of God's grace. Third, in this definition there is no mention of miracles going contrary to nature. We will also revisit this view in greater detail below.

In *De Trinitate*, Augustine tries to distinguish between the natural and the miraculous as follows: Natural things are those that happen in a continuous and flowing succession. Miracles, however, are natural things that get thrust into the flow by an unusual changeableness—happening for the admonition of humans.[104] The unusual changeableness that Augustine discusses comes from the hidden causes in nature. Therefore, the changeableness is natural but rare rather than contrary to nature. But such events are unusual from our perspective, because we are unable to grasp the nature of the hidden powers of nature. However, when seen from God's perspective, they are part of nature. Thus, in reality, miraculous events are events that happen in accordance with nature.[105]

Augustine divides miracles into two kinds.[106] Those that cause only wonder and those that bring great favor and good will.[107] An example of

102. Augustine, *On the Profit of Believing*, 364.
103. Augustine, *Letters*, 162.
104. Augustine, *De Trinitate*, III, VI, 11.
105. Ibid.
106. Augustine, *On the Profit of Believing*, 364.
107. Ibid.

the former would be a man flying. According to Augustine, inasmuch as that brings no advantage to the spectator, the spectator only wonders. An example of the latter would be the instant healing of a person afflicted with sickness. Here, the healed person will go beyond the wonder of healing. In addition to the wonder, he will be devoted to the one who heals.[108] Miracles of this kind, Augustine observes, happened when Christ was revealed in human flesh. He healed the sick, the lepers, the lame, the blind, and the deaf.[109] When we consider Augustine's description of the first kind of a miracle, there does not appear to be much of a distinction between a miracle and an act of magic. As we shall see, Augustine does not seem to think that such a distinction is available.

Nevertheless, the hidden cause of miracles is an issue Augustine pursues at considerable length. According to Augustine, the Creator himself is hidden and incomprehensible to humans in much the same way that his manner of creation is hidden.[110] It is worth noting, he observes, that creation is a standing miracle. But it is little thought of because it is always before us. However, when we bring ourselves to reflect on it, creation is a greater miracle than the rarest and unheard of miracles.[111]

Augustine does not think, therefore, that miracles are contrary to nature, given his doctrine of the hidden cause of miracles. According to him, what happens by the will of God cannot be contrary to nature. This is because the will of God is certainly the nature of each created thing. Therefore, a miracle happens, not contrary to nature, but contrary to what we know of nature. Augustine is contending that miracles are caused by certain hidden seeds already implanted in nature by God. Like the Stoics, Augustine contends that God is the Creator of certain hidden seeds of all things lying hidden in the physical elements of nature, and generated in a physical and visible way.[112] Rather than connecting these "seeds" to specific miracles, Augustine goes only as far as inferring that these seeds bring about the miracles in question.

Augustine maintains that only God is capable of ruling his creation from "the innermost and highest pivotal cause of all causation."[113] However,

108. Ibid.
109. Ibid.
110. Augustine, *City of God*, 10.12.
111. Ibid.
112. Augustine, *De Trinitate*, III.8.
113. Ibid., III.9.

God can grant his creatures the powers and faculties to perform miraculous deeds, presumably by making the powers of the hidden seeds of causation available to those very creatures.[114]

This explanation enables us to understand Augustine's treatment of magic and miracles that do not originate from God. Here, Augustine tries to explain why Pharaoh's magicians, for instance, were able to perform miracles as recorded in the book of Exodus. Augustine believes that the magicians were capable of performing their miracles because God allowed them to do so. But at a certain point, God's power kept them from performing any more miracles. What we find from Augustine, therefore, is that God can allow even wicked angels and wicked human beings to gain access to the powers of these hidden seeds and causes. But when they fail to perform their magic, it is because God has denied them access to these powers.

Nevertheless, Augustine's view that God has endowed nature with hidden miraculous powers is a curious one. In fact J. Houston observes that the sorts of wonders Augustine is talking about here may raise peculiar problems. This is because, on Augustine's view, magical acts cannot generally be explained as caused by any immediate exercise of God's power in order to corroborate divine truth or lift people's hearts and minds up to God.[115]

So where does this hidden seeds view of the miraculous powers of nature fit in Augustine's treatment of miracles? According to Houston, this view does not fall under Augustine's central characterization of miracle. In other words, it is at least possible that Augustine did not propose this view as applying generally to the properly miraculous.[116]

In contrast, Colin Brown, Benedicta Ward and Robert Grant all present the hidden seeds view as the motif underlying Augustine's treatment of miracles. Ward sees Augustine as claiming that God put hidden seeds in nature, hidden with the appearance of things, which at times caused miracles that seemed to be contrary to nature, but were in fact inherent in it.[117] To a lesser extent, but in clear agreement with Grant, Brown maintains that Augustine's philosophical background played a critical part in his treatment of miracles.[118]

---

114. Ibid.
115. Houston, *Reported Miracles*, 14.
116. Ibid.
117. Ward, *Miracles and the Medieval Mind*, 4.
118. Brown, *Miracles and the Critical Mind*, 8.

Grant's position is more explicit. According to Grant, the origin of the theory of "seeds" implanted by God in the universe can be traced back through Philo to the Stoics. It was Philo, Grant argues, who took the immanent seminal principles of the Stoics and asserted that they were placed in nature by the transcendent God.[119]

However, Houston argues that we must not be compelled to read Augustine's treatment of the miraculous in this way. Houston argues that this reading is only one of Augustine's conceptions of miracles.[120] For Houston, we need to take into consideration two more conceptions of the miraculous in Augustine's thought. Augustine's second conception of the miraculous is found in *De Genesi ad Litteram*. Here, Augustine contends that God possesses the hidden origin of specific things—things we do not find in creatures.[121] According to Augustine, when God first created the universe, he did not preestablish every cause. Rather, he retained some in his own will. The ones he retained are not contingent upon the necessity of created causes.[122]

According to Houston, this second conception ought not to be subsumed under or accommodated to the hidden seeds conception. It is a distinct conception. Moreover, it is related to Augustine's most significant examples of the miraculous, such as the creation of woman, rather than to a peculiar subclass of miracles. Therefore, Houston argues that this second conception has a good claim to be Augustine's central conception of miracle.[123]

But Houston also detects a third conception of the miraculous in Augustine's thought. It involves God's changing the nature of things, having first created these natures as he pleased.[124] For example, Augustine writes that in the resurrection of the dead, the human body shall be "constituted differently from its present well-known condition."[125]

For Houston, this is clearly a language of changing natures. Such language suggests that new causal factors, newly introduced by God, are not continuously present within nature itself. This leads Houston to conclude

---

119. Grant, *Miracle and Natural Law*, 219.
120. Houston, *Reported Miracles*, 15.
121. Augustine, *De Genesi ad Litteram*, IX, xiii, 33.
122. Ibid., VI, xviii, 29.
123. Houston, *Reported Miracles*, 16.
124. Ibid.
125. Augustine, *City of God*, XXI. viii.

that the third conception of nature fits ill with the hidden seeds view. For the causal principles thus newly and strikingly operative in nature were not implanted at first, but have been newly introduced by the will of God.[126] How different is this view from the second conception? According to Houston, this view may appear to go beyond the second understanding specifically because it entails the process of implanting somewhat permanent causal powers in nature—powers by which miracles happen. For this reason, Houston argues, when we seek to inquire whether miracles, on this understanding, possess a certain natural cause, our answer is neither clearly affirmative nor clearly negative. Perhaps, Houston thinks, we can best consider this last concept of miracle as a subclass of the second provided we wish to lower the number of Augustinian conceptions of miracle.[127]

A chief motivation for Houston to think in this way about the third conception is the fact that Augustine speaks in terms of God's rule over natures precisely in the context in which the second conception is explicit. Here, it looks as though Augustine regards what has been called the third conception as a variant on, or elaboration of, the second conception.[128]

What then should we make of Augustine's hidden seeds view? It seems to rest on a fallacious equivocation on "nature." It appears that, in his explication of miracle, Augustine unwittingly shuttles between two conceptions of nature. First, he speaks of nature as that which makes a thing *that* thing. In this case we can speak of the nature of anything in the universe, or even the nature of God. But Augustine also seems to speak of nature as God's creation, and this is the second conception. Unfortunately, Augustine seems to use both conceptions interchangeably. To see this let me recapture his argument here. He seems to argue as follows: "The will of God is certainly the nature of each created thing. Therefore, the will of God cannot be contrary to nature."

Notice that in the premise above, Augustine's use of "nature" implies the first conception elucidated above. Notice also, that his use of "nature" in the conclusion implies the second conception of nature elucidated above. My contention is that Augustine's attempt to explain miracles via the hidden seeds conception rests on a confusion of the two conceptions of nature, resulting in ambiguities. This is a confusion that neither Houston on the one hand nor Brown, Grant and Ward on the other recognize. However,

---

126. Houston, *Reported Miracles*, 16.
127. Ibid., 16–17.
128. Ibid., 17.

the Houstonian second and third conception of miracles in Augustine's thought has better promise, since it seems to avoid the confusion I have alluded to above, and can be seen to fit in our working definition formulated in the second section.

Let me now turn to Thomas Aquinas. Aquinas notes that the word miracle is taken from the Latin term *admiratio*.[129] Like Augustine, Aquinas argues that we experience wonder when an effect is obvious but its cause is hidden. For Aquinas, the word miracle connotes something altogether wondrous because it has its cause hidden absolutely and from everyone. This cause, Aquinas argues, is God. Thus God's works surpassing any causes known to us are called miracles.[130] This definition is different from Augustine's definition, to the extent that all miracles are events caused by God. For Augustine, some of these works are caused by hidden seeds God planted in nature, while others are the effects of causes hidden in God himself.

However, like Augustine, Aquinas argues that if we look to the world's order as it depends on the first cause, God cannot act against it. If he did, he would be doing something contrary to his foreknowledge, will and goodness.[131] But, unlike what we find in Augustine's first conception, Aquinas holds that if we take the order in things as it depends on any of the secondary causes, then God can act apart from it. Here, God is not subject to that order; rather, the order is subject to him—issuing from him not out of necessity of nature, but by decision of his will. In fact, God could have established another sort of pattern in the world.[132]

Therefore, when God wills, he can act apart from the given order, producing, for example, the effects of secondary causes without these causes or some other effects that surpass the power of these causes.[133] Thus for Aquinas, God never acts contrary to the normal course of nature. Moreover if he goes in any way contrary to the supreme law, he would be going against himself.[134] However, God so fixed the definite order in nature that he still reserved to himself what at times he wants to do differently for good

---

129. Aquinas, *Summa Theologica*, I. Q105, art. 7.
130. Ibid.
131. Ibid., art.6.
132. Ibid.
133. Ibid.
134. Ibid.

SUPERNATURALISM IN THE ANCIENT AND MEDIEVAL PERIODS

reasons.[135] This manner of doing things, Aquinas would say, turns out to be beyond the capacities of nature.

Therefore, Aquinas describes a miracle as difficult because it surpasses the capabilities of nature. It is considered unusual, not because it may not occur repeatedly, but because it seems to fall outside the normal pattern of nature. Something is said to surpass the capacities of nature not only on the basis of the kind of thing done, but also of the manner and order of its doing. A miracle therefore is said to be beyond the expectation of nature. But it is not beyond the expectation of grace.[136]

Aquinas parts company with Augustine when he contends, first, that with regard to secondary causes, God can act apart from nature, and when he contends, second, that no finite power, whether angels or humans, can perform miracles proper.[137] This belongs to God alone. According to Aquinas, whatever a creature does by its power cannot be called a miracle proper, even though what is done may be astonishing—especially to a person who does not comprehend the power of this creature.[138] However, "what is done by divine power, which, being infinite, is incomprehensible in itself, is truly miraculous."[139]

But how can we recognize a miracle? Aquinas writes that the event in question may be for our bodily health, thereby giving us the grace of healing; or it may be purely for the display of God's power, such as when the sun stood still or when God divides the waters of the Red Sea or the Jordan River.[140]

According to Houston, Aquinas did not suppose that the known occurrence of a miracle would compel anyone's belief in that which the miracle confirms. Rather, miracles are supportive or confirmative of faith. That is, they are reasons among other possible reasons, for a believer's faith.[141] In other words, Houston interprets Aquinas as follows: miracles do not produce faith in a person; they simply confirm the faith a person already has.

---

135. Ibid.
136. Ibid., art. 8.
137. Aquinas, *Summa Contra Gentiles*, 3. 102.3.
138. Ibid.
139. Ibid.
140. Aquinas, *Summa Theologica* I, II. Q111, art 4.
141. Houston, *Reported Miracles*, 30.

Houston's contention here seems to be misleading. What Aquinas seems to be saying here is that some people do come to faith when they witness a miracle; others do not. In other words, contrary to Houston, miracles do produce faith in some persons, although not necessarily in all.[142]

Conclusion

From the ancient and medieval theologians, then, we are able to provide a fuller view of the context in which it is possible to show that an alleged miracle actually took place. Their supernaturalistic view maintains, as we have seen, that God is the creator of everything there is, including nature. And it would not be irrational to think of God as interacting with his creation, since it belongs to him. Such an interaction is considered miraculous.

But how do we know that there is at least one event e such that e is a miracle and e has happened? The best answer, in my view, is to consider the starting point of the ancient and medieval theologians. First, consider that they believed our world is the product of an intelligent, wise, loving and most powerful Mind, properly called God. Second, consider that in section B we located a uniform understanding of nature that led us to define it as the empirically and scientifically detectable physical and material universe, which, according to the ancient and medieval theologians and philosophers we surveyed, was designed by God. Third, consider that a miracle involves God having interacted with nature in a manner apprehended as going contrary to nature, or above nature, or alongside nature. Fourth, consider that all these happen in a way that nature could not have done by itself. Fifth, notice that God's creation of the universe as explicated in our first consideration satisfies the third and fourth consideration above. I refer here to the claim that the creation of the universe involved God having interacted with (or should we say, "acted upon") nature, demonstrating powers in a way that nature could not have demonstrated by itself.

We are now ready to give a fuller definition of a miracle: it is an event in nature understood as occurring contrary to nature, above and beyond nature, or in accordance with nature, but in all cases capable of being authenticated, as mysteriously caused by God in a way that nature could not have done by itself. Such authentication comes through the prophetic context, the moral context or both. With regard to the prophetic context miracles not only confirm supernaturally revealed truths, but represent

---

142. Aquinas, *Summa Theologica* I, II, Q6, art.1.

those truths as well.[143] With regard to the moral context, the dignity of the miracle itself, the character and content of the human agent, the good effects of the miracle, all point to God as the cause of the miracle. Morally good circumstances point to a divine origin. Evil circumstances point to a diabolic origin.[144]

The upshot of all this is that it is a mistake to view miracles in isolation without considering the various contexts in which the miracles are claimed to occur. The richer definition of miracles we have offered provides us with a clearer view of a world in which the supernatural can reasonably have a place. This view was not limited to the ancient and medieval period alone. It carried itself over into the modern period as well. It is to this period that we turn in the next chapter.

143. Patterheads, "Miracles," 665.
144. Ibid., 669.

3

Supernaturalism and Epistemology in the Early Modern Era

HAVING SHOWN, IN THE previous chapter, that the ancient and medieval theistic supernaturalists viewed miracles within specific contextual frameworks, I proceed to show, in this chapter, that despite clear disagreements about their epistemological methodology, the skeptics, Descartes and the evidentialists demonstrated striking agreement in their supernatural commitments. This will show that most of the scientists we will investigate did not see any conflict arising between their scientific and religious views. Supernaturalism was part of their world-view in their scientific and epistemological enterprise. At least this seems to be the case with the scientific views of the New Pyrrhonists, Descartes and the evidentialists.

To see this, let me begin with the New Pyrrhonists. I begin with this group of thinkers specifically because they provide a chronological continuity from the medieval theologians considered in the previous chapter. From the New Pyrrhonists, we will turn to Descartes. His rationalistic method attempted to counter the skeptical claims of the New Pyrrhonists. After Descartes, we will examine the view of the evidentialists. Their position is important because, as Brown and Burns have shown, they adopted a middle ground between the New Pyrrhonists' view on the one hand, and Descartes' on the other. We will then discover that irrespective of the disagreement between their epistemological views, they all had a major concern to maintain their theological position, which for the most part, was identical in its key postulates.

SUPERNATURALISM AND EPISTEMOLOGY IN THE EARLY MODERN ERA

The New Pyrrhonists

Let me begin with the New Pyrrhonists. According to Colin Brown, a new version of Pyrrhonism developed during the Reformation period as a response to the Reformation theologians' insistence on the authority of the Bible as the word of God.[1] This was brought about, as R. M. Burns notes, by the debate over one of the major intellectual issues of the 1630s, namely, the nature of the rule of faith. Burns correctly notes that the Protestant Reformation began with a repudiation of the claim that Christian belief involved submission to the authority of the pope or, for that matter, the Church, in matters of interpretation of the faith. Protestants believed that their position was valid specifically because they appealed to Scripture as the only rule of faith.[2]

For example, one problem that Calvin had with the Catholic Church was the claim that their faith was confirmed by miracles.[3] To be sure, Calvin believed that the miracles in the Bible were authentic. For example, he argued on behalf of the miracles of Moses as follows. First, Moses performed all these miracles before the congregation, who were eyewitnesses of the events. For this reason, there was no opportunity for fraud. Second, whenever Moses referred to the miracles themselves, there was, at the same time, "disagreeably conjoined things that could stir up the whole crowd" to contradict him, had the occasion presented itself. Therefore, according to Calvin, the crowd had been led to assent to the miracles solely because they were quite enough convinced by their own experience. Third, the miracles could not have been works of magic because Moses himself shrank from this superstition; for he ordered that anyone who merely consulted magicians and soothsayers should be stoned to death.[4]

We can restate Calvin's arguments in the form of a question, as follows: what are the odds that hundreds of thousands of people will be consistently deceived for forty years by magic, without at least one of them detecting fraudulent maneuvers attending the magical art in question? According to Calvin, if Moses' actions were fraudulent, eyewitnesses would have declared them to be so. This is because, all things being equal, it is extremely difficult to consistently tell and live a lie for forty years without detection.

---

1. Brown, *Miracles*, 24–25.
2. Burns, *Great Debate on Miracles*, 38.
3. Calvin, *Institutes of the Christian Religion*, 16.
4. Ibid., 86.

Therefore, more than likely Moses performed, by the power of God, the miracles attributed to him by Scripture.

Thus we find in John Calvin a firm belief in what he took to be the authenticity of the biblical miracles.[5] But when it came to the Catholic Church's claim to the miraculous, we find a different story. It seems the Catholic Church had demanded Calvin to prove, with miracles, that the Protestant position mentioned above was authentic.[6] But Calvin felt that claims attesting to miraculous happenings, besides those recorded in the Bible, amounted to satanic delusion. He writes, "Those miracles which our adversaries point to in their own support are sheer delusions of Satan, for they draw people away from the true worship of God."[7]

This Protestant position prompted a Catholic counter response. Burns notes that Catholic apologists turned to Pyrrhonistic skepticism in order to demolish the claims that any individual could reliably trust his own judgments to interpret Scripture.[8] As Brown points out, the major reason for the growth of interest in Pyrrhonistic skepticism in the late sixteenth century was the use with which Catholic apologists made of it in their attacks on Protestantism. It was forged for the destruction of Calvinism.[9] According to Brown, it also sought to undermine all human claims to rational, objective knowledge.[10]

In order to grasp the skeptics' position more fully, let me draw from a summary of their views outlined by R. J. Hankinson. According to Hankinson, fundamental to the Pyrrhonists' method was the collection of cases in which things seem different under different circumstances.[11] Thus, if we trace the root of skepticism back to ancient philosophy, we find that Sextus Empiricus classified these different circumstances into "modes." For example, in the first mode, things appear differently to people as opposed to animals. Thus muddy water appeals to pigs but not to us. In the second, they appear differently to different groups of people. Thus Indians enjoy different things from the Greeks. In the third mode, things appear differently to different sense-modalities. For example, paintings seem bumpy to

---

5. Ibid.
6. Ibid., 16.
7. Ibid., 17–18.
8. Burns, *Great Debate*, 39.
9. Brown, *Miracles*, 24.
10. Ibid., 25.
11. Hankinson, "Pyrrhonism," 850.

visions but smooth to touch. In the fourth, they appear differently to the same sense-modality on different occasions.[12] For example, honey seems sweet to the healthy but bitter for the jaundiced. In the fifth, the appearance of things varies according to the distance and standpoint from which they are viewed. For example, a straight oar looks bent in water. Sixth, our apprehension of things differs according to how familiar we are with them. For example, naked bodies become unexciting after a while. Also, consider that different cultures have varying ethical practices. To be sure there were ten modes of such appearances.[13]

But what we see here, according to Hankinson, is the belief that everything appears to be relative. In fact, there is no second-order commitment to the truth of the claim that everything is relative; even that is a matter of appearance. The relativity apparent in all these modes share the following basic form: x appears F relative to a; x appears F^* relative to b; at most only one of the claims "x is F" and "x is F^*" can be objectively true; no uncontroversial decision procedure tells decisively either for "x is F" or for "x is F^*"; so we should suspend judgment as to what x is really like. But Hankinson clarifies that the range of x is broad and varies from mode to mode, as do the predicates covered by the variables F and F^*. What substitutes for a and b is determined by the particular nature of each mode. Thus, in the first mode a will be humans, b other animals; in the second a and b will be different individuals or groups of humans, and so on for the other modes.[14]

Having received this summarized understanding of skepticism in its initial formulation, we are able to draw parallels with the New Pyrrhonism of Galileo, Montaigne, Gassendi, Pascal and Bayle. Let me begin with Galileo. Galileo held that in matters of speculation the true and internal essence of substances cannot be known.[15] For example, if I seek to know the precise essence of clouds, someone will tell me that the substance of clouds is a moist vapor. But if I seek, further, to know what vapor is, the same person will tell me that vapor is "water attenuated by heat." But I will then seek to know what water is. At best, the answer I will get is that water "is the fluid body which runs in our rivers, which we constantly handle." This final information, Galileo observes, is "no more intimate" than what I know about clouds in the first place. Galileo's failure to account for essence in this way

12. Ibid.
13. Ibid., 851.
14. Ibid., 850.
15. Galilei, *Letters on Sunspots*, 59.

leads him to seek refuge in theology. He thus contends that knowledge of the true essences of earth, fire, moon or sun is not to be understood until we reach "that state of blessedness."[16]

Despite his skepticism about our ability to have knowledge of the true essence of things, Galileo maintained that we can know some of the properties of things. That is, we are able to know the location, motion, shape, size, opacity, mutability, generation and dissolution of bodies. Knowledge of properties of things, in turn, becomes the means by which we "philosophize better about the more controversial qualities of natural substances." For Galileo, the aim of such knowledge is to keep us steadfast, so that we will hopefully learn every other truth in God.[17]

It appears, for Galileo, that the primary qualities he discusses are objective to the extent that most humans can agree on the location, shape, size, opacity, dissolution and generation of external objects. However, we get the impression that the secondary qualities are subjective, from Galileo's point of view. He maintains that the qualities of taste, color, odor and so on reside only in the consciousness. If the living creature were removed, Galileo contends that all these qualities would be wiped away and annihilated.[18]

Consequently, Galileo maintains that if ears, tongues, and noses were removed, shapes, numbers and motions would remain, but not odors, taste or sound. Thus whereas the primary qualities appear to be real phenomena, the secondary qualities of sensation are not real. In other words, they have no real existence except in us. Beyond us or outside us, they are mere names.[19]

Having briefly considered Galileo let me turn to Michel de Montaigne. Montaigne argues that humans acquire knowledge through sense experience. He believes that we would know no more than inanimate objects if we did not know that there is sound, smell, light, taste and so forth—all of which are "the base and principles of all edifice of our knowledge."[20] However, Montaigne questions whether humans have been provided with all the senses of nature.[21] It is possible, Montaigne seems to argue, that humans lack "two, three or many other senses," which would enable them to know

16. Galilei, *Letters*, 60.
17. Ibid.
18. Galilei, *Assayer*, 65.
19. Ibid., 67.
20. Montaigne, *Apology for Raimond Sebond*, 77.
21. Ibid.

more about the world than they already know. Moreover, it is likely that there are sensory faculties in nature suitable to judge and perceive the occult properties that occur in nature. So far, the knowledge we have has been acquired only by the consultation of our five senses. But perhaps we needed the contribution of more faculties, which we do not have, to gain a more comprehensive truth about our world.[22]

Montaigne also calls into question the reliability of the five senses we already have. Here, he contends that our empirical perception of objects in the external world does not include the essence and nature of those objects. Otherwise we would receive impressions of those objects in the same way. To see this, consider for example, the fact that wine tastes differently in the mouths of sick people than it does in those of healthy ones. Another example he gives is that there is not one thing in the world on which we find universal consent among human beings.[23] Turning to the science of sound, Montaigne argues that when we are in a valley, the echo of the sound of a trumpet seems to come in front of us when, as a matter of fact, the trumpet is played from a league behind us.[24] Thus the impressions we receive from the external world come to us already falsified and altered by our senses, which accommodate things to themselves.[25]

These and a few more examples Montaigne cited lead him to conclude that the operation of the senses is laden with error and uncertainty.[26] For Montaigne, if the senses are our first judges, then we should not consult them alone; we should also consult the faculties of animals since some animals have keener hearing, sight and smell than humans.[27] Therefore, in order to determine whether or not the senses have given us reliable information, Montaigne suggests that we should first of all be in agreement with the animals, and second, with ourselves. The problem is that we are not in agreement in this way in the least.[28] In spite of this skepticism about the reliability of our senses to furnish us with information about the external world, Montaigne maintains that he has, by God's grace, kept himself

22. Ibid., 78.
23. Ibid., 74.
24. Ibid., 77.
25. Ibid., 75.
26. Ibid., 77.
27. Ibid., 78.
28. Ibid., 79.

intact, without agitation or disturbance of conscience in the ancient beliefs about his religion.[29]

According to Richard Popkin, Montaigne suggested that people should suspend judgment on all matters, and then wait until God reveals principles to them. Until then, one should just follow customs, traditions and social rules undogmatically, being tolerant of other people's views. Religious beliefs should be based solely on faith rather than on dubious evidence. Thus Montaigne's fideism rests upon the claim that since all is in doubt, we should accept Christianity on faith alone.[30]

What we find in Montaigne, therefore, is a kind of faith in his religion that does not depend on reason. Rather, it seems to come before reason. Ironically, Montaigne himself is skeptical of human rationality despite the fact that he relies on reason to show that reason is unreliable.

However, let me draw attention to a significant claim Montaigne makes. Recall his contention that, unknown to us, there could be sensory faculties, possessed by other creatures, to judge the occult properties that occur in nature. Of course those sensory faculties unknown to us would also be part of nature. But in Montaigne's view, such senses would be capable of *detecting* occult properties occurring in nature. Thus here we find in Montaigne, as we did with Galileo, some sort of commitment to supernaturalism. We also find a version of skepticism reminiscent of Pyrrhonism as initially formulated.

Let us now turn to Pascal. In order to understand Pascal's skepticism, we must put it in the context of his religion. Pascal's religious commitment can be traced back to the death of his father. Ian MacLean reports that after his father died, Pascal's sister became a nun at the convent of Port-Royal—the center of Jansenist doctrine and religious practice in France. Pascal opposed his sister's vocation strongly. Indeed, for two years thereafter, Pascal led a life very different from his sister's. He consorted with freethinkers, gamblers and libertines of fashionable Parisian society.

However, on the night of November 23, 1654, Pascal underwent a profound spiritual experience which altered his life irrevocably. It was so profound that Pascal sewed into his clothes a record that he made of it at the time of the event itself as a permanent memento, where it was found at his death. The document records an experience of conversion; it was not an intellectual experience. Rather, it was one which persuaded Pascal of the

---

29. Ibid., 75.
30. Popkin, "Montaigne," 488.

superiority of instinctive belief. This conviction was strengthened two years later when his niece was cured miraculously at Port-Royal of an apparently incurable fistula.[31]

As a result of this experience, Pascal went to Port-Royal-des-Champs for a two-week retreat in 1655. There he met Isaac Le Maistre de Saci, a Jansenist theologian, with whom he had a debate. This debate indicates not only that Pascal had conceived of an apology of the Christian religion in terms which would speak most powerfully to the very libertines and gamblers of the Parisian society which he had just forsaken, but also that he felt that one of the most powerful voices with which he had to contend with was that of Michel de Montaigne. It is also clear that he felt the need to reassure those who had been shaken in their faith by new scientific developments, especially those in astronomy.[32]

In light of this background religious experience, Pascal is able to say that we know truth, not only by reason, but also "by the heart." In fact, it is by the heart that we know first principles, as space, time, motion and number. But reason has no part in this way of knowing truth, though reason itself tries to challenge the first principles already acquired in this way. And however impossible it is for us to prove these first principles by reason, this inability only succeeds in demonstrating the weakness of our reason. But it does not affirm the uncertainty of all our knowledge. This is because the knowledge of first principles is as sure as any of those which we get from reasoning. Therefore, reason must trust these intuitions of the heart.[33]

For example, we have intuitive knowledge of the tri-dimensional nature of space, and of the infinity of number. Here, reason shows that there are no two square numbers one of which is double of the other. Thus, first principles are intuited and propositions inferred. Although these happen in different ways, it happens with certainty. Therefore, it is both useless and absurd for reason to demand from the heart proofs of her first principles in order to admit them. Similarly, it would be absurd for the heart to demand from reason an intuition of all demonstrated propositions before accepting them. This ought to humble reason. But it also ought not to call our certainty into question, as if reason were the only thing capable of instructing us.[34]

31. MacLean, "Pascal," 243.
32. Ibid.
33. Pascal, *Pensées*, 282.
34. Ibid.

For Pascal, the chief arguments of the skeptics are that only faith, revelation and intuitions of the heart make us certain about the truth of these first principles. This is because having no certainty, apart from faith, whether humans were created by a good God, or by a wicked demon, or by chance, it is doubtful whether these principles given to us are true, or false, or uncertain. Again, no person is certain, apart from faith, whether he is awake or asleep. For it is evident that during sleep we believe that we are awake as firmly as we do when we are awake. When we are asleep we believe that we see space, figure and motion; we are aware of the passage of time, measuring it as if we were awake. In this way we have no idea of truth, half of our life being passed in sleep.[35]

Who knows then, Pascal asks, whether the other half of our life in which we think we are awake, is not another sleep a little different from the former, from which we awake when we suppose ourselves asleep? Also, he continues, since we often dream that we are dreaming, is it not possible that the half of our life wherein we think we are awake is itself only a dream on which the others are grafted, and that we only wake up when we die? Is it not possible that at death, the few principles of truth and good that disturb us turn out to be illusions, the vain fancies of our dreams?[36] Once we are in this state, what should we do? Pascal says we cannot doubt everything. This makes him contend that there can never be a real complete skeptic. For Pascal, then, nature sustains our feeble reason, and keeps it from raving to the extent of complete skepticism. Thus nature confutes the skeptic and reason confutes the dogmatist.[37]

According to MacLean, a notable feature in Pascal's view of human nature is the very low assessment of the moral nature of humanity, whose self is said to be hateful. Pascal then turns to the paradox that in the very wretchedness of humans lie the seeds of greatness. Although the passions and imagination pervert and oppress them, humans also possess reason and self-awareness, and can even attain to certain knowledge about their environment through their intuitive grasp of geometric axioms. Such intuition, which, as we have already seen, Pascal locates in the heart, is also where true faith in God is to be found; the function of Pascal's apology is to persuade the reader rationally that the Christian religion is true because its

---

35. Ibid., 434.
36. Ibid.
37. Ibid.

description of the human condition is accurate, but it cannot do more than predispose the reader to receive the gratuitous divine gift of faith.[38]

In Pascal then we are faced with a person who freely juxtaposed his supernaturalism with his scientific enterprise. Of course he did not claim that one supported the other. Rather, he believed that each had its own important function. Thus on the one hand we see Pascal the mathematician concerned about discovering important mathematical truths; on the other we see Pascal the apologist concerned about the human condition with respect to the afterlife which he believed was inevitable.

Let us now turn to Pierre Bayle. According to Charles Larmore, Bayle was one of the most important skeptical thinkers of all time, as well as a notable moral philosopher and advocate of religious toleration. The fundamental motivation of his skepticism was religious; his aim was to curb the pretensions of reason in order to make room for faith. This will become apparent when we return to the issue of faith. But in terms of his skepticism, Bayle did not have any serious doubts that straightforwardly empirical questions admit of rational solutions. Indeed he frequently urged that philosophy should recognize the validity and importance of historical knowledge.[39]

Bayle's skepticism was therefore restricted to speculative questions of principle. He argued that no good philosopher will doubt that the skeptics were right in maintaining that the qualities of bodies that strike our senses are only appearances. We all can justly say, for example, that we feel heat in the presence of fire. But we cannot say that we know that fire is in itself such as it appears to us. For Bayle, heat, smells, colors and the like are not in the objects of our senses. They are modifications of our souls.[40] Moreover, sense objects cannot be the cause of our sensations. It would be possible for us to feel heat and cold, see colors, shapes, extensions and motions, even though there were no bodies in the universe. Therefore, we have no good proof of the existence of bodies. Whereas the skeptics we have outlined so far did contend that bodies exist, Bayle seems doubtful here.[41]

In order to conquer the skeptics' contention, Bayle argues that one must appeal, for example, to self-evidence as a mark of truth.[42] However,

38. MacLean, "Pascal," 245.
39. Larmore, "Bayle," 673.
40. Bayle, *Historical and Critical Dictionary*, 342.
41. Ibid.
42. Ibid., 343.

he observes that some things we reject as false are as evident as can be. For example, the idea of space is incoherent on any of the interpretations one might give of it. Space cannot consist ultimately of mathematical points, since the addition of extension-less entities to another cannot produce extension. Nor can it consist of extended but indivisible physical points, since anything extended is divisible. Here we find a perfect specimen of Bayle's theme that reason tends inevitably to undermine itself.[43]

According to Larmore, Bayle believed that human reason suffers from the fact that it is more a negative than a positive faculty. That is, it lends itself better to the refutation of opposing views than to the justification of one's own position.[44] According to Bayle, reason is better able to demolish than to build. When reason is instead put to the use of defending some particular position, it tends naturally to undermine itself. Reason is essentially destructive because it excels in uncovering the self-contradiction into which its positive employment inevitably falls.[45]

For Bayle, the logic of suspending judgment is the greatest effort of subtlety that the human mind has been able to accomplish. Suspension of judgment, Bayle says, is the most proper one of all for convincing us that our reason is a path that leads us astray.[46] Notice how this suspension of judgment comes into play in Bayle's treatment of bodies. He contends, for instance, that since the same bodies are sweet to some men and bitter to others, one is right in inferring that they are neither sweet nor bitter in themselves, absolutely speaking. Moreover, we should have no doubts that bodies appear to us to be small or large, round or square, according to the place from which they are viewed. Notice, further, that bodies that seem very small to us appear very large to a fly.[47]

Therefore, regarding bodies, Bayle concludes, only faith can convince us that they exist. For whether bodies exist or not, God is equally able to communicate to us all the thoughts that we have. The fact that our senses furnish us with information about bodies is no proof at all that these bodies exist. Our senses deceive us with regard to all of the corporeal qualities, without excepting the magnitude, size, and motion of bodies. It is not true that anything like hardness, fluidity, cold, heat and the like exist outside our

---

43. Larmore, "Pierre Bayle," 674.
44. Ibid., 673.
45. Bayle, "Historical and Critical," 347.
46. Ibid.
47. Ibid., 348.

minds. And concerning the mysterious matters of the gospel, reason gets us nowhere. Therefore, we ought to be completely satisfied with the light of faith.[48]

The idea that in its positive employment reason is ultimately self-destructive also shaped Bayle's attitude towards the fundamental conflicts between reason and faith which, to use Larmore's words, he doggedly uncovered. If reason were in agreement with itself, we should be more worried that it agrees so poorly with some of our articles of religion. Bayle's skepticism took a form of fideism, intended to confirm his belief in the radical disparity between God's ways and our own.[49] He argued that if we follow reason alone, proportioning all our beliefs to the available evidence, we will end up doing away not only with superstition and barbarism, but eventually with every sort of conviction. For Bayle, man's fate is so bad that the knowledge that delivers him from one evil throws him into another.[50]

It would be correct to think of Bayle as willing to renounce reason in favor of faith. This, of course, seems to take him beyond the other skeptics studied so far, some of whom were willing to use reason for pragmatic purposes rather than for the purposes of delivering truth. However, I think it is safe to conclude that, for the most part, the key skeptical thinkers of this period upheld the importance of maintaining their theological views alongside their epistemological enterprise. Notice, though that none of the skeptical thinkers attempted to give rational arguments for the existence of God. This was so for obvious reasons. The rational faculty could not be trusted to deliver indubitable truth. Instead, they contended that knowledge of God is an epistemological enterprise graspable only by faith.

Descartes

Whereas the skeptics-cum-scientists hitherto observed maintained that belief in God is arrived at by faith, Descartes responded to the skeptics by showing that such a belief is derivable by reason. In his *Meditations* Descartes tries to formulate an epistemological method based on firm unshakeable principles.[51] Descartes began by rejecting every claim he considered doubtful and would accept only those he believed were clear and distinct,

---

48. Ibid., 349.
49. Larmore, "Pierre Bayle," 673.
50. Ibid., 674.
51. Descartes, *Meditations on First Philosophy*, I.

based on a solid foundation. His aim was to see if, by his method of doubt, he could arrive at any infallibly true claims.[52] By systematically rejecting all claims he believed were ill-founded, his meditative project resulted in the discovery of an infallibly true proposition, namely: He doubted, and because of this doubting, it followed that he was thinking. Therefore, it had to be the case that he existed. Since this claim was clear and distinct, it became the foundation for building other infallibly true propositions.[53]

As a "thinking thing," Descartes classified his ideas into three categories: adventitious, factitious and innate.[54] Adventitious ideas originated from impressions caused by perceiving external objects. Factitious ideas were those he believed originated from his imaginations. But innate ideas involved the power of perceiving truth. They originated from his nature.[55] According to Descartes, adventitious ideas were not clear and distinct, and therefore could not be trusted; at least the skeptic would not trust them. Also, factitious ideas could not be trusted owing to the fact that they originated from his imagination.[56] But innate ideas could be trusted because they were clear and distinct to him. Upon these innate ideas, he built what he took to be infallibly true claims.

By positing innate ideas in this way, Descartes arrived at specific conclusions about his religious beliefs. He first of all observed that among his ideas, some of them include those that presented *him*, as a person, to himself; others represented God, corporeal and inanimate things, angels, animals and finally other human beings. As for those ideas that displayed other human beings, animals and angels, Descartes held that they could be fashioned from the ideas he had of himself, of corporeal things and of God, even if no humans, no animals and no angels existed in the world.

As for the ideas of corporeal things, Descartes found nothing in them to prevent them from having originated in him. That is, he found nothing in them to keep them from being factitious. Only the primary qualities of the things they represented could be perceived clearly and distinctly. But one cannot determine whether their secondary qualities were true or false. Moreover, Descartes found no reason to assign to these ideas an author distinct from himself.

52. Ibid.
53. Ibid., II.
54. Ibid., III.
55. Ibid.
56. Ibid.

Thus Descartes was left with the idea of God. By "God" Descartes referred to a certain substance that is infinite, independent, supremely intelligent and supremely powerful, that created him along with everything that exists, assuming something else exists besides him. Here, Descartes asked if there was anything in the idea of God that could have originated factitiously. The more Descartes carefully considered the idea of God, the less possible it seemed that this idea could have arisen from Descartes alone. Therefore, Descartes concludes that God necessarily exists.

Moreover, Descartes found more reality in an infinite substance than in a finite one. For there was no way Descartes could understand that he doubted, that he desired, or more accurately, that he lacked something and was not perfect, unless there was some idea in him of a more perfect being—a being by comparison with which he recognized his defects. Therefore, for Descartes, his perception of the infinite, of God, was somehow prior in him to the perception of the finite, that is, of himself. Descartes writes: "For how could I know that I doubt, desire, or that something is wanting to me, and that I am not wholly perfect, if I possessed no idea of a being more perfect than myself, by comparison of which I knew the deficiencies of my nature?"[57] Thus Descartes concluded that the certainty and truth of every science depended exclusively upon the knowledge of God. Prior to his becoming aware of God, Descartes believed he was incapable of achieving perfect knowledge about anything else. In other words, for Descartes, true science was only possible under supernaturalistic presuppositions.

It would appear, for Descartes, that the mistake the Pyrrhonist made is that he limited the origin of his knowledge to adventitious ideas, and perhaps, to the factitious ideas. If this is true, Descartes would urge the Pyrrhonist to look inward more deeply and discover that the acquisition of infallible truths is possible when we build them on our innate ideas. This seems to be the case when, in the synopsis of his *Meditations*, Descartes maintains that the usefulness of doubting, in general, is located in its ability to deliver us from all prejudice and afford for the epistemologist the easiest route by which his or her mind may withdraw from the senses. Afterward, upon the discovery of truth, the mind will no longer be susceptible to doubt.

Notice that whereas some Pyrrhonists accepted the possibility of such innate truths, they did not believe we could build any sound system of thought on them. For instance, like Descartes, Montaigne believed that first principles are given us by God. But unlike Descartes, Montaigne argued

57. Ibid.

that beyond the first principles, we find "nothing but dreams and smoke."[58] For Montaigne, then, whether or not we have the first principles, certain types of knowledge are beyond our reach. Perhaps such kinds of knowledge are those that could have been derived from those first principles if we had the requisite faculties. Unfortunately we do not, since, according to him, it is doubtful whether we have been provided with all the senses of nature. However, Montaigne does not say what those first principles are. Perhaps, we may guess here, that belief in God's existence is one of them.

Now, the strength of Descartes' method, insofar as it is a response to the New Pyrrhonists, is his claim that we can know some truths clearly and distinctly, such as those relating to our own existence. Descartes claimed that the mere fact that "we doubt" is demonstrable proof of our existence. And this inference is indubitably certain. Notice that whereas Descartes arrived at the certainty of these first principles through rational reflection, Pascal arrived at the certainty of first principles by "the intuitions of the heart." Recall his claim that first principles such as space, time motion and number can be known in this way, and that the knowledge of these first principles is as sure as any of those we get from reasoning. Notice, however, that whereas Descartes believed that we could build clear and distinct truths upon these first principles, Pascal and his skeptical cohorts were doubtful of such an endeavor.

Even more significant, for my purpose here, is what we find in Descartes' attitude toward science and religion. As we have already seen, true science for Descartes is not possible without the knowledge of God. This is somewhat similar to the skeptics' claim, which also contended that knowledge of the first principles is put in place by God. In Descartes, then, we find that his epistemology was clarified through the "findings" of his religion. But Descartes' view, as well as the skeptical position, drew a response from a third group of thinkers, namely, the evidentialists. It is to them that I now turn.

Evidentialism

In order to understand the history of evidentialism, we need to understand, following R. M. Burns, the history of the Liberal Anglicans. They were a relatively small group of English theologians of the mid-century. According to Burns, they came to supremacy in the Anglican Church by the end of the

58. Montaigne, *Apology for Raimond Sebond*, 74.

seventeenth century. But in the 1630s through the 1650s, they were a small despised group of moderates. Unfashionably they preached toleration and ecclesiastical comprehensiveness in an age of religious extremism and dogmatism. Consequently, both fideists and rationalists despised them.[59]

In terms of epistemology, the Liberal Anglicans' position can be formulated as a critique of the skeptic's position, as we shall see below. More broadly, however, their view was as much a response to the Cartesian rationalists as it was to the Pyrrhonists. Moreover, Burns argues that they also tried to find a middle ground between the Pyrrhonists and the Cartesians.[60] But despite their critiques of skepticism and rationalism, their religious beliefs and their scientific enterprise were not mutually exclusive.

The Liberal Anglicans broke with the tendency to embrace fideism as the basis of belief. At the root of both Catholic and Protestant fideism, such as those we find in Luther and Calvin, for example, was the notion that authentic faith must be characterized by an absolute, flawless, infallible certitude—analogous to philosophical certitude. The Liberal Anglicans denied this assumption. They argued that absolute certitude belongs to God alone.[61] Therefore, it was entirely appropriate and reasonable for human beings to allow their minds to rest in well-grounded probability judgments in the sphere of religious belief. All the leading writers of this school repeatedly expound, with reference to theological issues, that theory of probability judgments characteristic of the English scientists.[62]

Against their Cartesian opponents, they asserted that not even mathematical propositions can be accepted with absolute confidence. This is because of the known possibility of error in computation.[63] Apart from mathematical certainties, metaphysical certainties and physical certainties, the highest kind of certainty of which humans were capable was "practical" or "moral" certainty. The Liberal Anglicans were therefore the first writers in English to use this term as well as the phrase "beyond reasonable doubt." It was a phrase that was later borrowed by scientists and eighteenth-century legal theorists.[64]

---

59. Ibid., 38.
60. Ibid., 19–20.
61. Ibid., 40.
62. Ibid.
63. Ibid.
64. Ibid.

In reference to theological issues the Liberal Anglicans urged that we should not expect a personal, loving God, desiring a free response of love from his creatures, to provide them with coercive proof of his reality.[65] By coercive proof I think Burns refers to the attempt to formulate deductive arguments of the sort that purport to provide compelling proofs for the existence of God. Moral (or practical) certainty is the result of the balancing of the probabilities and will therefore not be obtained without serious effort. A complex, sustained activity of carefully weighing the evidence (for and against God's existence) may be required in order to produce moral certainty in a given sphere. But only the man ready to believe will work patiently through the evidence with adequately open and responsive attitudes.[66]

Burns then points out that the above-mentioned sort of probability that plays a central role in Liberal Anglican theology is identical to that found in the work of the English scientists. Moreover, he argues, it would seem a reasonable hypothesis that the latter was derived from the former.[67] Also, a study of the biographical facts about the leading personalities of these two movements shows that there was a connection between them, and that it was a deep one. This is because these theologians and scientists were in the closest of contacts with one another. And many of them were equally distinguished in both the theological and scientific spheres.[68]

In fact, Burns contends, no one who reads carefully the works of men such as Boyle can fail to recognize the profound interpenetration of the religious and scientific aspects of their thought. An unprejudiced reading of the writings of these men reveals only repeated proof of a thoroughgoing harmony between the two aspects of their thought, namely, the scientific and the religious aspect.[69] Burns finally concludes here that not only was there harmony, but a vital interdependence and symbiosis between the theistic convictions of these men and their scientific outlook.[70]

But who were the English scientists? Burns contends that they were the leading lights and thinkers of their age. They were founders of the theological tradition which produced the emphasis on miracles. But they were also prominently involved in the development of the scientific outlook.

65. Ibid., 41.
66. Ibid., 41–42.
67. Ibid., 42.
68. Ibid.
69. Ibid., 43.
70. Ibid., 43–44.

They included thinkers like Bishop John Wilkins, founder of the Royal Society, Sir Robert Boyle, Sir Isaac Newton and John Locke.[71] They were also variously called "the evidentialists,"[72] "the empiricists"[73] and "the orthodox theologians."[74]

Their philosophical assumption was not simply a response to the Pyrrhonistic skepticism that characterized the Roman Catholic Church; it was also an attempt to strike a middle ground between that very skepticism, and the rationalism of Descartes.[75] According to Burns, both the skeptics and the rationalists were declared guilty, by the English scientists, of bringing unwarranted *a priori* assumptions to their investigation of experience. These assumptions warped their capacity for discovering truth, and the root cause of this mistake was alleged to be an extravagant overconfidence in the powers of the human intellect.[76]

To be sure, if this charge is aimed at the rationalists, perhaps it is plausible. However, it appears implausible if aimed at the fideists for at least one reason: the fideists demonstrated little or no confidence in the powers of the human intellect. If anything, they were ready to believe religious postulates but only insofar as such postulates were based on faith.

However, Burns points out that the evidentialists' notion of scientific method firmly precluded any notion of a methodological *a priori*. That is, they were strongly opposed to laying down any rigid rules for scientific research. Rather, they stressed that types of explanation and methods of discovery must always remain flexible in order to accommodate the diversities of phenomena.[77]

Burns also observes that the English scientists emphasized the weakness of the human intellect. Robert Boyle, for example, had enthusiasm for the labors of the intellect. According to Burns, Boyle's belief in the intellect's ability to attain truth cannot be questioned. But Boyle manages to combine this positive attitude with constant expressions of extreme epistemological diffidence. Burns, as we shall see, correctly interprets Boyle's comments by observing that scientific knowledge presents us only with "respective and

71. Ibid., 14.
72. Ibid., 50.
73. Ibid., 19.
74. Ibid., 14.
75. Ibid., 19–20.
76. Ibid., 15–16.
77. Ibid., 15.

probationary truths" and that theories should not be accepted as true until the most exhaustive analysis and experimentation has taken place.[78]

In the following survey, I will outline the religious-cum-scientific views of four of the leading thinkers of this group, namely, John Wilkins, Robert Boyle, Isaac Newton and John Locke. I selected John Wilkins because he was the founder of the Royal Society.[79] And Robert Boyle sponsored the scientific-cum-theological lectures that, in a way, propelled this society into the limelight of scientific thought, lectures which subsequent thinkers called "Boyle's Lectures." Also, I selected Isaac Newton because of his major influence and impact on the scientific community to this day. Finally, I selected John Locke because the deists picked their cue from him in their attempts to place reason over revelation. Also, in his objection to miracles, it seems David Hume borrowed quite substantially from John Locke's ideas, as Burns rightly contends.[80]

Let me begin with John Wilkins. According to Popkin, Wilkins became a leading advocate of the New Science, which started with the Copernican Revolution, embraced by Galileo, Gassendi, Descartes and Pascal.[81] Popkin observes that Wilkins was the first to popularize Galileo's work in England, and also encouraged the work of Boyle and Hooke. For Wilkins and his theological cohorts, the study of nature in mechanistic terms enhanced one's knowledge, understanding and appreciation of God.[82]

In Wilkins's *Of the Principles and Duties of Natural Religion*, first published in 1734, Wilkins proposed what he called foundational principles indispensable for any discussions with critical thinkers concerning the first bases for religion.[83] The first of these is his claim that there are some things which are equally true and certain in themselves, but are not yet capable of the same kind or degree of evidence to us.[84] For example, that there was such a man as King Henry VIII or that there are such places as America or China are claims we get only from the testimony of others, and from human traditions.[85] But mathematical propositions, such as the claim that a

78. Ibid.
79. Popkin, "Skepticism," 11.
80. Burns, *Great Debate*, 63.
81. Popkin, "Skepticism," 11.
82. Ibid., 11–12.
83. Wilkins, *Of the Principles and Duties*, 38.
84. Ibid., 22.
85. Ibid., 22–23.

triangle necessarily has three sides, require a different kind of proof. Given this possibility nothing can be more irrational than for a man to doubt or deny the truth of anything simply because it cannot be established by particular kinds of proofs of which the nature of such a thing is not capable.[86]

A second principle Wilkins suggests is that things of several kinds may admit and require several sorts of proofs, all of which may be good in their own kind.[87] This is because according to the diverse nature of things, so must the evidences for them be. To fail to acknowledge this, in Wilkins's opinion, is an argument of an "undisciplined wit." For example, mathematical conclusions can be demonstrated by the clearest and most unquestionable proofs. But it would be unreasonable to expect similar proofs in moral issues.[88] This is because moral issues do not belong to the same category as mathematical truths. Rather, they depend upon circumstances, and are therefore incapable of such kind of demonstrative proofs. Moreover, Wilkins argues that this being the case, a similar demonstration should not be expected about divine things or matters of facts concerning times, places and actions.[89]

Wilkins then states his third principle as follows: When a thing is capable of good proof in any kind, we should be satisfied with the best evidence for it, which that kind of thing will bear, and beyond which better evidence could not be expected supposing it were true.[90] According to Wilkins, people ought not to expect either sensible proof, or demonstration for such matters as are not capable of such proofs, supposing them to be true. Otherwise, we will be unable to assent to or believe anything except that which has the highest evidence; and we will look upon all other things as uncertain, doubtful, and completely exclude them from all possibility of being known—including things whose existence we are usually unquestionably sure of but whose natures we are unable to explain.[91] For example we do not doubt whether there be such things as motion, sensation and continuity of bodies. But these things are commonly esteemed inexplicable. Thus, our inability to see to the bottom of things and to give a distinct

---

86. Ibid., 23.
87. Ibid.
88. Ibid., 23–24.
89. Ibid., 24.
90. Ibid.
91. Ibid., 25–26.

account of the nature and manner of them can be no sufficient cause to doubt their being.[92]

But Wilkins's contention here, admittedly, begs the question against the skeptic, for the skeptic says we ought to doubt these very things. However, according to Wilkins, if we doubt these things, it will be impossible to live our normal daily lives, or to carry out our day to day activities. I will return to this later.

Wilkins then advances a fourth principle—namely, the human mind may and must give a firm assent to some things, without any kind of hesitation or doubt of the contrary, where the evidences for such things are still not so infallible as to leave room for the possibility the thing may be otherwise.[93] That is, there may be an indubitable certainty where there is not an infallible certainty. For the intent and purpose of conducting our day-to-day lives, Wilkins thinks that indubitable certainty may serve us just as well as infallible certainty.[94]

For example, Wilkins asks: Who is so skeptical as to question whether the sun will rise in the east rather than in the west, or whether it will rise at all, because the contrary is not impossible and does not entail a contradiction?[95] But it is possible that the sun may not rise. The implication here is that evidence from custom, though indubitable, is not infallible. By contrast, Descartes seemed to think that evidence from custom is dubitable. Moreover, Hume also contended that just because the sun has always, in the past, risen from the east and set in the west is no proof that it will do so the next day. Wilkins subscribed to this sort of indubitability for pragmatic purposes, namely, to be able to live our normal day to day lives, which, surprisingly, is quite similar to the skeptic's position, as we shall see below.

According to Wilkins, skeptics in religion make the mistake of suspending their assent merely because some arguments for it do not so infallibly establish its truth. But a person who will cherish any real doubts according to the mere possibility of things will not be able to determine himself to the belief or practice of anything. Such a person will not stay indoors for fear the house shall fall on him. He will not go out, lest the next man that meets him should kill him; for that is also possible. Thus the

92. Ibid., 26–27.
93. Ibid., 27.
94. Ibid.
95. Ibid., 27–28.

skeptic is sure to be deceived in very many things where it is possible he may be deceived.[96]

Notice, though, that the skeptics maintained that belief and practice can be separated: one can follow "appearances" rather than adopt belief. However, this sort of recourse to follow appearance is as much a stance taken for pragmatic value as the stance Wilkins would have us take. In other words, I contend here that the skeptic chooses to follow appearance because it seems to have worked for him, for the most part, in the past. But the logical conclusion following the skeptic's view on the *nature* of things, as Wilkins sees it, is that the skeptic will be unable to "determine himself to the practice of anything." That is, the skeptic will be unable to carry out his normal day to day life.

Recall my contention above that the skeptic follows appearances for pragmatic purposes specifically because following appearances in this way has worked, for the most part, for the skeptics' normal day to day life. Interestingly, this is the very thing that Wilkins is urging us to do in his fourth principle, namely: to assent to things where the evidences for such things are still not so infallible, allowing for the possibility the thing may be otherwise. Thus, in the final analysis, both the skeptics and Wilkins end up adopting the same stand with regard to the issue of custom. It is an assent that comes from the realization that though the uniformity of nature is not guaranteed with absolute certainty, it is indubitable to the extent that it has always worked in the past.

Wilkins' fifth principle states that it is sufficient that matters of faith and religion be propounded in such a way as to render them credible such that an honest and teachable man may willingly and safely assent to them; and that according to the rules of prudence, such a person may be justified in making such an assent.[97] However, Wilkins notes that it is neither necessary nor convenient, that such matters be established by the sort of cogent pieces of evidence that necessitate assent; for this would not leave any place for the virtue of believing, or the freedom of our obedience. It would not even leave any ground for reward or punishment. It would not be thankworthy for a man to believe that which of necessity he must believe, and cannot otherwise choose. This is because rewards and punishments properly belong to free actions rather than to necessary actions. There is no more reason to reward a man for believing that four is more than three,

---

96. Ibid., 29.
97. Ibid., 30.

than for being hungry or sleepy, because these do not proceed from choice but from natural necessity.[98]

Is Wilkins merely claiming that beliefs in matters of faith are rationally permissible? If he is then we must admit that it is a fairly weak claim. But to answer this question it is best to consider this claim in the context of Wilkins's overall claim about assenting to religious claims. As we shall see below, Wilkins is anticipating the sort of "safe" assent suggested by Pascal's wager. In other words, the recourse to safeness is not motivated by the fear of committing an intellectual blunder. Rather, it is a free moral choice made after considering the consequences that follow the choice of not assenting to just this kind of faith. Properly construed, therefore, it is as rational as it is obligatory. It strikes a middle ground between assent that is merely rationally permissible on the one hand and assent that seems necessary and compelling on the other. This middle ground of assent is taken, as we shall see, for the sake of one's future well-being.

According to Wilkins, this principle will appear unquestionable, and the deductions from them demonstrable, to anyone careful enough to preserve his or her mind free from prejudice. There would be little reason for Scripture to magnify the grace of faith as being a great virtue acceptable to God if every person were necessitated to it. Therefore, God is pleased to propose these matters of belief such that we give some testimony to our teachable dispositions, and of our obedience to them.[99]

Sixth, Wilkins suggests that when there is no evident certainty to take away all kind of doubting, we must make an equal and impartial judgment that inclines to the greater probabilities.[100] This happens in ordinary affairs where human beings guide their actions by this rule. That is, they incline themselves to that which is most probable and likely when they cannot attain to any clear unquestionable certainty. Thus, suppose that some of the principles of religion should not seem evident and demonstrable. Here, they must still assent to the greater probability. They should seriously attend to, and consider the evidence proposed to them in order to take a just estimate of it.[101]

Seventh, Wilkins suggests that if in any matter under consideration the probabilities on both sides appear equal, even in this case people are

---

98. Ibid., 30–31.
99. Ibid., 31–32.
100. Ibid., 34.
101. Ibid., 35–36.

obliged to order their actions in favor of that side which appears to be most safe and advantageous for their own interests.[102] To demonstrate the importance of this principle, Wilkins uses it, in a manner reminiscent of Pascal's wager, to urge us to "see" the safety in believing in the existence of Deity.

If, for example, the probabilities on both sides are equal, one must ask the question: on what side lies the danger of mistaking? If on the one side, all the inconveniences of believing will be such that we are tied to needless restraints during this short time of our lives, then our error shall die with us and we will not have to account for our mistake. But, on the other side, if there should be a Deity, we must expect vengeance and indignation from him to those who have made it their business to banish him out of the world.[103]

In light of these seven principles, Wilkins argues that affirming the existence of God ought to be seen as a rational alternative. But it is rational not in a merely permissible way; it is rational in some obligatory way, since, according to Wilkins, failing to make the choice comes with painful consequences. Here, we see that among other possibilities, the likelihood that God exists is a claim evidenced by the fact that there seems to be universal consent to it among the world's different nations.[104] Also, different nations have records depicting recollections about how the universe was made. Moreover, that the universe was caused is a claim consistent with the principle that every event must have a cause. According to Wilkins the cause of the universe is God. Therefore, the belief that God exists is a belief that can be assented to both from rational and empirical evidence.[105] Notice, though, that Wilkins provides no intermediate premises allowing him to infer that the cause of the universe is God from the premise that every event must have a cause. Either he sees no need for such intermediate premises, or he assumes the reader will supply them.

Now, Robert Boyle's argument was somewhat different from that of Wilkins, though comparisons could be drawn between them. Boyle observed that we are sometimes confronted by things above reason. According to Boyle, things above reason are not false or absurd. They are such that the intellect sees sufficient cause to assent to them owing to experience, authentic testimony from others, or mathematical demonstration.

---

102. Ibid., 37.
103. Ibid., 97.
104. Ibid., 41.
105. Ibid., 62.

However, once we are conversant with them, the intellect finds itself unable to sufficiently comprehend them, or unable to reconcile them with some other thing we are persuaded to be a truth.[106]

Boyle called these "things above reason" and categorized them into three different classes: incomprehensible, inexplicable and unsociable.[107] For Boyle, incomprehensible things are those whose natures are not distinctly and adequately comprehensible to us. For example, from the consideration of nature, we may know that God exists, and we may also know what God is not. But though one may know that God exists, it is impossible for one to understand God thoroughly.[108]

Inexplicable things consist of things we cannot deny to be true, but cannot clearly and satisfactorily understand how they can be such as we acknowledge them to be. For example, we cannot know how matter can be infinitely divisible. Mathematical demonstrations assure us that this is so. But we are unable to clearly conceive how this should be possible.[109]

Finally, unsociable things consist of those to which the rules, axioms and notions by which we judge the truth and falsehood of ordinary things seem not to agree. They have something belonging to them that cannot be reconciled with some very manifest or acknowledged truth. Take the case of two lines of different lengths, namely, two feet and one foot. These are infinitely divisible as shown in geometry. But this results in interesting implications; for either a line one foot long remains divisible into as many parts as a line two feet long, or else a line two feet long remains divisible into as many parts as a number of parts greater than the infinite.[110]

Of course this sounds bizarre and awkward. But upon closer scrutiny, we must admit that this claim follows logically. Boyle's implication here is that if any line whatever is infinitely divisible, then it matters not what length of a line one deals with, for all are equally infinitely divisible. Thus, a one-foot line is as infinitely divisible into as many parts as a two foot line. And even if one is confronted by a line that can be divided into parts greater than an infinite number of parts, call it line ∞, a two-foot line is just as infinitely divisible as line ∞!

---

106. Boyle, "Things above Reason," in *Works*, 9:366.
107. Ibid., 367.
108. Ibid.
109. Ibid.
110. Ibid., 367–68.

Boyle concludes that this reasoning enables us to see that we must be reduced either to reject its inferences legitimately drawn from granted truths, or admit conclusions which will appear absurd. Therefore, there may be things that surpass our reason such that they are not to be evaluated by the same standards and rules by which we judge ordinary things. This is the elusive nature of "things above reason," which Boyle also called "privileged things."[111] What Boyle is trying to show here is the fact that logic can sometimes lead us to see that some postulates we accept as true, when scrutinized further, exhibit mysterious features incomprehensible to the very logic that located them in the first place.

Boyle then draws our attention to the following objection: it is probable that the obscurities attending privileged things will be cleared in the future, given the great progress made in science.[112] According to Boyle, this objection has two problems. First, it is grounded upon hope, or at most, a conjecture about which we need not trouble ourselves until new discoveries about the things in question engage us to a new consideration of them. Moreover, Boyle does not expect that we will solve all metaphysical difficulties in which neither matters of fact, nor hypothesis of subordinate parts of learning avail much. Finally, even if our inquisitiveness may, in the future, extricate some of those difficulties hitherto perplexing to philosophers, it is possible that this may still lead us to discover new difficulties more capable of baffling human understanding than the previous ones.[113]

Boyle argues that reason operates according to certain notions or ideas, and certain axioms and propositions. And when we say that a thing of a given sort is consonant with reason, we mean that it is immediately or mediately deducible from reason, or at least consistent with it. But when we say it is repugnant to reason, we mean it is contradictory to one or other of those standard notions or rules. And if these rules and notions are such that they are abstracted only from finite things, they may prove useless or deceitful to us when we stretch them beyond their measure and apply them to the infinite God, or to things that involve infiniteness either in multitude, magnitude or littleness.[114]

Also, as we shall see below, Robert Boyle does not think that faith and reason are mutually exclusive. Christianity, Boyle argues, has not reduced

111. Ibid., 369.
112. Ibid.
113. Ibid., 373–74.
114. Ibid., 375.

God to a mere postulate. It not only argues philosophically for the existence of a deity. It has "peculiar historical proofs" as well. The historical proofs that Boyle has in mind here are "the miracles performed by Christ and his followers." According to Boyle, if these miracles are well stated, they not only prove the rest of Christianity. They will also show that God caused them.[115] Boyle does not quite explicate his understanding of what counts as well stated claims. At any rate, he proceeds, much later, to provide an argument for the possibility of miracles, quite similar to those we encountered in the first chapter.

To begin with, Boyle claims that natural theology is enough to evince the existence of Deity. Consider, for instance, that many of the ancient philosophers discovered and confessed that God exists. However, Boyle admits that if such a being exists, it is reasonable to see that there may be many things about his nature that are beyond the grasp of reason. This leads us to see that there may be some things about God's nature that have no perfect analogy with inferior beings[116]—things that could not be discovered by the light of reason. Such things can only be discovered by divine revelation. And the person who believes divine writings of this sort would not be renouncing his reason. Instead he would be allowing his reason to be the pupil of an "Omniscient Infallible Instructor, who can teach him things that his reason cannot."[117] To buttress his claim, Boyle draws from Descartes and Galileo as follows: If both mathematicians such as Descartes and Galileo find themselves forced to confess that not only their reason but also the entire scope of human reason may be confused about natural objects such as quantity, why should we think we can find ourselves able to understand fully and clearly the subject concerning the attributes of God?[118]

To clarify his contention further, Boyle draws distinctions between doctrines that seem repugnant to the general well-weighed rules of reason, and those that disagree with axioms which, when established, were not supposed to be applied to that doctrine. According to Boyle, rules are of great use when confined to things on which the rules themselves are meant to be used. But those rules are not meant to overthrow divine doctrines that do not seem consistent with them. This is because the framers of those rules generally built them upon the observations they made of natural and moral

---

115. Boyle, "Reconciling," 246.
116. Ibid., 248.
117. Ibid., 249.
118. Ibid., 251.

things. Therefore, it is not impossible that there may be rules which will hold in all inferior beings for which they were made, but which will fail to apply to God and to divine matters not taken into consideration when the rules were framed.[119]

Suppose, Boyle continues, we grant that God is the author of the universe and the free establisher of the laws of motion. We must acknowledge that by changing these laws of motion, God may invalidate most, if not all, the axioms and theorems of natural philosophy.[120] For example, it is a rule in natural philosophy that necessary causes always do as much as possible. But if God chooses to withdraw his power from the operation of flames, it will not follow that fire must necessarily burn Daniel's three companions or their clothes. Also, that a dead person cannot be brought back to life has been, in all ages, a doctrine of mere philosophers. And this is true according to the course of nature. In fact, it is unreasonable to believe a miraculous effect when attributed only to a mere physical agent. But the same thing may reasonably be believed when ascribed to God or to agents assisted with his absolute or supernatural power.[121] Boyle argues how making one's belief irrational by holding that the things believed cannot be true according to the course of nature does not seem to be of much help. Instead, one must show either that those things are impossible even with respect to God's power to which they are ascribed, or that the records available remain insufficient to engender belief in the nature of a testimony.[122]

These considerations lead Boyle to grant that physically speaking, it is impossible that a virgin should bring forth a child miraculously without any form of intercourse with a man. But this does not signify any more than the claim that such a thing cannot happen according to the course of nature. However, when we speak "absolutely and indefinitely," that is, without confining the effect to mere physical agents, we may safely conclude the following: philosophy does not pronounce it impossible that the sort of virgin described above should be a mother. This is because there is no reason why the author of nature should be confined to the ways of working of dependent finite agents.[123]

---

119. Ibid.
120. Ibid.
121. Ibid., 252.
122. Ibid.
123. Ibid., 253.

Jan Wojcik summarizes Boyle's position in the following way: Boyle contended that the Christian should not withhold assent from the truths of revelation simply because they are mysterious. The fact of the matter is, nature itself is filled with mysteries. If we acknowledge causality in the natural world, even without understanding it fully, we should also acknowledge supernatural causality, even when we do not have a full comprehension of it.[124]

Thus, when dealing with things above reason, and deciding whether or not we should assent to propositions about such things, Boyle suggests six principles he believes we should follow. First, he suggests that we must not admit any assertions about privileged things without proofs, sufficient in their kind, to evince them.[125] According to Boyle, privileged things have such peculiar affections and attributes that demand the employment of notions and rules congruous to their particular conditions. We may well grant in general that a privileged thing may have some attribute belonging to it that is still above reason.[126]

Second, Boyle suggests that we must not be hasty to frame negatives about privileged things, or to reject propositions or explications concerning them as if they were absurd or impossible.[127] Boyle maintains that it is unreasonable to be quick to resolve upon negative propositions about things which we ourselves acknowledge to be above the reach of human reason. Our own sharing in the disability of penetrating such abstruse things should keep us from being over-confident—that we may also not be mistaken—and incline us to tolerate other people's opinions about matters in which we only have an opinion.[128]

Third, Boyle suggests that a matter of fact or other truth about privileged things being proved by arguments competent in their kind ought not to be denied merely because we cannot explain what appears to be mysterious about them.[129] For example, in some cases we do not clearly and distinctly understand how the property of a subject belongs to that subject, or performs its operations; as exemplified by the way the mind exercises

---

124. Wojcik, "Due Degree," 372.
125. Boyle, "Advice," 396.
126. Ibid.
127. Ibid., 400.
128. Ibid., 400–401.
129. Ibid., 402.

power over the human body, or by the way the understanding and the will act upon one another. All these have not been intelligently explained.[130]

Fourth, Boyle suggests that when dealing with privileged subjects, we are not bound always to deem everything false that seems to thwart some received dictate of reason.[131] Suppose, for example, that some positive dictates of reason contain limited truths. Suppose, further, that they come to be unduly extended to privileged things. It may very possibly happen that a thing which appears false may be really true, owing to the fact that its truth is limited, and assuming it is judged by its congruity to one of those limited but respective dictates of reason.

Fifth, Boyle suggests that where privileged things are concerned, we are not always bound to reject everything as false that we know not how to reconcile with some thing that is true.[132] Boyle observes that the reason why we judge things to be repugnant is that the notions or ideas we have of them seem to us inconsistent. That is, if either of these notions are wrongly framed or judged by an unfit rule, we may think those propositions to be contradictory that are really not contradictory.[133]

Sixth, Boyle suggests that in privileged things we ought not always to condemn that opinion which is liable to ill consequences and encumbered with great inconveniencies, provided the positive proofs of it be sufficient in their kind.[134] These six suggestions allow Boyle to include claims about the supernatural in his scientific enterprise.

Thus in Boyle's view there is no reason to doubt that anyone assenting to belief in God is acting rationally. In fact, belief in the existence of such a being was seen as rational, in Boyle's view. For example, in *The Metaphysical Foundations of Modern Science* Edwin Arthur Burtt quotes Boyle's version of the design argument as follows: When an intelligent and unprejudiced person considers the vast beauty and regular motion of the solar system as well as the structure of animals and plants, he or she may justly conclude, as a rational entity, that a supremely powerful, wise and good author formed this system.[135]

---

130. Ibid., 403.
131. Ibid., 406.
132. Ibid., 414.
133. Ibid., 415.
134. Ibid., 421.
135. Burtt, *Metaphysical Foundations*, 189.

From Robert Boyle, we now move to Isaac Newton. Like that of Boyle, Newton's scientific method did not simply presuppose the supernatural; it assented to the supernatural. For instance, in one of his writings, Newton observes that the primary planets revolve around the sun in circles concentric with the sun, "and with motions directed toward the same parts and almost in the same plane." Newton observes that ten moons revolve about Earth, Jupiter and Saturn in circles concentric with these planets, with the same direction of motion, and nearly in the planes of the orbits of those motions.[136] Newton then observes that one must not think that mere mechanical causes could produce so many regular motions, specifically because the comets range over all parts of the heavens.[137] According to Newton, blind metaphysical necessity, which is certainly the same always and everywhere, fails to account for such a variety of things.[138] Rather, this most beautiful system of the sun, planets and comets could only have been caused by the counsel and dominion of an intelligent and powerful Being, namely, God.[139]

Newton adds that the Supreme God exists necessarily. And by the same necessity, God exists always and everywhere. However, although we have ideas of God's attributes, Newton holds that we really have no idea of the substance of God. In fact, we really do not have an idea of what the real substance of anything is.[140] This fact remains because when dealing with bodies, we countenance only their primary and secondary qualities (i.e., solidity, shape, volume and colors). However, their inward substances and natures remain cognitively inaccessible to us.[141]

How does Newton arrive at the belief that God exists? Newton argues that we know God only by what he has created.[142] To show exactly what he means Newton draws our attention to the cosmic order of things. Take, for instance, the material elements of the sun, the planets and those of the universe in general. Newton observes that these elements divide themselves into different sorts. Some of them divide themselves in such a way that they compose a shining body and thus make a sun. Others would

136. Newton, "God," 42.
137. Ibid.
138. Ibid., 44.
139. Ibid., 42.
140. Ibid., 44.
141. Ibid.
142. ibid.

compose themselves and form other little bodies like planets and so forth. Suppose the sun at first were an opaque body like the planets; or suppose the planets initially were lucid bodies like the sun. According to Newton, natural causes cannot explain how the sun alone could be changed into a shining body while the planets all continue as opaque bodies. And if we go by the second supposition, natural causes cannot explain how the initially lucid bodies would be changed into opaque ones while the sun remains unchanged.[143]

Newton's conclusion here is that all these can happen only by the power of a voluntary agent. According to Newton, the power which placed the sun and the planets in their actual places could not have been a blind one "without contrivance or design."[144] Had this been so, the sun would have been a body of the same kind with Saturn, Jupiter, and Earth, that is, without light and heat. Newton argues that the only reason why "there is one body in our system qualified to give light and heat to all the rest" is this: the Author of the system thought it convenient.[145] Consider his argument: The motions of the planets could not have arisen from natural causes alone. God caused them. Consider, for example, that comets move in all manner of ways as they descend into the region of planets. Sometimes they go in tandem with the planets, and sometimes they go contrary to the planets, and still, at other times, they go perpendicularly to the planets. Clearly, no natural cause could determine all the planets to move the same way and in the same plane without any serious variation. This reality must have been the work of divine counsel.[146]

Moreover, for Newton, no natural cause could give the planets just those degrees of velocity in proportion to their distance from the sun and other central bodies, which were requisite to make them move in such concentric orbs about those bodies.[147] Rather, Newton believes that in order to make a system like this with all its motions, it would require a cause that understood and compared together the quantities of matter in the several bodies of the sun and the planets and the gravitating powers resulting from thence. The cause would also have to understand the several distances of the primary planets from the sun and of the secondary ones from Saturn,

---

143. Newton, "Four Letters," 47.
144. Ibid.
145. Ibid.
146. Ibid., 47–48.
147. Ibid., 48.

Jupiter, and Earth, and the velocities with which these planets could revolve about those quantities of matter in the central bodies.[148]

Thus for Newton, God's design is the best explanation for the complexity seen in the cosmic order. God, in the beginning, formed matter in solid, massy, hard, impenetrable, movable particles, of different sizes and figures, of different properties, and in different proportions to space such that they were most conducive for the end for which he formed them.[149] It pleased God to set all these in order. Therefore, it is unphilosophical to seek for any other origin of the world, or even to pretend that it arose from chaos by the mere laws of nature. However, once formed in this way, it may continue by those laws for years.[150]

The upshot of all this for Newton is that a Being exists who made all things, who has all things in his power and who should therefore be feared. All humans must see their need for God in the following way: humans must acknowledge on infinite, eternal, omniscient, and omnipotent creator of all things who remains most wise, just, good and holy. Humans must love, fear and honor him. They must trust in him, pray to him, thank him, praise him, hallow his name, obey his commandments, and consecrate times for his service.[151]

Turning to John Locke we find in him a thinker who accepted the supernatural as a reasonable way of formulating his epistemology. In his *Essay concerning Human Understanding* Locke's supernaturalism is seen when, first, he draws distinctions between faith and reason. He defines reason as the discovery of the certainty or probability of truths which the mind apprehends through deductions made from ideas it acquires through the use of its natural faculties. He then defines faith as the assent to any proposition made upon the credit of the proposer as coming from God in some extraordinary way of communication, namely, through revelation.[152]

Second, Locke distinguishes between propositions that are according to reason, those that are above reason and those that are contrary to reason. Propositions according to reason are those whose truth we can discover by examining and tracing ideas we have from sensation and reflection; and by natural deduction we find them to be true or probable. Propositions above

---

148. Ibid.
149. Newton, "Universal Design," 175.
150. Ibid., 177.
151. Ibid., 65.
152. Locke, *Essay concerning Human Understanding*, IV. XVIII, 2.

reason are those whose truth or probability we cannot by reason derive from those principles. And propositions contrary to reason are those inconsistent with or irreconcilable to our clear and distinct ideas.[153]

What does this mean for faith? Locke argues that faith can never convince of anything that contradicts our knowledge; for we cannot have any assurance of the truth of faith being a divine revelation greater than our knowledge, though it is founded on the testimony of God who cannot lie revealing any proposition to us. The whole strength of the certainty depends upon our knowledge that God revealed it. But in this case, the proposition supposedly revealed contradicts our knowledge of reason. Thus it will always face the objection that we cannot tell how to conceive that the proposition in question came from God, which if accepted as true, must overturn all the principles and foundations of knowledge God has given us. Therefore, in all things where we have clear evidence from our ideas, reason is the proper judge. Revelation confirms the dictates of reason by agreeing with reason. However, revelation cannot invalidate the decrees of reason.[154]

Also, Locke continues, there are many things in which we have very imperfect notions, or none at all. And there are others of whose past, present or future existence we can have no knowledge at all by the natural use of our faculties. These lie beyond the discovery of our natural faculties. And since they are above reason, they are the proper matters of faith when revealed.[155]

Just the same, in giving us the light of reason, God has not thereby tied up his own hands from affording us, when he thinks fit, the light of revelation in any of those matters in which our natural faculties are able to give a proper determination. Therefore, according to Locke, where God has been pleased to give revelation, it must be carried against the probable conjectures of reason. Since the mind is not certain of the truth of what it does not evidently know, and instead yields to those probabilities that appear in those truths, it is bound to give up its assent to the kind of testimony that comes from an infallible God, one who cannot deceive. Nevertheless, it still belongs to reason to judge the truth of any given revelation. Indeed, if anything purportedly coming by revelation is contrary to the plain principles of reason, then here reason must be hearkened to.[156]

153. Ibid., IV. XVII, 23.
154. Ibid., IV. XVIII, 5–6.
155. Ibid., IV. XVIII, 7.
156. Ibid., IV. XVIII, 8.

Locke then considers the following case: suppose we are faced with matters in which the mind has uncertain evidence and is persuaded of their truth only upon probable grounds. And suppose these matters still admit a possibility of the contrary to be true, without doing violence to the certain evidence of its knowledge, and overturning the principles of all reason. Locke suggests that in such probable propositions an evident revelation ought to determine our assent, even against probability. In certain instances, where the principles of reason may not confirm whether a proposition is true or false, revelation, as another principle of truth may establish such truths. Thus here it is a matter of faith and is also above reason; for reason, in this matter, was able to reach no higher than probability. Therefore faith gave the determination where reason came short; and revelation uncovered on which side the truth lay.[157]

By arguing in this way Locke is satisfied that faith can come this far in matters of epistemology without doing violence or hindrance to reason. Here reason is not injured or disturbed, but is assisted and improved by new discoveries of truth, coming from the eternal foundation of knowledge. After all, whatever God has revealed is certainly true and no doubt can be made of it. But whether it be a divine revelation or not, reason must judge; for reason cannot permit the mind to reject a greater evidence to embrace what is less evident. In fact, the greatest evidence that any traditional revelation is of divine origin is the requirement that it be as clear and as certain as the principles of reason. Anything that is of divine revelation ought to overrule all our opinions, prejudices, and interest and has a right to be received with full assent. This does not shake the foundation of reason. Rather, it leaves us the use of our faculties for which they were given us.[158]

Locke strongly contends that the existence of God is the most obvious truth that reason discovers.[159] Belief in God in this way permits Locke to argue for the possibility and occurrence of miracles. He sees miracles as the credentials of a messenger delivering the precepts of a divine religion. Therefore miracles have no place except upon the supposition of the existence of God. Locke maintains here that divine revelation is attested to by miracles.[160] That is, miracles prove that God delivered the revelation in question.

157. Ibid., IV. XVIII, 9.
158. Ibid., IV. XVIII, 10.
159. Ibid., VI. X, 1.
160. Locke, *Reasonableness of Christianity*, 80.

Having made this contention, Locke further observes that the heathen world believed in an infinite and uncertain jumble of deities, fables and worship. But their doctrines had no room for divine attestation of one deity against the rest. They were at liberty in their worship. And none of their divinities pretended to be the only true God. Therefore, none of the deities could be supposed in the pagan scheme to make use of miracles to establish his worship alone or to abolish that of the other deity. Much less, was there use of miracles to confirm any articles of faith. This is because none of them had such articles to propose as necessary to be believed by their votaries.[161]

According to Locke, what is claimed of Zoroaster or Brahma is so obscure and manifestly fabulous that no account can be made of it. Only three figures of history came in the name of one true God: Moses, Jesus and Mohammed. And when we consider Mohammed, he never pretended to perform any miracles for the vouching of his mission, since he had no miracles to produce. The only revelations that come attested by miracles are those of Moses and Christ, and they confirm each other. Therefore, the business of miracles, as Locke sees it, provides us with no difficulty. This means that the most scrupulous or skeptical person cannot raise, from miracles, the least doubt against the divine revelation of the gospel. The person coming with a message from God to be delivered to the world cannot be refused belief if he vouches his mission by a miracle, because his credentials have a right to it.[162]

But what enables us to take any extraordinary operation to be a miracle? In other words, what enables us to conclude that the operation in question comes from God as an attestation of revelation from God? Locke's answer is simple: the operation carries with it the marks of a greater power than what appears in opposition to it. According to Locke, God would not allow that a lie, set up in opposition to a truth coming from him, should be backed with a greater power than he demonstrates for the confirmation and propagation of a doctrine which he has revealed. The Egyptian magicians and Moses were able to produce the same miracles. But it was clear which of them had greater power. Therefore, "the superior power is an easy, as well as a sure guide to divine revelation, attested by miracles where they are brought as credentials to an embassy from God."[163]

---

161. Ibid., 80–81.
162. Ibid., 81–82.
163. Ibid., 82–83.

According to Locke, no mission can be seen as divine when it delivers things derogating from the honor of God, or things inconsistent with natural religion and the rules of morality. This is because having revealed himself to human beings, God cannot be supposed to back the contrary by revelation. Doing so would destroy the evidence and use of reason, without which men cannot distinguish divine revelation from diabolical imposture.[164]

Implications for Supernaturalism

What should we make of these three major groups of philosophers? Clearly, their epistemological commitments are different. But even clearer is the fact that they were all committed to belief in the supernatural. That is, it would be safe to say that the epistemological enterprise of the skeptics, Descartes and the evidentialists did not call their supernaturalistic commitments into question. Nothing in their scientific findings undermined their religious beliefs. What we find in almost all of them is a clear interpenetration of their religious views with their scientific views.

As we have already seen, their epistemological methods are quite different. The skeptics, for the most part, believed that only the appearance of things, rather than their nature, could be known. And what we know of their secondary qualities is neither clear nor distinct. Whereas some skeptics maintained that the primary qualities can be known with some degree of probability, others held that even these could not be known for sure. In short, even the skeptics differed among themselves about their own principles of knowledge. But notice that they all seemed to be in agreement about their supernaturalistic views. Given their skepticism about objects of the external world, it should strike us as interesting that they maintained a belief in God and the doctrine of divine revelation with relative firmness.

Also, recall that Descartes' epistemology was radically different from the skeptics'. He attempted to show how the skeptics' method of doubt can be turned around to build infallibly true claims, namely, that one doubts and therefore one most certainly thinks. The striking thing about this feature of Descartes' epistemology is the following: despite its notable distinction from the epistemology of the skeptics, his view of the supernatural is relatively similar to the skeptics' view.

164. Ibid., 84.

When we turn to the evidentialists the findings are just as striking. In Wilkins, Boyle, Newton and Locke, we find an epistemological system that tries to strike a balance between Descartes and the skeptics. All the evidentialists agreed, with minor variations, that things in life could be seen as being according to reason, contrary to reason, or above reason. In maintaining that some things were according to reason, they were, on the one hand, agreeing with Descartes but on the other disagreeing with the skeptics. They agreed with Descartes to the extent that both believed that some things could be rationally demonstrated by following the principles of reason. Some skeptics, like Montaigne, thought this was very questionable.

But how is it that even with these differences of opinions, they unblushingly weaved their assent to supernatural claims into their epistemology? Why is it that they were willing to differ in terms of deciding on how to arrive at reliable knowledge about the world we live in, but were all in agreement, for the most part, about the supernatural world?

Typically, in matters of this sort (that is, of the supernatural), we would understandably expect variations of opinion, and perhaps inconsistent ones as well. In fact, the atheist Michael Martin points to just such inconsistencies when he observes that a general problem with religious experiences is that they are concerned with non-public objects.[165] These experiences, according to Martin, tell no uniform or coherent story, and there is no plausible theory to account for discrepancies among them.[166]

In light of Martin's contention, the fact that the skeptics, Descartes and evidentialists agree on the claim that a being created the universe is fundamentally striking. This leads me back to the question already posited above: how is it that these epistemologists agree on this very issue where we would reasonably expect them to disagree? More accurately, how is it that on the one hand they agree on issues and areas we would expect them to disagree, and on the other they disagree in the very areas we expect them to agree?

One specific answer has dominated recent scholarship on this issue, namely: it was as much a matter of political correctness as it was of personal safety for these thinkers to somehow declare their religious stand, especially if they wanted to remain in the intellectual arena of their day. The assumption here was that had the political environment allowed them to

---

165. Martin, "Critique," 44.
166. Ibid., 45.

safely disavow belief in the supernatural, perhaps their writings would have been permeated with fewer theological postulates.

This answer has some plausibility. Popkin observes, for instance, that the seventeenth century was dominated by severe religious struggles. All the philosophers at that time were affected by them. People were killed for religious mistakes and behavior, not for bad philosophy.[167] According to Popkin, the mathematician, the philosopher and the scientist lived and worked in a world in which the theologians and their positions dominated the intellectual scene.[168]

But I doubt that this is the whole story. Consider that a thinker like Pascal underwent what he took as a firsthand religious experience that transformed him morally. His belief in the supernatural cannot be accounted for by matters of political or ecclesiastical safety alone. My contention is that something beyond political and ecclesiastical safety motivated assent to claims about the supernatural. For these philosophers, the consequences of believing or not believing that knowledge comes to the perceiver through the senses are not as severe as the consequences of believing or not believing in God.

For the skeptics, Descartes and the evidentialists, matters of religion were matters of life and death. But matters of epistemology did not come with similar demands. That is, there were no serious consequences that would follow one's abandonment of rationalism for skepticism, skepticism for evidentialism, or evidentialism for rationalism. However, the philosophers themselves seemed to believe that serious consequences would follow one's abandonment of belief in theism, traditionally understood, for anything less. As Pascal, Wilkins, and Boyle contend, faith or belief in God cannot be abandoned without putting oneself at risk.

My contention is that the epistemologists in question, namely, the skeptics, Descartes and the empiricists, were rational in giving assent to their theistic beliefs in this way. To be sure, when faced with the possibility of either eternal damnation or eternal salvation of one's soul, it would be irrational to opt for the former, especially when the seemingly reliable means for avoiding it and opting for the latter are available.

Therefore, it is only half the story to postulate that religious views penetrated the scientific enterprise to facilitate political-cum-ecclesiastical correctness that guaranteed the personal safety of the epistemologists in

---

167. Popkin, "Religious Background," 37.
168. Ibid., 38.

question. The epistemological concerns went beyond merely a concern for a "this-world" safety. The epistemologists were also concerned about "getting it right" eschatologically.

Notice that if we compare the views of the thinkers examined in this chapter with the views of those examined in chapter 2, we discover that both groups of thinkers attributed the origin of the universe to an intelligent designer. This in turn enabled them to envision a world in which the miraculous could have a place. Of course the skeptics did not try to logically prove the existence of the intelligent being, given their distrust for the reliability of human reason. But Descartes and the evidentialists endeavored to provide just such a proof. We also discover that the thinkers of the early modern era, like the ancient and medieval philosophers, were open to the possibility of miracles. Indeed, having believed that God was the first cause of the universe, they had to follow such a belief to its logical conclusion, namely, that the causation of the universe was miraculous, given our definition of "miracle" formulated in chapter 2. Thus from the seventeenth- and eighteenth-century epistemologists we get the impression that both science and religion have an important role to play in the overall epistemic enterprise of the human being. But as we shall see in the following chapters, this theological role was called into question by the deists, Hume and Darwin.

4

Deism and Supernaturalism

IN THE PREVIOUS CHAPTER I argued that compared to the striking differences attending their epistemological enterprise, the New Pyrrhonists, Descartes and the rationalists agreed, for the most part, in what they took to be fundamental beliefs about the supernatural. Recall that New Pyrrhonism initially developed from the Catholic Church's reaction to the theological claims postulated by the Protestant Reformation. In turn, the theological claims of this new form of skepticism prompted a philosophical reaction from Descartes' rationalistic method. We also saw that the evidentialists tried to strike a middle ground between the rationalism of Descartes and the skepticism of the New Pyrrhonists.

In this chapter, I intend to outline a different philosophical view that developed in reaction to the supernaturalism we have been considering in the previous two chapters, namely, deism. I will show here that the anti-supernaturalism of the seventeenth-century deists is ineffective as a critique of revealed religion. Exactly how this failure comes about is evidenced by the following observations: First, their rational belief in God from the testimony of nature seems to be at odds with their anti-supernaturalistic critique of revealed religion. Second, the critique of miracles by a select group of deists is unsuccessful. The importance of this survey will help us see, in chapter 5, how the deists' controversy with the British evidentialists provided an eye-opening background for David Hume's argument against miracles.

Following Dr. Samuel Johnson's eighteenth-century work entitled *Dictionary of the English Language*, Colin Brown defines a deist as a person who follows no particular religion, though acknowledging the existence of God. Deism had never been an organized school of thought. Its leaders, as we shall see from Anthony Collins, were free thinking, idiosyncratic individuals who shared a common distaste for institutional religion and a belief in reason and humanity. As they died off, their religion also died with them.[1]

Burns agrees with Brown's characterization of deism above. Beyond the claim that deism was not an organized ideological movement, Burns further observes that deists were in disagreement on many theoretical issues. However, he notes, they all agreed that revelation was unnecessary. They affirmed that natural religion was all-sufficient in matters of faith and conduct. According to Burns, some deists did affirm that God revealed himself in Jesus Christ. But they still differed from the evidentialists in their insistence that there was no essential need for such a revelation. They argued that the evidentialists' notion of revelation was incoherent; for to believe in Christ's divinity would require prior possession of criteria for recognizing a doctrine to be of divine character. But those very criteria, so they held, are already a "republication" of the religion of nature, which a rational God must have engraved in every man's mind.[2] This position will become apparent when we consider below the writings of the more prominent deists.

Owing to the vast differences of opinion in their religious epistemology alluded to above, it follows that a genuinely unifying position on religion to which all the deists granted their assent is almost impossible to formulate. Perhaps the best course to follow, in view of this consideration, is to select a few of the more prominent deists in the seventeenth century, in the hope that an adumbration of their views will help to shed light on their attempt to explain—or explain away—the supernatural of the sort endorsed by Christianity. I will first outline the role of reason in natural religion among the deists, and will then proceed to outline the deistic views on miracles. I will then argue that in none of these areas do the deists formulate a forceful critique of supernaturalism.

Deism and Reason

Let me begin with Charles Blount. Blount is considered, by Brown, as one of the most zealous propagators of deism.[3] In *The Oracles of Reason*, pub-

1. Brown, *Miracles*, 47.
2. Burns, *Great Debate*, 13.
3. Brown, *Miracles*, 49.

lished in 1695, Blount argues that all human beings have a native right to reason on things of fundamental concern to them. This is because God has furnished the human mind with reason as a guide sufficient to direct it to the end of man's being. In Blount's view, God and nature are identical. This is a reflection, not only of the Stoics' position already encountered in the first chapter, but also of Spinoza's view in the *Tractatus Theologico Politicus*. For Blount, reason is the light that brings clarity to those things that will contribute to or oppose our happiness. Without reason, the mind is bound to make choices that could prove harmful.[4]

Second, Blount observes that religion and eternity are sacred truths, and every man's enjoyment and loss of eternal happiness depends on his own faith. If we admit this, then all people, including Christians, should allow every human person to exercise this native right to reason on matters of religion. Thus, a person has the liberty to take his own methods of security when he commits himself to any cause, including the liberty to interpret the Holy Scriptures according to reason. This liberty, contends Blount, is a right of every reasonable person.[5]

Third, Blount contends that the liberty he is talking about is the liberty to examine the interpretation of others by the severe and just rules of reason. Blount thinks this is significant in light of the fact that the passions and interests of men have not only emboldened them to misinterpret Scripture to their own ends; it has also added to and detracted from the very text itself.[6]

Anthony Collins expresses views very similar to Blount's, though in a more comprehensive way. Collins was a confidant of John Locke in Locke's last years. According to Waring, a number of Collins' works were centers of controversy in his time.[7] In *A Discourse of Free-Thinking*, published in 1713, Collins argues that freethinking is a necessary epistemological method for rational beings. In his argument, Collins gives a more comprehensive definition than that of Blount. Collins begins by observing that freethinking is the use of our understanding in endeavoring to discover the meaning of any given proposition, considering the evidence for or against it, and judging it according to the seeming force or weakness of the evidence.[8]

---

4. Blount, *Oracles of Reason*, 4.
5. Ibid.
6. Ibid.
7. Waring, *Deism and Natural Religion*, 56
8. See Collins, "Discourse," 56.

Second, besides thinking freely about scientific questions, human beings have a right to think freely about religious questions. And where a right opinion is necessary, there human beings should have the greatest concern to think for themselves. The surest and best means of arriving at truth lies in freethinking. The person who thinks freely does his best toward being in the right. Should that person prove mistaken, he must be as acceptable to God as if he received none but the right opinions.[9]

Third, by freethinking, we can understand, for instance, the unreasonableness of superstitious fears. We know that God governs the world; and that God can require nothing from human beings in any country or condition of life except to be convinced by evidence and reason.[10]

Fourth, the large number of pretenders to the supernatural makes freethinking on this subject absolutely necessary. They pretended to revelations from heaven, supported by miracles, containing new notions of deity and so on. The only way to distinguish between the true messenger from heaven and the impostor is by considering the evidence produced by one as freely as the other. Moreover, the Holy Scriptures everywhere imply and press the duty of freethinking.[11]

Finally, the conduct of priests makes freethinking unavoidable. This is because the priests, whether of different sects or of the same sect, are infinitely divided in opinion about the nature of God, and the authority and meaning of Scriptures. According to Collins, the only way of setting ourselves in a right notion is to cease to rely on them.[12]

Blount and Collins formulated their views at a time when Protestantism vigorously argued for the laity's rights to interpret Scripture, a position that sharply negated the views of the Roman Catholic Church. As noted in chapter 3, the Roman Catholic Church maintained that the clergy, under the guidance of the pope, had the power to correctly interpret Scripture in a way that would articulate the rules of faith and conduct for the laity.

It would seem, for Blount and Collins, that the Protestant divines adopted, in their hermeneutic discipline, a criterion of scriptural interpretation comparable to their Roman Catholic counterparts. Thus even though Protestantism vigorously argued for the laity's uninhibited right to interpret Scripture, the Protestant Clergy made a similar mistake by claiming

---

9. Ibid., 59.
10. Ibid., 59–60.
11. Ibid., 60.
12. Ibid., 61.

exclusive rights to interpret Scripture on behalf of the laity. This idea, or something similar to it, bore the brunt of Blount's and Collins' objection. Both aimed to level the playing field between clergy and laity in terms of biblical interpretation. That is, by virtue of the fact that humans are rational creatures, all people should have the right to exercise their rational faculties in their attempts to arrive at all truths, including religious truths.

Let me now turn to John Toland. He was an Irishman reared in childhood as a Roman Catholic. But he became a Protestant dissenter in his adolescent years. In his later years as an academician he was acquainted with John Locke, and shared many of Locke's ideas, though Locke made a point of disavowing any identity of opinion between him and Toland.[13]

Christianity not Mysterious, published in 1696, is one of Toland's most well known works. In arguing for the employment of reason in matters of religion, Toland contends that the Christian religion is, after all, not as mysterious as popularly claimed by its adherents. This is because, first, reason is not as dangerous in religion as commonly thought;[14] for religion is meant for reasonable creatures.[15] But since it is possible to take a questionable proposition for an axiom, and a moral certitude for divine revelation, we need some infallible rule, or guide by which it is impossible for us to err, namely, evidence.[16] Reason is the faculty of the soul which discovers the certainty of anything dubious or obscure by comparing it with something evidently known, upon considering the evidence adduced.[17]

Second, Toland argues that Christianity is not mysterious because its doctrines conform to reason; they are not contradictory. According to Toland, if the gospel is God's word, the doctrine of the gospel cannot be contrary to reason.[18] According to Toland, whatever we find repugnant to clear and distinct ideas or to common sense remains contrary to reason. Toland finds this view very intelligible. From this vantage point, he proceeds to prove that if the gospel is the word of God, it cannot be contrary to reason. Toland could not think of any Christian who thought that the gospel and reason were mutually exclusive.[19]

13. Waring, *Deism and Natural Religion*, 1.
14. Toland, "Christianity," 1.
15. Ibid., 2.
16. Ibid., 6–7.
17. Ibid., 5.
18. Ibid., 8.
19. Ibid.

For example, the New Testament does not simultaneously insist that *p* and *not-p*.[20] If it does, this would throw us into religious skepticism.[21] In fact, all New Testament doctrines must agree with natural reason and our ordinary ideas, if those doctrines are divine.[22] In other words, New Testament doctrines are clear and distinct.

Thus, by reason we arrive at the certainty of God's existence; we discern God's revelations by their conformity with our common notions; and we discover that Scripture has the highest character of divinity. This is because reason is the tool that finds them out, examines them, approves them, and pronounces them sufficient. Our belief in the divine inspiration of Scripture must be justified by rational proofs and evident consistency.[23]

Toland's use of the phrase "clear and distinct" and his observation that religious claims could be verified by reason reflects Cartesian epistemology. It is possible that by arguing in this way Toland was quite likely recapitulating Descartes' argument in the fourth meditation.

Toland's third reason for contending that Christianity is not mysterious is his observation that Christianity is intelligible of itself, though veiled by other things such that it could not be known without special revelation. Here, Toland admits that the gospel is covered with figurative words.[24] However, he notes, God reveals in Scripture wonderful matters of fact; we receive God's revelation because it is intelligible and possible.[25] And to be sure that we leave no room for doubt in this matter, God proves his authority by miracles.[26] This is a curious admission on Toland's part, which I will revisit below.

Toland observes that the word "mystery" can be understood in two ways. The first is what he calls "the early understanding." This understanding portrays mystery as a thing intelligible of itself, but so veiled by other factors that it could not be known without special revelation. The second understanding of mystery should be construed as a thing inconceivable however clearly revealed.[27]

20. Ibid., 9.
21. Ibid., 10.
22. Ibid., 12.
23. Ibid., 9–10.
24. Ibid., 18.
25. Ibid., 12.
26. Ibid., 13.
27. Ibid., 19.

From Toland's perspective, Christianity is not of this second sort. It should be understood in the first way. Toland maintains that the doctrines of Christianity cannot be called mysteries. This is because we cannot call something a mystery simply because we have no adequate idea of it. If we did, then everything would be a mystery; for we never have a full conception of whatever belongs to something.[28]

Toland advances this claim by drawing a distinction between what he calls the "nominal" essence and the "real" essence of a thing. The former is a collection of properties we principally observe in a thing. The latter is the "intrinsic constitution" of a thing; it is the "ground of all its properties." According to Toland, we know that the real essence exists; but we are ignorant of what it is.[29] As we shall see below, John Locke uses these very terms, but creates further distinctions than Toland.

For Toland, nothing can be called a mystery just because we are ignorant of its real essence. This is because the real essence is neither knowable in itself nor even thought of by us. According to Toland, when we apply this concept to our understanding of God, we discover that we know God's attributes very well. But we do not know the essence of God wherein infinite goodness, love and power coexist. Thus God cannot with more reason be accounted mysterious in this respect than the most contemptible of his creatures.[30]

Toland seems to be saying that we have clear and distinct ideas of the nominal essence of things, including God. For instance, we get clear and distinct ideas of God from Scripture. If the nominal essence of any entity can be grasped, then the entity in question is not mysterious. The nominal essence of religious entities, such as God, can be apprehended. For this reason, religious entities, such as God, should not be deemed mysterious.

Before proceeding further, let me return to an observation made above, namely, that Toland's distinction between "the nominal essence" and the "real essence" is one that Locke made in his *Essay concerning Human Understanding*. Locke completed his *Essay* in 1690. Therefore it might be reasonable to conclude that Toland derived this distinction from Locke since Toland's work was completed in 1696. But this suggestion is not quite conclusive, since there is always the possibility that both Locke and Toland could have derived this idea from a third source. To see this, consider the

---

28. Ibid.
29. Ibid., 21.
30. Ibid., 22.

fact that the skeptics and the evidentialists had already made a similar distinction, only that they used different terms, namely "appearance" and "the real nature" of a thing.

A second reason why Toland could have drawn this conclusion independently of Locke is that Toland seems to ignore what Locke says concerning the real essence. We find, for example, that Locke's treatment of real essence distinguishes between essence as an immaterial entity and essence as a material entity, which, however, is undetectable by the senses. For Locke, the real essence is concealed in individual material substances because it is composed of particles of matter too small for our organs to perceive. In his explication of the real essence of things, Toland makes no such distinction. This suggests that Toland might have been ignorant of Locke's view.

Toland's view of "mystery" was criticized in *A Letter* by Peter Browne, an Irish academic cleric. Whereas Toland did try to judge all matters of religion by reason, it does not seem, as Browne would want to argue, that Toland adopted a stand that eliminated mystery out of religion altogether; for on the one hand Toland holds that God reveals wonderful matters of fact in Scripture. On the other, he adds that God confirms this revelation with miracles.

By making this admission, Toland may very well be giving us a Lockean argument already presented in the previous chapter. There we cited Locke's contention that some things were according to reason, others contrary to reason, and still others above reason. It would be correct to say that for Toland, just as for Locke, things above reason reflect the sort of mystery, intelligible of itself, but hidden in other factors that can only be known with special revelation.

Browne's *Letter* was so widely read that Toland later boasted that he had been responsible for Browne's becoming a bishop.[31] Browne begins his attack on Toland by observing that in Christian mystery, there is something we do understand, and something we are wholly ignorant of. According to Browne, the question is not whether one can believe what one does not know. The question is whether we have good reasons to believe that there are some things in the gospel that have much more in them, above and beyond what we are now able to comprehend.[32]

---

31. Waring, *Deism and Natural Religion*, 27.
32. Browne, *Letter*, 28.

Browne believes that this question can be answered in the affirmative. To see this, Browne draws our attention to Toland's assertion that clear and distinct ideas are the basis of all our knowledge, assent and belief. To challenge this position, Browne postulates what he calls "adequate ideas," full and comprehensive knowledge of anything including all that is knowable about it. According to Browne, it is impossible to determine how far clear and distinct ideas fall short of "adequate ideas." He argues that we are far from having clear and distinct ideas of those things of another world which are revealed to us. However, even though we have no proper or immediate idea of them, we are bound to believe them. By proper or immediate idea, Browne refers to a conception or notion of the thing as it is in itself.[33]

Seemingly, Browne uses "adequate ideas" synonymously with "proper or immediate ideas." In Browne's perspective, we have no proper ideas of things of another world. For example, he objects to Toland's claim that "we can know God's attributes very well." Browne argues that our imagination can frame no likeness or resemblance of God as it can of material and sensible objects. Also, by the claim "God is spirit," we understand nothing more than that he is a being that is not matter. And as for God's omnipresence, it is utterly impossible for us to conceive how the same thing should be here and there and everywhere at the same time. That is to say, in every attribute of God, we make ourselves some representations of them by compounding and enlarging those ideas we have either of sensible objects or of the operations of our minds.[34]

Browne's conclusion is this: If, as Toland contends, we must give our assent to nothing but what we have clear and distinct ideas of, then farewell to all religion. For all religion, whether natural or revealed, is founded upon belief in a deity, the soul's immortality, and rewards and punishments in another world. But we have no clear and distinct ideas of these.[35] And by arguing in this way, Browne seems to be taking an anti-Cartesian conclusion here.

From Browne and Toland let us consider Matthew Tindal. His major work, *Christianity as Old as the Creation*, published in 1730, became the focal center of the deist controversy very soon after its publication. The work is often termed the deist's Bible because almost every argument, quotation

---

33. Ibid., 28–29.
34. Ibid., 30.
35. Ibid., 33.

and issue raised for decades can be found in it.[36] Tindal argues that the Christian religion has existed from the beginning, and that God has given mankind sufficient means to know it, namely, reason, though the name Christian is of a later date.[37] According to Tindal, God has from the beginning given mankind a perfect rule or law of conduct, namely, reason. That law is perfect, since only the absolutely perfect can come from a being of infinite wisdom and perception.[38]

How does Tindal advance this claim? He argues that all men at all times must have had sufficient means to discover whatever God designed they should know and practice.[39] If God designed that all mankind should at all times know what he wills them to know and has given them no other means for this but the use of reason, then human reason must be that means; for if humans sincerely endeavor to discover the will of God, they will perceive there is a law of nature, or reason, and that this law, like its author, is absolutely perfect, eternal and unchangeable.[40]

Second, human beings will perceive that the design of the gospel was not to add to, or take from this law, but to free men from that load of superstition which has been mixed with it. So, true Christianity is a religion that God dictated at the beginning. Tindal takes for granted that there is sufficient evidence of a person being sent from God to reveal it.[41]

Third, Tindal observes that humans do live immorally. This means they can do what God has forbidden them to do. But it is also clear that humans do live virtuously and piously in other instances. Once again, this means that they can do what God has commanded them to do. These observations and their implications lead Tindal to conclude that there has always been a universal law, fully promulgated to human beings, a universal law which humans are aware of and by which they live.[42]

Fourth, Tindal argues that it is evident by the light of nature that God exists, and that he is absolutely perfect, infinitely happy in himself, and that he is the source of all other beings. Whatever perfections God's creatures have, they are wholly derived from God. And the creatures can neither

36. Waring, *Deism and Natural Religion*, 107.
37. Tindal, "Christianity," 109.
38. Ibid., 108.
39. Ibid., 109.
40. Ibid., 110–11.
41. Ibid., 111–12.
42. Ibid., 112.

add to nor take away from the happiness of that being. Moreover, the only motive that God could have in relation to his creatures is the motive of promoting their own good. Therefore, nothing can be a part of the divine law except what advances the common interest and mutual happiness of God's rational creatures.[43]

Fifth, considering the variety of circumstances human beings are under, it is impossible to have rules laid down by any external revelation for every particular case. Moreover, most of the particular rules articulated in the gospel for our direction are spoken in a figurative manner such that unless we judge their meaning by what the law of nature antecedently declares to be our duty, they are apt to mislead us. But God's will is so clearly and fully manifested in the book of nature that anyone may read it.[44]

Sixth, Tindal argues that the religion of nature is an absolutely perfect religion. Therefore external revelation can neither add to nor take from its perfection; and true religion, whether internally or externally revealed, must be the same.[45] This means that if we maintain that Christianity is indeed a new religion, and that the gospel is incapable of any additions specifically because God is immutable and his law too perfect to need any such additions, we argue inconsistently; for we would be maintaining that from the time Christianity commenced, God is mutable and that additions to his laws have been made to the already presupposed all-perfect laws of infinite wisdom.[46]

But the law of nature, Tindal argues, is immutable because it is based on the unalterable reason of things. And in truth all laws, whether the laws of nations, or those of particular countries, are only the law of nature adjusted and accommodated to circumstances. Thus, the religion of nature was so perfect that nothing could be added to it. The truth of all revelation is to be judged of by its agreement with the religion of nature.[47]

What seems to motivate Tindal's overall argument is, I believe, the attempt to show that Christian divines are mistaken in contending that Christianity is unique when compared to natural religion. Tindal contends that Christianity does not really bring anything new to the table, and therefore does not have this special status commonly attributed to it.

43. Ibid., 114.
44. Ibid., 118–19.
45. Ibid., 125.
46. Ibid., 127.
47. Ibid.

From the aforementioned deists, we get a picture of their view concerning faith and reason, and its implications for the supernatural. What should appear striking is that none of the deists hitherto examined called into question claims about the existence of God, which, in my view, is an important factor in determining whether miracles can and do occur. However, notice that we do find objections to miracles once we focus on different deistic treatments on the subject. I consider the nature of the debate below.

Deism and Miracles

Nowhere is the deists' objection to established Christian religion more prominent than in the aspect of miracles. Burns notes, however, that the attack on miracles was not central to the deists' credo; for by no means all of them recorded their disbelief either in the possibility or in the reality of miracles. It is easy to find affirmation of Christian miracles in the writings of earlier and later deists like Blount, Tindal, Toland or Morgan.[48]

In his investigation of the deists' treatment of miracles, Burns makes an interesting observation. He argues (convincingly, I think) that Hume's argument against miracles borrows heavily from the deists. More accurately, Hume's argument against miracles is really a collection of different deistic arguments against miracles already given long before Hume wrote his essay on miracles.[49]

Following Burns, my intention here is to examine the original texts in which deistic arguments against miracles can be found, and compare them with Hume's argument. This will show, as Burns has argued, that Hume's argument against miracles was largely borrowed from the deists. Moreover, I will examine the response the evidentialists made against the different arguments presented by the deists. I will then try to determine whether the deists' arguments obtain, and whether the response from the evidentialists was adequate. This differs from the task in chapter 5, which will focus primarily on selected major responses that Hume's argument generated from Hume's time through the twenty-first century.

In the first part of his essay on miracles, Hume defines a miracle as a violation of the laws of nature. He adds that a firm and unalterable experience has established these laws. Therefore, the proof against a miracle, from the very nature of the unbreakable laws of nature, is as entire as any

---

48. Burns, *Great Debate*, 14.
49. Ibid., 72.

argument from experience can possibly be imagined. For Hume, there must be a uniform experience against every miraculous event; otherwise the event would not merit that appellation. But a uniform experience amounts to a proof. Therefore, a uniform experience is a direct and full proof against the existence of any miracle.[50]

Burns contends that Hume was not the first thinker to advance this claim. A number of deists before him already made this observation.[51] To see this, let me begin with the deist Peter Annet. In his *Supernaturals Examined*, published in 1747, Annet argues that God has settled the laws of nature by his wisdom and power, and therefore cannot alter them consistently with his perfections. Annet continues to say that this is a demonstrative proof of the impossibility of miracles *a priori*. Moreover, Annet continues, if we grant that *effects* change, then we must grant that the *cause* of those effects also change. Thus if the laws of nature are altered, so must be the law giver. This implies that God's will and wisdom are mutable, and thus not what we would expect from a most Perfect Being.[52]

According to Annet, miracles by definition violate the laws of nature. Therefore, the miracle worker, the work, and reporter, have not an equal right to be believed by those who would neither be imposed upon nor impose upon others; for miracles have been shown to be operations contrary to the course of nature. If that course has been confounded once, we know not how often it may be done, nor where the confusion may end, and then there can be no dependence on the course of nature. But the laws of nature are the only laws to a man of truth and certainty. If what is invariable fails and lies to us, we have nothing to depend on. Since inconstant miraculous interpositions do not agree with the constant course of nature by which the senses and reasons of men are directed, they destroy the rational principles that are based on them.[53]

Thus Peter Annet advances an argument against miracles that Hume would later use in the first part of his essay on miracles. For purposes of brevity of exposition, I will call Annet's argument the "uniformity-of-nature" argument. Burns also contends that Hume borrowed heavily from the deists when he formulated the second part of his essay on miracles.[54] To

50. Hume, "Miracles," in *Dialogues concerning Natural Religion*, 673–74.
51. Burns, *Great Debate*, 72.
52. Annet, *Supernaturals Examined*, 44.
53. Ibid., 67.
54. Ibid., 72.

see this, we will examine the four reasons that Hume gives against miracles in the second part of his essay, and compare them with the earlier arguments of the deists.

Hume's first reason is the claim that in all of history no miracle is attested by a sufficient number of credible witnesses "as to secure us against all delusion in themselves." By credibility here Hume refers to "unquestioned good sense," "education," and "learning." I will therefore call this argument the "credibility-of-witness" argument.

Burns holds here that Hume is really providing a veiled attack on the witness of the writers of the New Testament to the events which they relate. Therefore, what we find, according to Burns, is a summary of the characteristic position of the more extreme deists on the nature of the New Testament. A number of deists had presented a number of detailed and substantial criticisms of the Bible.[55]

Thomas Woolston is one such deist. In his *Six Discourses on the Miracles of our Savior*, published in 1727 and 1728 Woolston argues that the literal history of many of the miracles of Jesus, as recorded by the New Testament writers, implies absurdities, improbabilities, and incredibilities. For example, the New Testament writers report that Jesus cast demons out of a demoniac and allowed them to possess a herd of swine grazing in the region of Gadarene. Woolston did not find any good and justice of this act on the part of Christ. According to Woolston, the proprietors of the pigs suffered heavy losses. Moreover, we do not read that Jesus compensated them, or that they deserved such usage from him.[56]

Also, Woolston takes the instance where Jesus cursed a fig tree. Jesus was hungry, it seems, and being disappointed that there were no figs on the tree, he cursed the fig tree. Why was he so peevish and impatient? To curse the fig tree was as foolishly done as for another man to throw chairs and stools about the house, because his dinner is not ready at a critical time. Moreover, the evangelists report that the time of figs was not yet. Nothing is more unreasonable than for a man to expect fruit out of season.[57]

What Woolston is trying to do here is to undercut the reliability of the reports about the miracles of Jesus by calling the credibility of Jesus into question. Notice that whereas Hume only offered a veiled attack on the credibility of the miracles, as Burns contends, Woolston goes into specific

---

55. Ibid., 77.
56. Woolston, *Six Discourses*, I.
57. Ibid., III.

details. What Burns does not point out, however, is that Woolston's polemics against Jesus were also accompanied by frequent affirmations from Woolston himself that Jesus did perform some of the miracles as recorded in Scripture. Woolston holds that the messiah-ship of Jesus is only to be proved by his more mysterious works, of which those done in the flesh are but a type and figure.[58] When Jesus appeals to his miracles as to a testimony and witness of his divine authority, he was not referring to the miracles he is taken to have done in the flesh; rather, he referred to the mystical miracles he would do in the spirit.[59] Exactly what these mystical miracles are Woolston does not say. Admissions of this sort weaken Woolston's attack, as we shall see in my evaluation of deism.

Let us now turn to the second reason Hume gives in the second part of his essay. According to Hume, the many instances of forged miracles and prophecies and supernatural events, which, in all ages, have been detected by contrary evidence, or which detect themselves by their absurdity, prove sufficiently the strong propensity of mankind to the extraordinary and the marvelous and ought reasonably to beget a suspicion against all relations of this kind. This, Hume holds, is our natural way of thinking, even with regard to the most common and most credible events.[60] Thus I will call this the "credulity-of-witness" argument.

Do we find this argument among the deists? To answer this question, let us consider the words of Thomas Chubb. He contends, in his *Discourse on Miracles*, published in 1741, that religion awakens the passions and engages them in its favor. We are then more easily led to believe those claims to be true. In Chubb's view, honesty and integrity may secure us from imposing our passions on others. But these are not always a security against imposing those passions on ourselves. Chubb thus argues that even though a steady integrity should appear to run through the general course of man's action, his credibility must not be beyond suspicion when matters of religion are in consideration, given that to some people, religion seems to sanctify every action.[61]

Burns notes that this is a position that even the Christian writers admitted and cautioned against. For example, the evidentialist William Warburton, writing in 1727, noted in *A Critical and Philosophical Enquiry*

---

58. Ibid., I.
59. Ibid., I.
60. Hume, "Miracles," in *Dialogues concerning Natural Religion*, 674–75.
61. Chubb, *Discourse on Miracles*, 73–76.

DEISM AND SUPERNATURALISM

into the Causes of Prodigies and Miracles as Related by Historians that we experience admiration to be one of the most bewitching enthusiastic passions of the mind, and that every common moralist knows that it arises from novelty and surprise, which are the inseparable attendants of imposture.[62]

Thus, to answer the question posited above, we do find Hume's contention among the deists who wrote years before him. Notice also that the evidentialists were aware of this factor and drew our attention to it. Once again we find that Hume was not the first person to make this objection. The deists as well as the evidentialists before him were already discussing it.

The third reason against miracles that Hume advances in the second part of his essay is the observation that supernatural and miraculous relations are observed chiefly to abound among ignorant and barbarous nations. And if a civilized people have ever given admission to any of them, these people will have received the stories from ignorant and barbarous ancestors, who transmitted them with that inviolable sanction and authority which always attend received opinions.[63] For obvious reasons, I will call this the *ad hominem* argument.

Once again, as we shall see, this is not altogether an original claim from Hume. For example, Toland stated that the more ignorant and barbarous any people remain, the more their customs and practices are filled with tales of the miraculous.[64] But as we saw earlier in the first section of this chapter, Toland was not entirely skeptical of miracles altogether. He did admit that miracles do in fact happen.

Thomas Chubb's treatment of this very issue is almost as extensive as Hume's. Chubb contends that some things, according to the accounts that are given of them, take place in one age, and in one country and not in another country. But this happens (or does not happen) in proportion to the credulity of the people in a given country. This leads Chubb to conclude that such things probably did not take place in nature.[65]

Chubb observes that when men grow skeptical and incredulous with regard to these things, then stories of miracles are not likely to be imposed on them; neither will such people impose those stories on others. The result is that, presumably with the advent of civilization, things of this kind seldom happen. And this, in Chubb's opinion, seems to be the case in his

---

62. Warburton, *Critical and Philosophical Enquiry*, 82.
63. Hume, "Miracles," in *Dialogues concerning Natural Religion*, 675–76.
64. Toland, *Christianity Not Mysterious*, 148.
65. Chubb, *Posthumous Works*, 198–200.

day.⁶⁶ This very sentiment is reflected in Hume's words, who thought it strange that miraculous events never occurred in his days,⁶⁷ though he apparently contradicts himself when he describes at length recent such events in Paris.

Let us now turn to Hume's fourth and final reason for calling the miraculous into question. Here, Hume contends that there is no testimony for any miracle, including those that have been expressly detected, that is not opposed by an infinite number of witnesses, so that not only the miracle destroys the credit of testimony, but the testimony destroys itself. For example, in matters of religion, every miracle pretended to have been wrought in different religions has the direct intention of establishing the particular system of the religion in question. But that very miracle has the same force, though more indirectly, of overthrowing every other system. In destroying a rival system, it at the same time destroys the credit of those miracles on which that system was established. Therefore, all the miracles of different religions are to be regarded as contrary facts. And the evidences of those miracles, whether weak or strong, oppose each other.⁶⁸

According to Burns, Hume's fourth attack was by far the most common maneuver in the deistic polemic against the Christian miracles.⁶⁹ For example, Woolston claimed that he would not be so impious and profane as to believe that Jesus actually changed water into wine. This is because if Apollonis, and not Jesus, had been the author of the miracle, we should have criticized his memory with it.⁷⁰ Also, consider the miracle of raising Jairus' daughter from the dead, of raising the widow of Nain's son, and of raising Lazarus. If such miracles had not been reported of Jesus, but had been reported of Muhammad by three different historians, we all would have scented the forgery and imposture.⁷¹

Also, Thomas Morgan argued that there is no imposture, or false religion in the world, which might not be confirmed in the same way, that is, with miracles. According to Morgan, we would be arguing against fact and common experience to say, that God, in his wisdom and goodness, could never suffer any such cheat or imposture from miracles to pass, without

---

66. Ibid.
67. Hume, "Miracles," in *Dialogues concerning Natural Religion*, 676.
68. Ibid., 676–77.
69. Burns, *Great Debate*, 72.
70. Woolston, *Six Discourses*, I.
71. Ibid., V.

controlling them by more and greater miracles set over against them. For it is certain that God has suffered, and still continues to suffer, the greatest part of the world to be deluded in this way.[72]

Moreover, Morgan contends that from all history, the priests and politicians of all religions have always gained their point and established their different schemes of superstition among the people by the tricks of miracles. For Morgan, it is not even possible, even under the gospel itself, ever to guard against such imposture. This is because the ecclesiastics in all countries have their different and opposite schemes of revealed religion all equally proved by miracles and immediate revelation.[73]

Thomas Chubb argues very similarly. He contends that it is groundless to say that miracles are a proper fence and security against delusion and imposition.[74] Take, for example, the miracles reported by the Roman Catholic Church. For ages past, these miracles have been looked upon, and in general, treated by Protestants, as fraud and impositions. But it has been wholly out of the power of the Protestants to prove some of them to be such. Interestingly, some of these facts seem to be better attested than any of the miracles which were wrought or supposed to be wrought in the first century.[75]

According to Burns, Hume makes this exact point by drawing our attention to the story related by Cardinal de Retz, a French political leader. He fled into Spain to avoid persecution, and was shown a man who worked for seven years as a doorkeeper in the Cathedral of Saragossa, the capital of Arragon. The doorkeeper had lost one of his legs. But the story going around is that the doorkeeper recovered his leg by the rubbing of holy oil upon his artificial leg. According to Hume, this miracle was vouched by all the canons of the church, and all the company in town were appealed to for a confirmation of the fact. In fact, the cardinal examined the leg, and found it to be a true natural leg like the other. According to Hume, the cardinal found that the citizens of the town were thorough believers of the miracle.[76]

Hume notes that it is significant that the cardinal himself does not seem to give any credit to the miracle itself, though the witnesses were very numerous, all of them being spectators of the fact to which they gave

---

72. Morgan, *Letter to Eusebius*, 8–9.
73. Ibid., 9.
74. Chubb, *Posthumous Works*, 35–36.
75. Ibid., 227.
76. Hume, "Miracles," in *Dialogues concerning Natural Religion*, 677.

their testimony. The cardinal, according to Hume, felt that to be able to accurately disprove the testimony and to trace its falsehood through all the circumstances of knavery and credulity which produced it, was not requisite. Moreover, it was impossible to do this, anyway, given the short time he had and the place. But even more so, it was extremely difficult to disprove it even where one was immediately present, by reason of the bigotry, ignorance, cunning, and roguery of a great part of mankind. Therefore, Hume reports that such an evidence carried falsehood upon the very face of it and that a miracle supported by any human testimony was more properly a subject of derision than of argument.[77]

According to Burns, Hume's fourth reason was an argument used by almost every deist. At the very beginning of the movement, Charles Gildon, for example, remarked that every new god and prophet among people was to have miracles as credentials of his divinity.[78] Also, Peter Annet, one of the last deists, remarked in 1747 that the miracles of one party are never owned by another.[79] Burns contends that Hume's fourth reason for rejecting the miraculous is really a form of argument that would be perfectly familiar to anyone with even a partial acquaintance with the deistic writers.[80]

What we find in this section is that the key structure of Hume's attack on the credibility of testimonies about miracles is by no means original. He based his argument on presuppositions that were already widely available. These considerations provide the context in which Hume's argument against miracles, to be evaluated in the next chapter, can be seen. However, when the deists launched their attack on miracles, as presented in this section, it generated different responses from the evidentialists. I turn to these responses below.

The Evidentialists' Defense of Miracles

Once again, following Burns, we learn that each aspect of Hume's attack had already generated a response from the evidentialists.[81] Thus, in this section we will consider the response the evidentialists gave their deistic

---

77. Ibid., 678.
78. Gildon, preface to Blount, *Oracles of Reason*.
79. Annet, *Supernaturals Examined*, 89.
80. Burns, *Great Debate*, 75.
81. Ibid., 114.

opponents. We will begin by focusing on the attacks similar to the one Hume used in the first part of his essay.

According to Burns, Joseph Butler and Thomas Sherlock formulated their response in the period preceding the publication of Hume's attack on miracles. Their response was mostly focused on the uniformity-of-nature argument. For example, in *The Analogy of Religion*, published in 1736, Butler begins by observing the following: it is commonly supposed that there is some peculiar presumption, from the analogy of nature, against the Christian miracles. More accurately, it is argued that stronger evidence, than would be sufficient to convince us of other events, is necessary to prove the truth and reality of Christian miracles.[82]

According to Butler, however, the fact that things lie beyond the natural reach of our faculties, is no presumption against their truth and reality. This is because there are innumerable things, in the constitution and government of the universe, which are beyond the reach of our natural faculties. Similarly, there is no presumption at all that the whole course of things naturally unknown to us is similar to anything that we know. Therefore, we cannot have a peculiar presumption against anything in the former based upon the fact that it is different from anything in the latter.[83]

In Butler's view, miracles must not be compared to common natural events, or to events which, though uncommon, are similar to what we daily experience. Rather, they should be compared to the extraordinary phenomena of nature. In this way, the comparison will be between the presumption against miracles, and the presumption against such uncommon experiences, like comets, so contrary to the properties of the other bodies not endued with these powers. And before anyone can determine whether there is any peculiar presumption against miracles, more than against other extraordinary things, he must consider what, upon first hearing, would be the presumption against the last-mentioned appearances and powers to a person acquainted with only the daily, monthly, and annual course of nature respecting this earth and with those common powers of matter which we every day see.[84] Thus, Butler points out that an argument against miracles of the type Wollaston used, and which Hume would also use, would exclude very many unusual things from the possibility of belief.

---

82. Butler, *Analogy of Religions*, 142.
83. Ibid., 144.
84. Brown, *Miracles*, 130.

In the *Trial of the Witnesses of Jesus*, published in 1729, Thomas Sherlock gives a different response. In this work, Sherlock tries to defend the disciples of Jesus against the charge that they were guilty of fraud in claiming that Jesus rose from the dead. According to Sherlock, those who formulated the charge argued as follows. They claimed that although in common life we act in a thousand instances on the faith and credit of human testimony, yet the reason for doing so is not the same as in the case of the resurrection. This is because in common affairs, where nothing is asserted except what is probable and possible, a reasonable degree of evidence ought to convince every man, according to the usual course of nature.[85]

According to the charge, we know that this is so because the very probability or possibility of the thing is a support to the evidence. And in such cases we have no doubt that a man's senses will qualify him to be a witness. But when the thing testified is contrary to the order of nature, and at first sight at least, impossible, no evidence can be sufficient to overturn the constant evidence of nature, evidence that nature affords for us in the uniform and regular method of her operations. Thus, if a man says he has been to France, we ought to give a reason for believing him. But if the same man tells us that he comes from the grave, we have no reason to give for believing him.[86]

Sherlock responds to this charge as follows. A person must be understood as claiming that the testimony of witnesses is to be received only in cases which appear to us to be possible. For example, a man who lives in a warm climate and never saw ice ought on no evidence to believe that rivers freeze and grow hard in cold countries. This is because according to his notion of things, such events are impossible. But we all know that this is a plain manifest case discernible by human senses, of which they are qualified to be good witnesses. Nothing is more apparently absurd than to make one man's ability in discerning, and his veracity in reporting plain facts, depend on the skill or ignorance of the hearer. And what the charge against the resurrection is advancing is very similar to what the person who never saw ice might say against a hundred honest witnesses who assert that water turns into ice in cold climates.[87]

According to Sherlock, it is true that men do not so easily believe, on the testimony of others, things which to them seem improbable or

---

85. Sherlock, *Trial of the Witnesses of Jesus Christ*, 58.
86. Ibid., 59–64.
87. Ibid.

impossible. For instance, when someone tells you that he saw a stone go uphill of its own accord, you will probably question his veracity. However, you should not say that the thing admitted no evidence simply because it was contrary to the law and the usual course of nature. Whenever you see facts yourself, which contradict your notions of the law of nature, you admit the facts because you believe yourself; when you do not admit like facts upon the evidence of others, it is because you do not believe them, and not because the facts in their own nature exclude all evidence.[88]

Therefore, if someone would tell you that he rose from the dead, you would quite likely suspect his evidence. But what is it exactly that you would suspect? You would not suspect that he was not alive when you heard him, saw him, felt him and conversed with him. What you would call into question here is whether the man had ever been dead. But what you cannot say is that it is incapable of being made plain by human testimony that this or that man died a year ago. In other words, it is absurd to say that cases of this sort admit of no evidence when the things in question are manifestly objects of sense.[89]

Finally, Sherlock calls into question the objectivity of the notion "usual course of nature." According to Sherlock, every man, from the lowest countryman to the highest philosopher, frames to himself from his experiences and observation, a notion of a course of nature. Such a person is ready to say of every thing reported to him that contradicts his experience, that it is contrary to nature. But surely, those who advance the charge in question are not ready to say that everything is impossible, or even improbable, that contradicts the notion which human beings frame to themselves of the course of nature. Therefore, when men talk of the course of nature, they really talk of their own prejudices and imaginations. But when men admit things contrary to this presupposed course of nature upon proper evidence, they do not quit their own sense and reason. Rather, they truly quit their own mistakes and prejudices.[90]

In these ways, Butler and Sherlock formulate their response to charges like those advanced by William Wollaston and Peter Annet. But this is not the only response that the evidentialists brought against the deistic attack. Recall that the deists also presented four different attacks, all of which Hume would later use in the second part of his essay on miracles.

88. Ibid.
89. Ibid.
90. Ibid.

For example, in their response to the credibility-of-witness argument, which essentially called into question the moral credibility of the witnesses, we find John Conybeare and Joseph Butler appealing to the moral context, which we examined at length with Origen, in demonstrating that the workers of the biblical miracles did not perform them by fraudulent means. Conybeare maintains that neither Christ nor his apostles could have been guilty of any imposture in the facts related by the New Testament. According to Conybeare, persons of their character for virtue and integrity could never attempt it.[91] Joseph Butler also contends that it cannot be supposed, that such numbers of men should make so great, and to say the least, so inconvenient a change in their whole institution of life unless they were really convinced of the truth of those miracles.[92]

The deists' second attack was the credulity-of-witness argument. Recall that Thomas Morgan argued that all humans take pleasure in hearing and telling of wonders even when such events did not take place. Thomas Chubb also advanced a similar charge. Evidentialist Conybeare responds to this claim as follows. He notes that there is only one way of evading the evidence of the Apostles' sincerity and therefore of the truth of their claims, namely by affirming that the apostles were fanatics and thus madmen, and were therefore capable of believing anything which favored the great point they were possessed with. According to Conybeare, this may be affirmed. Unfortunately, he observes, there seems to be no evidence for it.[93] According to Warburton, these persons did not betray anything in the form of credulity.[94]

However, Warburton and Conybeare are not the only people to formulate a response to this second attack. Butler summarized his response in the following way. He begins by observing that enthusiasm greatly weakens the evidence of testimony, even for facts in matters relating to religion. Some people think it totally and absolutely destroys the evidence of testimony upon this subject.[95] However, Butler states that human beings are naturally endued with reason, or a capacity of distinguishing between truth and falsehood. And naturally they are endued with veracity, or a regard to truth in what they say. To be sure, from many occasions human beings are

---

91. Conybeare, *Discourse on Miracles*, 21.
92. Butler, *Analogy of Religions*, 212.
93. Conybeare, *Defence of Revealed Religion*, 451.
94. Ibid.
95. Butler, *Analogy of Religions*, 215.

liable to be prejudiced, biased and deceived. They are also capable of intending to deceive others. But notwithstanding all these, human testimony remains still a natural ground of assent, and this assent remains a natural principle of action.[96]

For Butler, this means that nothing can destroy the evidence of testimony in any case except a proof or probability that the persons are not competent judges of facts to which they give testimony, or that they are actually under some indirect influence in giving it in a particular case. Unless this be made out, the natural laws of human actions require that testimony be admitted. For Butler, it can never be sufficient to overthrow direct historical evidence indolently and then say that there are so many principles from which human beings are liable to be deceived themselves and disposed to deceive others, especially in matters of religion.[97]

We now turn to the third attack, namely, the *ad hominem* argument. It contended that believers in miracles are predisposed to argue for the occurrence of miraculous events owing to the circumstances that influenced their beliefs, namely, the barbarous circumstances under which they thrived.

In *An Enquiry into the Rejection of the Christian Miracles by the Heathens*, W. Weston argues that many of the most extraordinary wonders of antiquity were not only disregarded, but held in the utmost detestation by the heathens themselves.[98] Conybeare presented a similar argument when he contended that if anything suggesting the miraculous had been attempted it could never have escaped the discovery of so many nice enquirers in such a learned and curious age.[99]

What Weston observes is important and more will be said about it in my evaluation. We now focus our attention on the fourth attack which suggested that alleged miracles of any religion call into question alleged miracles of other rival religions. Consequently, the attack concluded, all reports of miracles cancel each other out. According to Burns, this objection received the most attention from the evidentialists.[100]

For example, in *A Vindication of the Christian Religion*, published in 1725, Samuel Chandler argued that every pretender to a divine revelation is not to be immediately believed even if his miracles be real. According to

---

96. Ibid., 216.
97. Ibid., 218.
98. Weston, *Enquiry*, 385–86.
99. Conybeare, *Defence of Revealed Religion*, 21.
100. Burns, *Great Debate*, 114.

Chandler, the person's character and message must also be considered.[101] Also, in *Eusebius*, published in 1739, Chapman contends that every miracle is not of itself an incontestable argument of truth in doctrines. According to Chapman we do not attribute this power to every miracle as such, or merely because it is a miracle. Rather, miracles of a certain quality and kind, and with certain circumstances attending them, have this effect.[102]

With this sort of response in place, what did the evidentialists make of miraculous events allegedly occurring outside Christianity? Chandler noted that both Simon Magus and Apollonius Tyanaeus are reported to have done many strange and surprising things. But the fact that these were imposters might be as certainly known as almost any truth whatsoever. This is because they taught doctrines inconsistent with true piety, and they did many things contrary to plain morality.[103]

In a similar vein, deist John Leland surprisingly argues as follows: it does not follow that because there have been many miracles falsely pretended, therefore there have been no real ones, and that because this kind of proof has been made use of by cheats and impostors, therefore it can in no case be depended on at all; no more than it follows, that because all parties pretend to have truth and right reason on their side there is no such thing as truth and right reason.[104]

Evaluation of the Deist-Evidentialist Debate on Miracles

What should we make of this debate? There seems to be some tension between the deists' admission, on the one hand, that the "findings" of natural theology allow us to cogently infer the existence of God, and on the other, their use of the "uniformity-of-nature" argument to call reports of the occurrence of miracles to question. As we saw in chapter 1, admitting the former quite rationally allows us to infer what Augustine calls the standing miracle of creation. Here, God is understood to have interacted with nature in a manner properly deemed miraculous.

Moreover, Butler and Sherlock correctly observe that the "uniformity-of-nature" argument is mistaken in important ways. First, it is a rule formed under the supposition that one has access to every phenomenon

---

101. Chandler, *Vindication of the Christian Religion*, 33.
102. Chapman, *Eusebius*, 82.
103. Chandler, *Vindication of the Christian Religion*, 33.
104. Leland, *Defence of Christianity*, 56–57.

available in nature, which is clearly false. Second, it rules out other aspects of nature which, to the best of our knowledge, still remain mysterious. The "uniformity-of-nature" argument can be seen to apply only to "what we think we know of nature" rather than to "what nature really is in itself." If these two considerations are taken along with the oddity I located above, the uniformity-of-nature argument is seen to be clearly inadequate.

Next is the credibility-of-witness argument. As we have already seen, this argument was advanced by Woolston, and received a response from Butler and Conybeare. I have already noted the obscurity in Woolston's argument, and there is no need to repeat that point here. Suffice it to say that it is not clear what standard Woolston uses by insisting that some of the biblical miracles should be taken allegorically and that others literally happened.

By contrast, I think Butler and Conybeare are right in demonstrating that workers of the biblical miracles did not perform them by fraudulent means. Both appealed to the moral test originally used by the church fathers we surveyed in chapter 1, but largely ignored by the deists and subsequently by Hume.

Third is the credulity-of-witness argument. Warburton and Butler argue that there is no evidence to support the claim that the New Testament authors were credulous. The New Testament itself shows that a good number of the miracles were received with skepticism and subjected to scrutiny. For example, when St. John records that Jesus healed a man blind from birth, the scribes, Pharisees and teachers of the law became skeptical, and began to investigate the healing. It seems to me that Warburton and Butler have good reasons for maintaining that credulity was always challenged by skepticism and that the New Testament writers were aware of the challenge and expected it. But they proceeded with reporting the miraculous events anyway. They believed that such events, which they took to be supernatural truths, actually happened. This is a claim St. Luke, the physician, makes in the first few verses of his gospel. It is also repeated by St. John and St. Peter. But this is a claim that the deists overlook, for they fail to show why the position of the New Testament writers excludes a critical examination of the facts.

Of course it is possible that on the one hand, a person could claim that a miracle happened, and that the person actually witnessed the miracle, but on the other the person could fail to correctly report the event. Indeed, this could have been a possibility with the New Testament writers if they presented their claims in a different environment. But given the hostile religious and political environment, it is highly unlikely that they would have risked making claims to the miraculous if they believed that those claims were false. This is because those very claims militated against the already preestablished religious and political beliefs. One would hardly die for claims one believes to be false. But if one is convinced of the veracity of those claims, it is quite understandable that one should die for them. Moreover, history showed that they did in fact pay with their lives for holding such beliefs.

Finally, there is the *ad hominem* argument. As the name suggests, to argue that one is predisposed to argue in a certain way owing to the circumstances in which one was raised is indeed to advance a circumstantial argument against the person. Any standard logic text, such as Patrick Hurley's *Concise Introduction to Logic*, will show that to argue against your opponent in this way is really no argument at all. The arguer is instead attempting to discredit his opponent's argument by alluding to certain circumstances that affect the opponent.[105]

This essentially is what Toland and Chubb are doing. If we go by Hurley's explication, Toland and Chubb are maintaining that those who argue for the veracity of miracle reports do so because they are uncivilized and barbarous, or at least have been influenced by uncivilized and barbarous presuppositions. But this clearly is fallacious. For the connection between the premises of Chubb's argument and the purported conclusion, is emotional rather than logical. For example, Toland and Chubb would argue as follows: the evidentialists believe that miracles happen. But the evidentialists are members of modern civilization. Therefore, we should not reject the arguments for miracles as presented by the evidentialists. As noted, the connection between the premises and the conclusion of this argument is emotional rather than logical.

We are now ready to consider the final argument. This argument could be restated as follows. Miracles are used by adherent of rival religions to establish the doctrine of those religions. But the doctrines of any given religion contradict the doctrines of its rival religions. That means the miracle of any given religion will contradict the miracles of its rival religion. Therefore, miracles cannot be used to establish any given doctrine.

As we have already noted, this conclusion was accepted, to some degree by the evidentialists. We also discovered, in chapter 2, that some

---

105. Hurley, *Concise Introduction to Logic*, 119.

church fathers did agree that miracles could not be used to establish specific doctrines. In fact some of them, like Origen, observed that counterfeit miracles could be performed by beings other than God. In order to determine whether or not an authentic miracle had happened the context in which the miracle was wrought had to be taken into consideration as well. Thus, in the second chapter we saw that there had to be a moral test and the prophetic test. We saw that within such tests, the authenticity of miracles could be established, provided we understood that a miracle is authentic if it was caused by God.

The argument presented by the deists here makes the mistake of ignoring the importance of such contextual considerations, and rules out, *a priori*, the possibility that some miraculous events could be genuine. In effect they argue that from the fact that miracles of different religions cancel each other out, we should reject reports of the miraculous altogether. But this vantage point misses out on the possibility that genuine miracles could in fact happen. It is an argument that essentially "throws out the baby with the bath-water." In my view, the deists leave us with no more than a closed-minded demand motivated by an intentional refusal to examine each miraculous claim on its own merit. But this is hardly a suitable framework for arriving at truth.

If my evaluation of the deists' position is correct, it should be clear that their arguments against miracles fail, and cannot be taken, cumulatively or individually, as forceful objections to miracles. But this raises an interesting issue. If David Hume built his argument against miracles, as Burns contends, on the deistic objection to miracles, does this imply that Hume's objection to miracles also fails? This is a question I intend to answer in the fifth chapter.

5

Hume's Argument Against Miracles

WE NOTED, IN THE previous chapter, that the deistic arguments against miracles can be classified into five different types: the uniformity-of-nature argument, the credibility-of-witness argument, the credulity-of-witness argument, the *ad hominem* argument, and the claim that miracles of any religion contradict those of its rival religions. We noted that Hume structured his argument against miracles around these five arguments. The task of this chapter is to highlight the different responses to Hume's argument from Hume's time to the twenty-first century. Some responses drew attention to a number of flawed assumptions that Hume made. Others tried to defend Hume's argument, contending that it was forceful. We will see that Hume's rescuers have failed to defend him adequately.

Let me begin this section by summarizing Hume's argument. Hume defines a miracle as a violation of the laws of nature. An unalterable experience, he argues, has established these laws. Therefore, the proof against miracles is as entire as any argument from experience can possibly be. It is no miracle that an apparently healthy man should suddenly die; for such has been frequently observed to happen. But it is a miracle that a dead man should come to life; for this has never been observed in any age or country. Therefore, there is a uniform experience against every miraculous event. But a uniform experience amounts to a proof. Therefore, there is here a direct and full proof against the existence of any miracle. Therefore, no testimony is sufficient to establish a miracle, unless the testimony is of such a kind that its falsehood would be more miraculous than the fact which it endeavors to establish.[1]

---

1. Hume, *Enquiry*, X.I.

In the second part of his argument, Hume gives further reasons why he believes the evidence for miracles is weak. First, the witnesses must be of unquestioned good sense, education and learning, and they must be of good credit and reputation in the eyes of humankind. But this has never been the case with religious miracles. Second, the many instances of forged miracles and supernatural events prove sufficiently the strong propensity of humankind to the extraordinary and the marvelous. Third, miraculous events are observed chiefly to abound among ignorant and barbarous nations. Fourth, all testimonies of miracles are opposed by an infinite number of witnesses of rival religions such that the miracle destroys the credit of testimony and the testimony destroys itself. The conclusion is that no human testimony is sufficient to prove a religious miracle.[2]

Throughout this chapter I will outline, in a chronological order, different but major responses to Hume's argument. The first section will deal with responses made in the eighteenth and nineteenth centuries, and the second section with those made in the twentieth and twenty-first centuries.

Eighteenth- and Nineteenth-Century Responses to Hume

In 1751 Thomas Rutherford's *The Credibility of Miracles Defended against the Author of Philosophical Essays* was published in response to David Hume's essay on miracles. Rutherford contended that no special degree of testimony is necessarily required to prove a miracle. He argued that in cases where we do not know the facts about, say, *p*, we measure *p*'s credibility in three ways: first, by its consistency with our experience; second, by its consistency with our knowledge in general; and third, by the testimony of others.[3]

Take the first way. According to Rutherford, some events occur steadily at stated times in certain places without exception. Their existence is taken for granted, and we assure ourselves that they will happen at the usual time. For example, we never think of disputing whether the sun will rise tomorrow morning, or of disbelieving that the tide came in yesterday.[4] We admit these facts as true without any testimony to vouch for them.[5]

---

2. Ibid., X.II.
3. Rutherford, *Credibility of Miracles*, 22.
4. Ibid.
5. Ibid., 24.

What about the second way? According to Rutherford, some events have a less exact likeness of truth. We find them conformable to our experience in most respects. But they are not conformable to all our experiences. The general resemblance of the truth of such events makes us think them likely to be true. However, sometimes they fail and are therefore inconsistent with truth in some points. The credibility of events in such cases does not amount to a full proof of their experience. Thus when we cannot ascertain their existence by the evidence of our senses, we are ready to believe them upon the evidence of our former experience. But our belief is not so fixed as to be raised to any degree of assurance or confidence without the help of testimony.[6] For example, whatever probability we may have from experience, that there will be frost in England on a certain week in December, and thunder on a certain week in June, we have the same probability from our knowledge of the globe that, in the opposite southern latitude, there will be frost in some particular week of June, and thunder in some particular week of December.[7]

In the third way, we measure p's credibility by the testimony of others who vouch for the evidence of their senses. This is because with respect to some events we have equal experience in both ways already stipulated above: that is, they are consistent with our experience and consistent with our knowledge in general. But with respect to other events, we have no experience either way. That is, we have not experienced them in order to judge whether they are consistent with our experience or with our knowledge in general. In such cases, we rely on the testimonies of others, who in turn, rely on and vouch for the evidence of their senses.[8]

For example, that Julius Caesar existed in Rome is a fact about which we have no experience at all. But it is seen as credible in itself because it furnishes no case of doubt about the nature of the thing. Notice also, argues Rutherford, that it furnishes no cause of belief either. However, whether we call it credible or indifferent, it is capable of being proved by a fair testimony.[9] Facts of this sort do not have credibility in themselves that can make us either believe or doubt them. But they are credible insofar as they are consistent with our knowledge.[10]

6. Ibid., 23.
7. Ibid., 24.
8. Ibid., 22–23.
9. Ibid., 23.
10. Ibid., 24–25.

From these parameters, according to Rutherford, we can see that all our reasoning about the laws and order of nature will be precarious unless it proceeds upon experiments and observation. However, once we gain some ground to stand on, our reason can survey many parts of nature, which our senses were unable to discover. For example, suppose we have determined, by observations, the proportion between the respective distances of the planets from the sun, and the periodical times of their orbits. According to Rutherford, our experience of facts stops here; but our rational knowledge of them reaches farther. That is, based upon this information furnished to our senses, our reason demonstrates the law of that force, which continually urges the planets toward the sun. This fact remains because some truths that relate to real existence are perceived immediately by our senses. But there are others which we discover by reason.[11]

Thus, according to Rutherford, experience is not the only way of discovering truth. Rather, events are made as credible by their conformity with our reason as they are by their conformity with our experience. When events conformable to and consistent with our rational knowledge are supported by a fair testimony, our assent to them is well grounded.[12]

Rutherford believes that we have a demonstrative knowledge of the existence, the power, the wisdom, and the goodness of God. This principle helps us to show that miracles do not require any supernatural degree of testimony to establish our belief in them.[13] Thus, Hume's experience of the ordinary powers of nature may be a decisive proof, with respect to those powers which are the immediate objects of experience. But they can be no proof at all, with respect to a power superior to nature, which is not the immediate object of experience, but of demonstrative knowledge.[14]

According to Rutherford, knowledge (reason) reaches further than experience, and reason leads us on from these powers to another power, that is, God's power, which is superior to the powers of nature. The existence of a miracle has a general conformity or consistency with our knowledge of such a power. This conformity or consistency with our knowledge gives it credibility enough to render it capable of being proved by a fair testimony.[15]

---

11. Ibid., 25.
12. Ibid., 25–26.
13. Ibid., 26.
14. Ibid., 27.
15. Ibid., 29–30.

Rutherford further argues that when we reject any well attested miraculous event as spurious, our reason for such rejection is not, and ought not to be, any pretended proof against the event from the general nature of all miracles. This is because if a miracle is considered merely as a supernatural change in the common course of things, then it is consistent with our knowledge of God's power.[16]

But if the circumstances of any particular miracle exclude, either directly or by necessary consequence, the power of any being that can change the common course of nature, then reports of such miracles ought to be rejected. Such a miracle, Rutherford argues, becomes inconsistent with our knowledge, from its own particular circumstances, and is incapable of being proved by any testimony whatever.[17]

From Thomas Rutherford, we proceed to William Adams. In his *Extract from an Essay on Mr. Hume's Essay on Miracles*, published in 1752, Adams draws our attention to Hume's presupposition about the uniformity of nature, namely that our reasoning about matters of fact depends wholly upon experience.[18] According to Adams, the uniformity of nature is in no way impeached by the supposition of miracles. By supposing an event to be miraculous, the uniformity of nature is preserved, and the miraculous facts are accounted for upon another principle entirely consistent with it.[19]

Moreover, according to Adams, the experience which Hume pleads is no argument at all. The experience only proves a course of nature, and whether this is ever interrupted, Adams thinks, is an open question. The experience Hume pleads teaches what may be ordinarily expected from common causes and in the common course of things. But miraculous interpositions are by their nature and essence extraordinary and out of the common course of nature.[20]

According to Adams, a great part of mankind has given its testimony to the credibility of miracles, actually believing them. In fact, by Hume's account, all the religions in the world have been founded upon this belief in miracles. If this is true, we have universal testimony to the credibility of miracles. How then can there be universal experience against them? Hume tells us we must judge of testimony by experience. But, according to Adams,

16. Ibid., 30.
17. Ibid.
18. Adams, "Extract," 40.
19. Ibid., 46.
20. Ibid., 46–47.

it seems more certain that we judge of the experience of men by their testimony.[21] Moreover, the powers of nature are so imperfectly known to us, that in most cases we argue with great uncertainty from this principle. Hence, testimony is, for the most part, of much greater force to establish the truth of past facts, than experience.[22]

However, Adams grants that there are many cases which we may from nature and experience pronounce to be impossible. For example, a physician may restore a dying man to health; but he cannot restore a dead man to life. Of all such events, as raising the dead or curing diseases with a word, we may fairly pronounce that they are impossible to human strength, and therefore when imputed to it are incredible. In this case experience decides with sufficient authority against the fact. And this is what Hume mistook for an argument against miracles.[23]

In response to Hume's credibility-of-witness argument, Adams notes that human beings are naturally made to love truth, and to hate and abhor falsehood and deceit. According to Adams, the shame of being detected in a lie, and the reproach that follows, is full proof of this.[24] Thus, we are assured that the witnesses in question (that is, the Apostles) renounce every known interest for the sake of their testimony, without any known prospect of advantage. The witness exposes himself to life-threatening circumstances, which he might have prevented by not attesting to the event in question; and the witness actually gives up his life for a painful and ignominious death. According to Adams, this is such a proof of sincerity that cannot be resisted.[25]

From Adams we proceed to Samuel Vince. Vince responds to Hume's essay on miracles in his work *Extract from "Remarks on Mr. Hume's Principles and Reasoning, in His 'Essay on Miracles,'"* published in 1809. According to Vince, the extraordinary nature of a fact is no argument against its admission upon authentic evidence. It only implies that such a fact was not to be expected. Improbability relates only to expectation. It offers nothing which can affect the proof of the fact. An inquiry into the truth of a matter of fact is a question of testimony, not of probability. The chances for

21. Ibid., 47–48.
22. Ibid., 49.
23. Ibid., 52–53.
24. Ibid., 54.
25. Ibid., 54–55.

and against the happening of an event, make no part of an investigation into its truth.[26]

According to Vince, Hume places the improbability of a miraculous event into a wrong account. He puts it in opposition to the evidence that supports the fact. But its proper office is only to influence our expectations, and thus to cause a suspension of our belief until evidence is produced. However, since evidence is not affected by the improbability of an event's occurrence, the mind ought to be left unbiased in respect to the proofs which may be offered.[27]

Also, by experience, Vince argues, Hume cannot mean personal experience only, for he includes past experience in his argument. This sort of experience must necessarily be derived from the reports of others. And it is this which must constitute the great bulk of direct evidence in the matter under consideration. Hence, this latter experience must be measured by testimony. We may then in the present question use the term experience for testimony. Therefore, contrary to what Hume has asserted, we have general experience, that is, testimony, in favor of Christian miracles.[28]

Finally, Vince questions Hume's further contention that there must be a uniform experience against every miraculous event, or else the thing would not merit that appellation. Thus, if the Deity were to work a miracle, then by Hume's definition, it ceases to be a miracle as soon as it is performed. In other words, a miracle in definition is not a miracle in fact. Thus, according to Vince, Hume frames his definitions so that they may lead him to the conclusions he wants to establish. But here, his definition is inconsistent with the existence of the thing defined.[29]

From Samuel Vince we proceed to James Somerville. In 1815, Somerville published his work *Remarks on an Article in the Edinburgh Review, in which the Doctrine of Hume on Miracles Is Maintained*. Here, Somerville treats the uniformity-of-nature argument more comprehensively than Vince. More specifically, Somerville focuses on the word experience and takes its implication to what he thinks is its logical conclusion.

To begin with, Somerville argues that the word experience can with no propriety be applied to anything except what falls under the personal observation of the epistemologist. The knowledge that any epistemologist

---

26. Vince, "Extract," 99.
27. Ibid.
28. Ibid., 101.
29. Ibid.

has of the regular rising and setting of the sun, from experience, is exactly commensurate with his own life. More exactly, it is commensurate with that part of the epistemologist's life in which he has been able to make observations. But with regard to all the time that elapsed before, the epistemologist has no experience. If he knows anything about "that time," he knows it solely by testimony. Granted, "that time" might count as "experience" with each of the successive generations which preceded the enquirer's present generation. But it comes to the present generation only in the shape of testimony. Therefore, it must be subjected to all the rules by which testimony is usually tried.[30]

In light of this, Somerville asks us to suppose, for the sake of argument, that history reaches back five thousand years. All the experience that exists in the world of the regular rising and setting of the sun is limited to the experience of the oldest men who are alive at a given time. The remainder of the given five thousand years depends entirely on testimony.[31] Thus, if Hume and his cohorts are determined to call "experience" what comes to us by testimony of persons who lived before our days, then they must in justice apply the same word to that testimony which has transmitted miracles to us. If it is by experience that we know the rising and setting of the sun from the beginning of the world, it is also by experience we know that in the days of Moses the Red Sea was divided, and many other similar facts. For Somerville, the ordinary facts which happened in those times, and these extraordinary ones, come to us precisely in the same way, by the testimony of persons who declare that they occurred within their personal experience. We must therefore give them all one denomination: either call them all experience, or call them all testimony.[32]

However, argues Somerville, if Hume does this, then Hume has to say either one of the following. First, he has to say that no testimony is to be credited against a man's personal experience. Second, he has to say that no testimony can prevail against uniform testimony. If Hume adopts the first, it will destroy all historical evidence, and all credibility of facts, except the few which have fallen under an individual's personal observation. If he adopts the second, it is perfectly harmless, though the reasoning would seem to be just. However, it assumes what is not true; for testimony is not uniform with regard to the great laws of nature. The testimony which

---

30. Somerville, "Remarks," 118.
31. Ibid., 118–19.
32. Ibid., 120.

attests the existence of miracles, whether that testimony be true or false, at all events, exists, and therefore destroys the uniformity of testimony on the other side.[33]

Therefore, Somerville concludes, miracles must be tried by the ordinary rules by which other testimony is tried. As it turns out, there is actually testimony for them. If there be any against them, Somerville contends, let it be brought forward and fairly weighed. But let them not be rejected by the sweeping assertion that uniform testimony is against them, an assertion evidently false.[34]

So far, the authors we have considered in this section rejected Hume's argument against miracles. But Hume was not entirely without defenders, one of them being Thomas Huxley. In 1881, Huxley published *The Order of Nature: Miracles*. Huxley contended that Hume's disquisition upon miracles may be safely declared to be indisputable. However, Huxley observes that Hume has "surrounded the kernel of his essay with a shell of very doubtful value."[35] To see this, Huxley draws our attention to the following argument made by Hume: According to Hume, a uniform experience exists against every miraculous event. If it did not exist, the miraculous event would not qualify to be called a miracle. Because a uniform experience against a miracle really amounts to a proof, the uniform experience serves as a real proof against the existence of any miracle. It is a proof which cannot be destroyed.[36]

Huxley contends that every one of these dicta appears to be open to serious objection. The word miracle in its primary and legitimate sense simply means something wonderful. And the source of the wonder which a miracle excites is the belief, on the part of those who witness it, that it transcends or contradicts ordinary experience. Thus, according to Huxley, the definition of a miracle as a violation of the laws of nature is, in reality, an employment of language which, on the face of the matter, cannot be justified. Every event must be taken to be a part of nature, until proof to the contrary is supplied. And such proof is, from the nature of the case, impossible.[37]

---

33. Ibid., 121.
34. Ibid.
35. Huxley, *Order of Nature*, 161.
36. Ibid., 162.
37. Ibid., 162–63.

For instance, Huxley argues, consider a piece of lead that remains suspended of itself, in the air. If such an event happened, the occurrence would be a miracle in the sense of a wonderful event. But no one trained in the methods of science would imagine that any law of nature was really violated thereby. He would simply set to work to investigate the conditions under which such a highly unexpected occurrence took place, and thereby enlarge his experience and modify his hitherto unduly narrow conceptions of the laws of nature.[38]

Huxley then draws our attention to Hume's contention that if any intelligible thing x can be distinctly conceived, then x implies no contradiction, and x can never be falsified by any *a priori* reasoning.[39] But a miracle, observes Huxley, in the sense of a sudden and complete change in the customary order of nature, is intelligible, can be distinctly conceived and implies no contradiction. Therefore, according to Hume's own showing, a miracle cannot be proved false by any demonstrative argument.[40]

Huxley believes that in making the claim cited above, Hume contradicts his own principles when he elsewhere states that a dead man coming back to life qualifies as a miracle specifically because that phenomenon has never been witnessed in any age or country. In truth, if a dead man did come to life, the fact would be evidence, not that any law of nature has been violated, but that those laws, even when they express the results of a very long and uniform experience, are necessarily based on incomplete knowledge, and are to be held only as grounds of more or less justifiable expectation.[41]

Therefore, Huxley concludes that the definition of a miracle as a suspension or contravention of the order of nature is self-contradictory. This is because all we know of the order of nature is derived from our observation of the course of events of which the so-called miracle is a part. On the other hand, no event is too extraordinary to be impossible. And therefore, if by the term "miracles" we mean only "extremely wonderful events," there can be no just ground for denying the possibility of their occurrence.[42]

But when we turn from the question of the possibility of miracles to that concerning the grounds upon which we are justified in believing

38. Ibid., 163.
39. Ibid.
40. Ibid., 163–64.
41. Ibid., 164.
42. Ibid.

any particular miracle, Hume's arguments have a very different value. For they resolve themselves into a simple statement of the dictates of common sense.[43]

However, Huxley wonders whether there are any miracles on record whose evidence fulfills the plain and simple requirements of elementary logic and elementary morality. Hume's answer can be found in the credibility-of-witness argument. In Huxley's view, Hume makes grave assertions in this argument, assertions which are least likely to be challenged by those who have made their business to weigh evidence and to give their decision under a due sense of the moral responsibility which they incur in so doing.[44]

Huxley's views were endorsed by Joseph Mazzini Wheeler in his *Introduction to Hume's Essay on Miracles*, published in 1882. According to Wheeler, everyone knows that both etymologically and popularly, the word miracle is equivalent simply to "a wonder." But Wheeler notes that Hume's argument was based on the theological definition of miracles as infractions of the laws of nature by a supernatural being or beings exterior to those laws.[45]

In Wheeler's view, a miracle in the theological sense denotes not simply the counteraction of one natural law by another, which is not opposed by experience, but the suppression of the law of uniformity of cause and effect, which experience shows to be universal. Thus, if by some unknown law, persons could, under given conditions, be raised from the dead, such facts, however wonderful, would take their place in the vast scheme of nature, and no more be properly entitled supernatural than any other.[46]

For Wheeler, the instance of the King of Siam rejecting accounts of ice has often been quoted against Hume by opponents who failed to notice the distinction between a discovery of the laws of nature and their suspension. If we could be taken to a region where the dead rise at command with the same certainty that water freezes when the temperature is below a certain point, the fact would be indubitable, but the miracle would be gone. We cannot admit a proposition as a law of nature and yet believe a fact in

---

43. Ibid.
44. Ibid., 166–67.
45. Wheeler, *Introduction to Hume's Essay*, 156.
46. Ibid., 156–57.

contradiction to it. We must disbelieve the alleged fact, or believe that we are mistaken in admitting the supposed law.[47]

Wheeler then considers the objection that once we assume a supernatural power, the antecedent improbability of supernatural visitations is removed. Wheeler contends that the existence of God is rather an additional difficulty to those who think that order was created by him and subsequently disturbed. The argument against miracles rests on our experience of the order of nature, and is therefore equally valid whether a cause of that order is assumed or not.[48] This is because the only test of the will or way of working of such a cause is to be found within the order itself. Any interference with that order still has to be proved by testimony. And the question remains whether it is more credible that men have been deceived, or that the laws of nature have been disturbed. Every individual has experience that men lie and make mistakes; none that miracles occur.[49]

Contemporary Responses to Hume

Having considered the eighteenth- and nineteenth-century responses to Hume, let us now turn to more recent responses, the first of whom is C. S. Lewis. In his book *Miracles*, first published in 1947, Lewis contends that the question whether miracles occur can never be answered simply by experience. According to Lewis, every event which might claim to be a miracle is, in the last resort, something presented to our senses, something seen, heard, touched, smelled or tasted. But our senses are not infallible. If anything extraordinary seems to have happened, Lewis contends, we can always say that we have been the victims of an illusion, provided we hold a philosophy which excludes the supernatural. In fact, what we learn from experience, according to Lewis, depends on the kind of philosophy we bring to experience. Therefore, it is useless to appeal to experience before we have settled, as well as we can, the philosophical question.[50]

According to Lewis, it is no use going to the texts arguing for miracles until we have some idea about the possibility or probability of the miraculous. Those who assume that miracles cannot happen are merely wasting

---

47. Ibid., 157.
48. Ibid., 157–58.
49. Ibid., 158.
50. Lewis, *Miracles*, 9–10.

their time by looking into the texts. For we know in advance what results they will find, since they have begun by begging the question.[51]

To begin with, Lewis addresses the subject of probability in Hume's treatment of miracles. Here, Lewis believes that Hume's version of probability is what may be called the majority vote of our past experiences. That is, the more often a thing has been known to happen, the more probable it is that it should happen again; and the less often, the less probable. Hume further contends that the regularity of nature's course is supported by something better than the majority vote of past experiences; it is supported by their unanimous vote, that is, by a "firm and unalterable experience." Therefore, there is in fact, "uniform experience" against miracles. Otherwise an event would not be a miracle, and it is always more probable that the witnesses were lying or mistaken than that a miracle occurred.[52]

However, Lewis notes that all the observations that human beings have made or will make covers only a minute fraction of the events that actually go on. Our observations would therefore be of no use unless we felt sure that Nature, when we are not watching her, behaves in the same way as when we are, that is, unless we believed in the uniformity of nature. Experience therefore, Lewis concludes, cannot prove uniformity because uniformity has to be assumed before experience proves anything. Unless nature is uniform, nothing is either probable or improbable. And the assumption which we have to make before there is any such thing as probability cannot itself be probable.[53]

According to Lewis, if we stick to Hume's method, far from concluding that all miracles are infinitely improbable, we get a complete deadlock. The only kind of probability Hume allows holds exclusively within the frame of uniformity. When uniformity is itself in question, this kind of probability is suspended. Thus, by Hume's method, Lewis concludes, we cannot say that uniformity is either probable or improbable. Equally, we cannot say that miracles are either probable or improbable. We have impounded both uniformity and miracles in a sort of limbo where probability and improbability can never come.[54]

From Lewis we turn to Alastair McKinnon. McKinnon's "Miracle and Paradox," first published in *American Philosophical Quarterly* in 1967, was

51. Ibid., 11.
52. Ibid., 134.
53. Ibid., 135.
54. Ibid., 136–37.

later republished by Richard Swinburne in his book *Miracles*. Here, McKinnon postulates two main supernaturalist senses of miracle, namely: an event involving the suspension of natural law, as well as an event conflicting with our understanding of nature. Consider the first conception. According to McKinnon, natural law involves highly generalized shorthand descriptions of how things do in fact happen, presumably within nature. On this conception there can be no suspensions of natural law rightly understood. Therefore, according to McKinnon and echoing Huxley, "miracle" defined as an event involving the suspension of natural law contains a contradiction in terms.[55]

Let us now turn to McKinnon's second conception. Here, if a miracle is seen as an event conflicting with our understanding of nature, then conceivably, the clash posited by this conception is not a clash within nature; rather it is between an event and our conception of nature. Hence, the idea of such a clash is not contradictory. This is because I might use "x is a miracle" to mean "x baffles me" or to mean "I know no laws that could account for x." Hence, there might be occasions here on which "miracle" could be used legitimately in this sense.[56]

However, McKinnon urges us to take note of the fact that people do not simply say that they do not know the appropriate laws accounting for x; rather, they use the term "miracle" to express their belief that there is no law accounting for x. If they did not use it in this way, it would be difficult to see how this term could have any distinctive meaning, or even the peculiar religious force it obviously has. Therefore, according to McKinnon, it seems that whereas the second conception could be a legitimate ascription to the term miracle, the meaning usually assumed has to reflect the first conception if it must retain its religious significance.[57]

Therefore, McKinnon concludes, one who insists upon describing an event as a miracle is faced with two equally impossible alternatives. First, if the person attempts to represent an event as an instance of the second conception, he is forced by the logic of his position to withdraw the term completely. Second, if the person attempts instead to present it as an instance of the first conception he forces himself to say that the event in question both is and is not a part of the actual course of events. Therefore,

---

55. McKinnon, "Miracle," 49–50.
56. Ibid., 50–51.
57. Ibid., 51.

according to McKinnon, all the properly descriptive senses of miracle are logically improper.[58]

Anthony Flew's article "Scientific versus Historical Evidence" takes a different approach from McKinnon's. According to Flew, there seems to be a lack, on the part of Hume, of an adequate conception of a law of nature. This makes it impossible for Hume to justify a distinction between the marvelous or the unusual and the truly miraculous. Consider, for instance, that in Hume's view, to say that A is the cause of B is to say that all A's are followed by B's, and that we habitually associate A's with B's. Hume would presumably have to say that a law of nature holds wherever A's are constantly conjoined with B's. According to Flew, if this were indeed all that a law of nature asserted, it would give no ground at all for saying that the occurrence of an exception to such a law is physically impossible. Thus any attempt to use our knowledge of such a merely numerical universal proposition as an evidential canon by which to justify the outright rejection of any testimony to the occurrence of a falsifying exception would be a preposterous piece of question-begging. According to Flew, Hume seems to be doing just that.[59]

Therefore, in Flew's view, Hume can provide no conception of law of nature sufficiently strong to allow for any real distinction between the miraculous and the extremely unusual. To dismiss out of hand all testimony to the occurrence beyond the range of our observations of a counter example, simply because such an occurrence would falsify the universal generalization based upon our observation to date, would indeed be arbitrary and bigoted.[60]

Flew suggests that we ought to achieve a better understanding of what the law of nature is. Once this is done, the way is open to a more adequate view of the sort of evidence needed to justify us in believing that some given candidate law actually does hold. As would now be expected, Flew believes that Hume can give us very little help here. However, Hume gives us hints. For example, after defining a miracle as a violation of the laws of nature, he argues that a firm and unalterable experience has established these laws, namely, nomological universal propositions. And since the criterion of the nomological is also a criterion of reliability, to be justified in asserting that

---

58. Ibid., 51–52.
59. Flew, "Scientific," 97–98.
60. Ibid., 98.

some law of nature in fact obtains you must know that the appropriate nomological statement has been thoroughly tested for reliability.[61]

So what option does Flew suggest for Hume? According to Flew, the nomological aspect of the laws of nature must serve as a fundamental canon of our historical criticism. Thus, finding what appears to be historical evidence for an occurrence inconsistent with such a nomological statement, we must always insist on interpreting that evidence in some other way. This is because if the nomological is true, then it is physically impossible that any event incompatible with it could have occurred. However, Flew observes, it is always possible that an accepted nomological may in fact be false, since we are all fallible. Therefore, it is theoretically possible that an occasion might arise in which in the light of historical evidence it would be rational to take another look at the credentials of what had previously been thought to be a law of nature.[62]

But then, Flew observes, this seems to be a conflict between science and history; for on the one side we have what purports to be a historical proof, while on the other the nomological is supposed to have been established by methods which might in a very broad sense be classed as scientific. However, Flew thinks that the antagonists in this contest are unevenly matched. To be sure, the historical evidence could constitute sufficient reason for reexamining the nomological. Under this reexamination, the nomological might fail to sustain its claim to be believed. But if, on the contrary, the nomological survived such testing, it would be rational, then, to reject the historical proof, though of course we could always be mistaken.[63]

In Flew's view, the justification for giving the scientific view ultimate precedence over the historical view lies in the nature of the propositions concerned, and in the evidence which can be deployed to sustain them. The candidate historical proposition will be particular, often singular, and in the past tense. But just by reason of this very pastness and particularity it is no longer possible for anyone to examine the subject directly for himself. All that is left to examine is the present detritus of the past, which includes the physical records of testimony. This detritus can be interpreted as evidence only in light of our present knowledge, or presumed knowledge, of men

---

61. Ibid., 98–99.
62. Ibid., 100.
63. Ibid., 100–101.

and things. This must always be the fundamental principle of historical interpretation.[64]

But Flew observes that this is not the case with the law of nature. The law of nature will, unlike the candidate historical proposition, be a general nomological. Therefore, in theory, it can be tested at any time by any person. Whatever falls within its scope is physically necessary, and whatever it precludes is physically impossible. It possesses, and is designed to possess, the logical strength required, when combined with appropriate particular premises, both to license and to demand inferences to substantial conclusions transcending those premises.[65] In this way, then, Flew thinks Hume's argument can be improved.

J. L. Mackie also tried to "improve" Hume's argument, though in a different way from Flew's. In *The Miracle of Theism*, published in 1982, Mackie contends that Hume's case against miracles is an epistemological argument. It does not try to show that miracles never do happen or never could happen, but only that we never have good reasons for believing that they have happened. According to Mackie, this argument must be clearly distinguished from the suggestion that the very concept of a miracle is incoherent.[66]

Perhaps then, Mackie suggests, we should consider whether there is a coherent concept of a miracle which would not rule out the occurrence of miracles *a priori*. If miracles are to serve their traditional function of giving spectacular support to religious claims, the concept must not be so weakened that anything at all unusual or remarkable counts as a miracle. We must keep, in the definition, the notion of a violation of natural law. But then, if it is to be even possible that a miracle should occur, Mackie suggests that we must stipulate a definition of a law of nature that contrasts the order of nature with a possible divine or supernatural intervention.[67]

Thus, we could take the law of nature to describe ways in which the world works when left to itself, when not interfered with. This notion of ways in which the world works is coherent and by no means obscure. However, Mackie suggests that, for purposes of explication, it is sufficient to

---

64. Ibid., 101.
65. Ibid., 101–2.
66. Mackie, *Miracle of Theism*, 19.
67. Ibid.

have an idea of the basic workings of the laws of nature, and to know in principle what it would be to discover them.[68]

Thus, using this idea, and the assumption that there are some such basic laws of working to be found, we can hope to determine what the actual laws are by reference to a restricted range of experiments. This opens up the possibility that we might determine that something is a basic law of working of natural objects, and yet also, independently, find that it was occasionally violated. An occasional violation does not in itself necessarily overthrow the independently established conclusion that this is a law of nature.[69]

Also, Mackie adds that there should be no obscurity in the notion of intervention within nature. This is because we have a clear understanding of how there can be, in "the closed system of the natural world," an external intrusion, which brings about changes that the closed system would not have produced of its own accord. For Mackie, if the laws by which the natural world works are deterministic, then the notion of a violation of them is quite clear-cut.[70]

Mackie further observes that if the basic laws of working are statistical or probabilistic, the notion of a violation of them is less precise. If something happens which, given those statistical laws and some earlier complete state of the world, is completely improbable, we still cannot say firmly that the laws have been violated: laws of this sort explicitly allow that what is extremely improbable may occasionally come about. Indeed it is highly probable, both physically and epistemically, that some events, each of which is very improbable, will occur at rare intervals.[71]

Nevertheless, Mackie contends that the full concept of a miracle requires that the intrusion discussed above be a purposeful intrusion, and that it should fulfill the intention of a supernatural being. For Mackie, this connection cannot be sustained by any ordinary causal theory; it presupposes a power to fulfill intentions directly, without physical means. In Mackie's opinion, the very possibility of such a power is highly dubious. Mackie therefore concludes that this requirement for a miracle will be particularly hard to confirm.[72]

---

68. Ibid., 20.
69. Ibid., 20–21.
70. Ibid., 21.
71. Ibid.
72. Ibid., 22.

Despite this contention, Mackie concedes that successful prophecy could be regarded as a form of miracle for which there could in principle be good evidence. Thus, if someone is reliably recorded as having prophesied at T_1 an event at T_2, which could not be predicted at T_1, on any natural grounds, and the event occurs at T_2, then at any later time T_3, we can assess the evidence for the claims both that the prophecy was made at T_1 and that its accuracy cannot be explained either causally or as accidental, and hence that it was probably miraculous. In Mackie's view, there is then a coherent concept of miracles. Their possibility is not ruled out *a priori*, by definition.[73]

What remains to be shown, however, is whether Hume's argument shows that we never have good reasons for believing that any have occurred. Mackie begins by claiming that Hume's general principle for evaluation of testimony is substantially correct. However, he holds that Hume's description of what gives support to a judgment about an unobserved case that would fall under some generalization, is very unsatisfactory. But Since Mackie's take on Hume's inductive generalization is almost identical to Flew's, I will not restate it here. It will be enough to point out Mackie's contention that a good deal of other information and background knowledge is needed before we can make the sort of generalizations that Hume makes. It is harder to arrive at well-supported inductive generalizations than Hume allows.[74]

For Mackie, then, these various qualifications together entail that what has been widely and reasonably thought to be a law of nature may not be one, perhaps in ways that are highly relevant to some supposed miracles. But, according to Mackie, this may create a problem for the defender of miracles, for he needs the very laws of nature in order to be able to say that the alleged occurrence is a miracle, a violation of that natural law, by supernatural intervention.[75]

Therefore, according to Mackie, the miracle advocate must identify the law of nature that has been violated in order to claim that the reported event is miraculous. That is, he must in effect concede to Hume that the antecedent improbability of this event is as high as it could be, hence that, apart from the testimony, we have the strongest possible grounds for

---

73. Ibid., 21–23.
74. Ibid., 25.
75. Ibid., 24–25.

believing that the alleged event did not occur. It is this maximal improbability that the weight of the testimony would have to overcome.[76]

For this reason, Mackie suggests the following as a way of improving Hume's argument: For one, the agreement of two or more independent witnesses constitutes very powerful evidence. This is because it is difficult for even a single liar to keep on telling a consistent false story; but it is much harder for two or more liars to do so. Of course if there is any collusion between the witnesses, or if either has been influenced, directly or indirectly, by the other, or if both stories have a common source, this question is easily answered. That is why the independence of the witnesses is important. On the one hand it means that a certain sort of testimony can be more powerful evidence than Hume's discussion would suggest. On the other hand, it means that where we seem to have a plurality of reports, it is essential to check carefully whether they really are independent of one another. The difficulty of meeting this requirement, urges Mackie, would be an important supplement to the points made in the second part of Hume's essay.[77]

Therefore, Mackie contends that where there is some plausible testimony about the occurrence of what would appear to be a miracle, those who accept this as a miracle have the double burden of showing both that the event took place and that it violated the laws of nature. But Mackie thinks it will be very hard to sustain this double burden. This is because whatever tends to show that it would have been a violation of natural law tends for that very reason to make is most unlikely that it actually happened.[78]

From Mackie, we turn to Richard Swinburne. In his article "Historical Evidence," Swinburne begins by identifying four kinds of evidence for the occurrence of a past event. First, we have our own apparent memories. According to Swinburne, "I remember, in my opinion, to some extent what I was doing yesterday, or last year, what happened to me, and what was going on in my neighborhood." Granted, I may be mistaken, and certain evidence may convince me that I am mistaken. However, if I remember that p in the usual use of "remember," then of logical necessity it was the case that p.[79]

Second, the testimony of others about their experience is also evidence about what happened in the past. This includes what the witnesses say they

---

76. Ibid., 26.
77. Ibid., 25–26.
78. Ibid., 26.
79. Swinburne, "Evidence," 133–34.

did and saw and what happened to them. This may be testimony spoken to us personally or written down long ago.[80]

The third kind of evidence involves the physical traces of what happened. Such physical traces are evidence for us that certain past events probably happened. The evidence of traces could be of considerable importance in assessing whether some miraculous event occurred. Thus, we might have evidence of footprints in soft mud that Jones was on the side of a broad river one minute ago, and evidence of Jones on the other side now, but not in the least wet or with the slightest indication of water having touched his body or clothes, and no bridge, boats, airplanes or rope by which he could have crossed. Hence, the evidence indicates he must have walked or flown across.[81]

The fourth kind of evidence involves our contemporary understanding of what things are physically impossible or improbable. That is, it involves such things as are ruled out or rendered improbable by the laws of nature or generalizations of what usually happens. This scientific knowledge serves as a check on the evidence of apparent memory, testimony and traces.[82]

Swinburne notes that whereas Hume says a great deal about evidence of the second and fourth kinds, he says nothing at all about evidence of the first and third kinds. Hume supposes that the conflict about what happens is a conflict between testimony and scientific knowledge. But sometimes the evidence available to an inquirer consists not merely of the testimony of others but of one's own apparently remembered observations.[83]

So what do we do when pieces of evidence seem to be in conflict with each other? Swinburne suggests three principles for weighing them against one another. First, evidence of different kinds ought to be given different weights. Thus, one's own apparent memory ought as such to count for more than the testimony of another witness, unless and until evidence of its relative unreliability is forthcoming.[84]

Second, different pieces of evidence ought to be given different weights in accordance with any empirical evidence which may be available about their different reliability, obtained by the procedure of "narrowing the evidence class." To see how this procedure would work in a particular

---

80. Ibid., 134.
81. Ibid., 136.
82. Ibid., 135.
83. Ibid., 135-36.
84. Ibid., 138-39.

setting, consider the following illustration: if the testimony of Jones conflicts with that of Smith, rather than investigating, broadly, the worth of testimony in general, Swinburne suggests we narrow our investigation by considering the worth of Jones' testimony and of Smith's testimony. This is done by seeing if, on all other occasions, when we ascertain what happened, Jones or Smith correctly described what happened. In so far as each did, his testimony is reliable.[85]

Third, Swinburne suggests that we must not reject coincident evidence unless an explanation can be given of the coincidence. Thus, if five witnesses all say the same thing and we wish to reject their evidence, we are in general not justified in doing so unless we can explain why they all said the same thing. Such explanations could be that they were subject to common illusions, or plotted together to give false testimony. For Swinburne, these subsidiary principles, perhaps with others he does not explicate, are the standards of investigation adopted by and large by all historical investigators.[86]

But what if pieces of evidence of the first three kinds conflict with evidence of the fourth kind? This is where Swinburne takes issue with Flew. In Swinburne's view, Flew seems to suggest, as we have already seen, that evidence of the fourth kind could never be outweighed by evidence of the first three kinds.[87]

But Swinburne thinks Flew is mistaken. This is because particular experiments on particular occasions only give a certain and far from conclusive support to claims that a purported scientific law is true. Any person can test for the truth of a purported scientific law; but a positive result to one test will give only limited support to the claim. Swinburne thinks exactly the same holds for purported historical truths. Anyone can examine the evidence, but a particular piece of evidence gives only limited support to the claim that the historical proposition is true. But in the historical as in the scientific case, there is no limit to the testing which we can do.[88]

Against Flew, Swinburne argues that claims that some formula L is a law of nature and claims that apparent memory, testimony or traces of certain types are to be relied on, are claims established ultimately in a similar kind of way. The claims will be strong or weak for the same reasons, and so

---

85. Ibid., 138.
86. Ibid., 139–40.
87. Ibid., 141–42.
88. Ibid., 142.

neither ought to take automatic preference over the other. To make the supposition that they are to be treated differently is to introduce a complicating *ad hoc* procedure for assessing evidence.[89]

According to Swinburne, if the law is universal, it will firmly rule out an exception. If statistical, it will merely show an exception to be highly improbable. Likewise, traces or testimony may, in virtue of the correlation used, either show to be certain or show to be highly probable the event in question. Here, Swinburne distinguishes between a statistical correlation and a universal correlation. A statistical correlation is of the sort that satisfies statements such as "witnesses of type n are reliable in 99% of the cases." A universal correlation is one that satisfies statements such as "witnesses of type n are invariably reliable." Thus, if the correlation between, for example, testimony of a certain kind of witness and the past event testified to is statistical, then it shows that the event in question having happened (that is, what the witnesses reported) is highly probable. And if the correlation is universal, then it makes certain the occurrence of the event in question.[90]

The point of Swinburne's distinction is this: whether the evidence on balance supports or opposes the occurrence of E is firstly a matter of whether the law or correlation in question is universal or statistical in form; it is secondly a matter of how well established the law or correlation is. A statistical law may have very strong evidence in its favor. On the other hand, some universal laws are, though established, not very strongly established. This includes, for example, many of the generalizations of biology or anthropology. Thus, suppose L is a law, universal or statistical, to which the occurrence of E would be an exception, and T is a trace of piece of testimony of the occurrence of E, shown to be such by an established correlation C. Whether the evidence on balance supports or opposes the occurrence of E is a matter of whether L and C are universal or statistical, and how well they are established.[91]

Suppose, therefore, that C is universal and better established than L. According to Swinburne, whether L is universal or statistical, the evidence on balance supports the occurrence of E. Whereas if L is universal and is better established than C, then, whether C is universal or merely statistical, the evidence is against the occurrence of E. If C and L are both statistical, and C is no less well established than L, and C renders the occurrence of E

---

89. Ibid., 143.
90. Ibid.
91. Ibid., 144–45.

more probable than L renders it improbable, then the evidence on balance supports the occurrence of E. If C and L are both statistical, and L is no less well established than C, and L renders the occurrence of E more improbable than C renders it probable, then the evidence on balance is against the occurrence of E.

The above considerations lead Swinburne to find it reasonable to suppose that in principle, the degree of support for any correlation C or disjunction of correlations could exceed the degree of support for any law, and hence render it more probable than not that the cited event E occurred. However, Swinburne admits that in general any one correlation C will be less well established than L. And since L will usually be a universal L, its evidence will in general be preferred to that of C. But Swinburne is quick to add that the more pieces of evidence there are that E occurred, the more such evidence by its cumulative effect will tend to outweigh the counterevidence of L.[92]

Therefore, although standards for weighing evidence are not always clear, apparent memory, testimony and traces could sometimes outweigh the evidence of physical impossibility. It is just a question of how much evidence of the former kind we have, and how reliable we can show it to have been.[93]

Almost a decade after Swinburne, J. Houston argued that Lewis' interpretation of Hume is mistaken; for, according to Houston, Lewis takes it that Hume regards a law of nature as describing what actually happens in its field, such that there can be no exception to a natural law (This, interpretation actually seems more relevant to Huxley than to Lewis). If taken in this way, Hume's definition of "miracle" would imply that there are no miracles. But Houston thinks this is not what Hume is saying.[94]

Rather, Hume errs in two ways, in Houston's view. First, Hume is at fault in maintaining that the evidence for the relevant law of nature is, in the overall dialectical context, undeniably relevant to an assessment of the probability that a reported putative miracle actually took place. The problem with this position is as follows: Suppose that there is reason to think that a god walked on water. On this supposition, a body of evidence, however vast, in favor of Archimedes Principle cannot without further

---

92. Ibid., 146–47.
93. Ibid., 151.
94. Houston, *Reported Miracles*, 128.

argument be taken as relevant to deciding the question of whether or not, on the reported occasion, a god walked on water.

But Hume reaches his conclusion that evidence for a supposed miracle will always be overridden because it will never outweigh the large body of undeniably relevant evidence in favor of natural law, only by *assuming* that no god has acted miraculously in such a way as to produce an event of a kind contrary to natural law. In Houston's view, the believer in miracles is not bound to recognize that assumption as necessary or well-founded. Thus, Hume's check appears to lack a firm anchorage here.[95]

Houston goes beyond Swinburne's view on witnesses by suggesting the possibility that some people will take particular care over what they say precisely when what they say seems surprising, questionable or unexpected. Thus, if such people were to witness "a walking on water," we can be sure that they would be carefully circumspect indeed before reporting the event. Thus, in Houston's view, the more *prima facie* unlikely the event, the more care will be taken by a person of this disposition that any account which he brings himself to give of it is accurate.[96]

Herein, according to Houston, lies Hume's second error. Hume erroneously maintains that the improbability of an event E counts against the likelihood that a report of E is true.[97] Hume could have continued to reason more soundly if he had continued by treating the improbability of what is reported. He should then have asked how, in our experience, a report's having an improbable content correlates with that report's being true. According to Houston, Hume's own view that having an improbable content in itself counts against the report's probability would be justified as a conclusion of such an empirical inquiry if indeed experience were to reveal a correlation between a report's having an improbable content, and that report's being found to be false. But Hume did not attempt this sort of necessary empirical justification.[98]

Houston maintains that when a report tells of something which would be contrary to natural law, this should prompt some careful assessment before the report is believed. However, suppose that what is reported is anomalous. This will not, on its own, determine the assessment that it is anomalous. Rather, the report, along with other facts, should be set against

95. Ibid., 133–34.
96. Ibid., 150–51.
97. Ibid., 151.
98. Ibid., 152.

experience of other similar reports of anomalous events. In this way, experience can guide the assessment of reports of putative miracles.[99]

More recently, John Earman provided an ingenious attempt to show that Hume's argument against miracles is fundamentally flawed. In *Hume's Abject Failure*, Earman contends that the structure of Hume's argument against miracles takes the form of Reichenbach's straight rule of induction, namely: if n A's have been examined and m have been found to be B's, then the probability that the next A examined will be a B is m/n. The consequence is that if $m = n$, then the probability that the next A will be a B is 1.[100]

Notice that this is essentially Mackie's and Flew's interpretation of Hume. But Earman goes further by citing his evidence for this contention. According to Earman, the evidence is found in Hume's writing alluding to the conclusion that a uniform experience must exist against all miraculous events and that such events would not be miracles if the uniform experience did not exist. Uniform experiences amount to a proof. Therefore, in these experiences, we find a direct and full proof against the existence of all miracles.[101] Additional evidence comes from Hume's letter of 1761 to Hugh Blair. In that letter, Hume argued how the proof against a miracle, owing to the fact that the proof is founded on invariable experience, remains complete and certain when taken alone specifically because it implies no doubt.[102]

But how does Hume define proof? To answer this question, Earman takes us back to Hume's treatment of probabilities in the *Enquiry*. Here, we find that Hume divides arguments into demonstrations, proofs and probabilities. Hume defines proofs as arguments from experience that leave no room for doubt. According to Earman, this definition seems to imply that when experience provides a proof, the conditional probability of the conclusion, given the evidence of experience, is 1. Only when experience is variable do we have room for doubt that the probability is less than 1.[103] Thus, by Hume's straight rule of induction, experience confers a probability of 1 on a presumptive law. Hence, the probability of a miracle is flatly zero. According to Earman, this proof works not only against resurrections, but

---

99. Ibid., 154–55.
100. Earman, *Hume's Abject Failure*, 22–23.
101. Hume, *Enquiry*, X.I.
102. Ibid., 23.
103. Ibid.

against, say, the "miracle" of a violation of the presumptive law of conservation of energy.[104]

Earman thinks that Hume's straight rule of induction is both descriptively inadequate to actual scientific practice, and stultifying to scientific inquiry. To see this, Earman asks us to consider that among the zillions of protons observed by particle physicists, none has been verified to decay. But particle physicists do not assign a probability of 1 to the proposition that the next proton to be observed will not decay. And they certainly do not think that they have adequate inductive grounds for probabilistic certainty with respect to the general proposition that no proton ever decays.[105]

According to Earman, there is positive evidence that Hume intended a consequence like this one. For example, in Hume's discussion in part 2 of his essay against miracles, he cites the hypothetical story of the resurrection of Queen Elizabeth. Here, Hume simply contends that such events have never been witnessed in any age or country. He also cites Cardinal de Retz's story of the recovery of a leg by rubbing holy water on it, as well as the Jansenists' miracle stories. Hume praises Cardinal de Retz for giving no credence to the story he related.[106]

However, Earman considers the possibility that Hume perhaps never intended a consequence of the sort cited above. The evidence that this, perhaps, was not Hume's intention is demonstrated by the fact that maintaining such a position seems dogmatic. And Hume does try to distance himself from such dogmatism. For example, when uniform experience supports a law statement L that is contradicted by testimony, Hume speaks of putting proof against proof, the strongest of which must prevail, but still with a reduction of its force, in proportion to that of its rival.[107]

At any rate, if the weighing of proof is to be done within the ambit of the probability calculus and the rule of conditionalization, then Earman thinks Hume's straight rule has to be dropped—his proof in favor of L by uniform experience cannot be taken to mean probability of 1 but at most a high probability that is short of 1. Consequently, uniform experience does not furnish a proof against a miracle in the sense of making the conditional probability of its occurrence flatly zero. Such a concession would mean that the distinction between a Humean miracle and a marvel is a matter

---

104. Ibid.
105. Earman, *Hume's Abject Failure*, 31.
106. Ibid.
107. Ibid., 32.

of degree rather than of kind. And once the concession is granted, Earman argues, it is natural to wonder how it can be that testimonial evidence can ground belief in marvels but not in Humean miracles.[108]

For example, take the case of the Indian Prince. According to Earman, Hume contends that the prince who refused to believe the first relations concerning the effects of frost reasoned justly. This is because the prince was right to be suspicious of reports of a solid form of water. In Earman's view, Hume seems to be saying that the solid form of water is not miraculous.[109]

Earman does grant Hume's contention here. Unfortunately, Hume's contention here is too broad because he cannot escape the consequence that his rule of induction which produces a proof against a resurrection also leads to a proof against ice.[110] Consider, for instance, that if, as is popularly maintained in science, *Homo sapiens* arose in the hot climate of Africa, then there was a stage in human history where the total collective experience of the species coincided in relevant respects with that of the Indian Prince. In these circumstances the collectivist version of Hume's straight rule (namely, that E must be universally attested) dictates a conditional probability of zero for the solid state of water, and consequently a dismissal of a report of such a state of affairs.[111]

Earman's position did not go unchallenged. Michael Fogelin has tried to rescue Hume from the sort of "misread" that he says has characterized most critiques, including that of Earman. In Fogelin's view, to claim that Hume ever said that no testimony could ever be sufficient to establish the occurrence of miracle is to misread Hume. Hume never says this in part 1 of his essay, though in part 2 he says that no testimony for any kind of miracle has ever amounted to a probability.[112]

According to Fogelin, we can think of Hume as offering two types of tests for evaluating testimony. The first of these is what he calls the direct test. Fogelin restates the direct test as follows: the witnesses must concur with one another, rather than contradict one another. The witnesses must be many, not few. The witnesses must be of unimpeachable, rather than of doubtful character. The witnesses must be disinterested, rather than interested, parties. The witnesses must present their testimony in measured

108. Ibid.
109. Ibid., 34–35.
110. Ibid., 35.
111. Ibid., 35–36.
112. Fogelin, *Defense of Hume on Miracles*, 2.

tones of confidence, rather than with hesitation or too violent asseveration. To these Fogelin adds that the witnesses must have special expertise relevant to the matter at hand. They must not be gullible, visually impaired, and so on.[113]

Fogelin calls the second test "the reverse test." Here, one should consider the probability that a reported event could have occurred without taking into account the testimony given on its behalf. If an event is extraordinary or marvelous, then the evidence resulting from testimony admits of a reduction, greater or less, in proportion, as the fact is more or less unusual. The improbability of the event's occurring gives us more grounds, though perhaps not decisive, for challenging the force of the testimony.[114]

Fogelin then proceeds by suggesting that satisfaction of the direct test is what, perhaps, amounts to what Hume is willing to call a proof. However, the decision rendered through the use of the reverse method also amounts to a proof, according to Hume. But just as unimpeachable testimony can supply strong support for the occurrence of an improbable event, the very high antecedent improbability of an event's occurring can supply strong support for asserting the nonoccurrence of that event. This sets the stage for the possibility of a clash of proof against proof. One proof is based on the direct method that the event did take place; and the other proof is based on the reverse method that the event did not take place.[115]

The upshot of this, according to Fogelin, is that we are now faced with a proof confronting a contrary proof. One is based on the reverse method, and the other on the direct method. It is tempting to think, according to Fogelin, that Hume holds that the proof using the reverse method would win, should such a situation arise. But Hume does not say this. Instead, Hume says that if the falsehood of a person's testimony is more miraculous than the event the person relates, then and not till then, would the person command Hume's belief or opinion.[116]

Fogelin then draws our attention to Hume's refutation of the miracle of Abbé Paris. According to Fogelin, Hume seems to concede, without qualification, that the testimony in behalf of these miracles amounts to full proof. We thus seem to have testimony amounting to a proof on one side, being overridden by some kind of *a priori* argument on the other. Fogelin

113. Ibid., 8.
114. Ibid., 7.
115. Ibid., 8–9.
116. Ibid., 15.

admits here that this is precisely the argument he contends Hume does not employ. However, Fogelin asks us to consider that Hume's further remark about the "cloud of witnesses" shows that he does not put the debate on *a priori* footing.[117]

Moreover, Fogelin adds, the eight days of darkness miracle shows that Hume's argument concerning miracles is not an *a priori* argument in character. This miracle shows that the contest between the direct method and the reverse method of evaluating testimony in support of a miraculous event need not always favor the reverse method. Moreover, there are no religious motives involved that might raise suspicions on that score.[118]

In Fogelin's view, the wise reasoner takes herself to be justified in rejecting reports of events that go against the laws of nature unless the evidence in favor of the events dominates the evidence in favor of the law. In such a conflict we have evidence facing evidence, and the matter can be resolved only through the weighing of evidence. Fogelin believes that this is precisely the situation Hume envisages when evaluating testimony on behalf of a miracle. And Hume's eight days of darkness miracle is intended to show that given the right sort of testimony, the balance can shift.[119]

In spite of this shift, Fogelin takes Hume to be contending that testimony concerning religious miracles is notoriously unreliable. On the basis of this general fact about the quality of such testimony, the wise reasoner has ample grounds to reject it. But this does not mean, Fogelin adds, that on *a priori* grounds no amount of testimony could ever establish the occurrence of a religious miracle. Suppose, for example, that for eight days all was dark, except for an illuminated face that simultaneously appeared throughout the world, speaking in a way intelligible to all, offering many proofs of his or her magnificence, and so on. Fogelin thinks that in such a case we could have a case that parallels Hume's example of a natural miracle. And it would be prejudice to reject the testimony in behalf of religious miracles while accepting the testimony in behalf of the natural miracle.[120]

Fogelin then turns his attention to Earman's critique of Hume. According to Fogelin, Earman's evidence for attributing the straight rule to Hume depends wholly on the occurrence of a number of strongly stated

---

117. Ibid., 23.
118. Ibid., 25–26.
119. Ibid., 27–28.
120. Ibid., 29.

conclusions. In Fogelin's view, the strong talk may seem to settle the matter, but it does not.[121]

To see this, Fogelin draws our attention to Hume's distinction between proof and probability as follows: To adapt our language more to common use, we ought to categorize arguments into demonstrations, proofs, and probabilities. By proof Hume refers to arguments from experience that leave no room for doubt. Fogelin urges us to take seriously Hume's expression to adapt our language more to common use. In Fogelin's view, if we take this quite literally, it concerns the way we speak. Here, Hume seems to say that when we speak of probabilities, we conversationally imply that some genuine, though perhaps small doubt remains. By using strong language, we cancel this conversational implication. Thus, Fogelin thinks it is a mistake to cite Hume's strong talk as the basis for attributing to him a commitment to the straight rule of induction.[122]

However, Fogelin is quick to admit that it would not be off the mark to say that sufficiently rich evidence could lead someone to speak and act as if, or almost as if a probability assignment of one (or zero) to a hypothesis is justified. In Fogelin's view, when the evidence is strong enough to make something a moral certainty, then a concern with further evidence ceases. This, Fogelin thinks, is the appropriate interpretation of Cardinal De Retz's behavior. But there is this difference. Cardinal De Retz's moral certainty, though robust, remains defeasible. It would take a great deal to budge De Retz from his skepticism, but it still remains possible he could be budged.[123]

Fogelin's point is that Hume's argument here is not an argument that someone committed to what Earman calls Hume's straight rule would produce. However, Fogelin admits that Hume's language in his relation of Cardinal De Retz's story is very strong. But the context in which it occurs is plainly concerned with religious miracles, and with respect to those sorts of miracles Hume holds that it is a moral evidential certainty that the miracle did not occur.[124]

---

121. Ibid., 44–45.
122. Ibid., 46.
123. Ibid.
124. Ibid., 50–51.

Evaluating Hume

In this section, I will evaluate Hume's argument against miracles, as well as those of his defenders. I will also evaluate the views of those who tried to defend the supernaturalist's position against Hume's attack. As noted at the beginning of this chapter, I will show that Hume's argument against miracles is weak. I will also argue that Hume's defenders do not quite succeed in trying to rescue Hume from the flaws attending his argument.

Let me begin with Hume. I contend here that our findings in chapter 2 can be used as a critique of key areas in Hume's essay on miracles. One such area is Hume's definition of miracle. As already noted, Hume defines a miracle as *a transgression of the law of nature by a particular volition of Deity, or the interposition of some invisible agent.*[125] If we compare this definition of miracle with the one we formulated in chapter 2, we at once discover that Hume's definition of a miracle is inadequate. We defined a miracle as an event in nature sometimes occurring contrary to nature, sometimes above or beyond nature and sometimes in accordance with nature, and in all cases, capable of being authenticated, as mysteriously caused by God in a way that nature could not have done by itself. We noted that such authentication comes through the prophetic context, the moral context, or both contexts.

Compared to our definition above, Hume's discussion is lacking in many ways. First, his definition of miracles views miracles in isolation by ignoring the various contexts in which the miracles are claimed to occur. We noted at the end of the second chapter that viewing miracles in isolation will result in a narrow understanding of the nature and purpose of miracles, and this would result in a misleading treatment of the whole question of miracles. Hume falls into precisely this kind of error.

We note, for example, that his understanding of the nature and purpose of miracles is narrow. One narrow feature we find in Hume's definition is that miracles are limited only to violations of the laws of nature. His definition does not take into consideration that miracles, besides being events that can happen contrary to nature, can also happen above nature without violating nature, as well as in accordance with nature. Another narrow aspect of Hume's definition is that he limits the purpose of miracles to "confirming systems of religion." But the different contexts explicated in chapter 2 show that confirming religious doctrine is not the only purpose of miracles. Miracles can also strengthen faith, or help to call one to moral

---

125. Hume, *Enquiries*, n1.

reformation. Since I dealt with these purposes at length in chapter 2, I do not need to repeat them here.

The second way in which Hume's whole discussion is lacking can be located in our discussion of context. Our definition of miracle is built on the predominantly theistic view of the ancient and medieval philosophers. We saw, in chapter 2, that belief in a supernatural, powerful and intelligent designer was seen as a rationally acceptable way of viewing our world. Once this viewpoint is conceded, then belief in miracles as possible and actual falls cogently into place.

Interestingly, Hume conceded this viewpoint in his *Natural History of Religion* as well as in his *Dialogues concerning Natural Religion*, but rejected its implication in his *Enquiries*.

In the *Natural History of Religion*, Hume postulates a belief seemingly uncharacteristic of a position for which he remains famous. He notes how every inquiry about religion remains supremely important. He draws our attention to two questions in particular. The first question concerns the foundation of religion in reason, and the second question concerns the origin of religion in human nature. According to Hume, the first question has a most obvious solution, namely, the whole frame of nature reveals an intelligent author. Therefore, after serious reflection, no rational enquirer can suspend his or her belief concerning the primary principles of genuine theism and religion.[126]

Toward the end of the same work, Hume contends that we have a universal propensity to belief in an invisible intelligent power. If this is not an original instinct, at least it remains a general attendant of human nature. According to Hume, it may be considered a kind of mark or stamp which God has set upon his work. Hume believes nothing can dignify human beings than to be selected in this way, from other parts of creation, and to bear the image or impression of God.[127]

In the *Dialogues concerning Natural Religion*, Philo, a character in the *Dialogues* widely regarded as Hume's mouthpiece argues how our question can never be concerning the *existence* of God in debates about such subjects. The question is only about the *nature* of God. The existence of God, argues Philo, is unquestionable and self-evident specifically because

---

126. Hume, *Natural History of Religion*, 134.
127. Ibid., 184.

nothing exists without a cause. The original cause of this universe, whatever it is, is God. We piously ascribe to God every species of perfection.[128]

In all these three instances, and several others not cited here, Hume unequivocally affirms belief in the existence of Deity, in much the same way that the ancient and medieval philosophers did. In the first two texts we quoted above, Hume subscribes to a version of design reminiscent of Del Ratzsch's argument, cited in chapter 2. When Hume claims that the whole frame of nature points to or reveals the work of an intelligent author and that after serious reflection, no rational inquirer can suspend his or her belief with regard to the principles of genuine theism, Hume seems to perceive marks of design in the works of nature. This fact is even more evident when Hume claims that the propensity to believe in God is a kind of stamp in human beings, placed there by God. Clearly we find in these words a contention similar to those Ratzsch made.

For Hume, the existence of God is unquestionable and self-evident. That Hume makes this claim in the very work that vigorously refuted the design argument for God's existence, is very significant. However, the important point to note here is that Hume was not an atheist, if we take atheism as the position that denies the existence of God. Hume was not an agnostic either, if we take agnosticism as a view advancing the claim that one cannot know whether God exists or not.

Hume concedes that God does exist, although we cannot know his nature. In spite of this concession, Hume remains unwilling to admit that miracles have happened. Hume's acknowledgment that God exists and his contention that all past reports of miracles are unreliable, I argue, are at odds with each other. To locate the oddity, let me revisit the argument I advanced in chapter 2. I argued that God's creation of the universe satisfies two conditions required in order to identify a miracle, namely: a miracle involves God causing an event in nature in a way that is contrary to nature, or above nature, or alongside nature, and in a way that nature could not have brought about by itself. Therefore, God's creation of the universe is a miracle. If Hume believes in God as the first cause of the universe, then Hume must of necessity believe in the occurrence of a miracle.

The considerations above bring us to perhaps the most important question of this chapter: how should we interpret Hume's essay? Should Hume's argument against miracles be seen as an *a priori* argument against miracles, or should it be seen as an *a posteriori* argument, or should it be

---

128. Hume, *Dialogues concerning Natural Religion*, II.

viewed as a combination of both? This is where our findings in chapter 4 come in. In chapter 4 we saw that Hume's argument against miracles was not original. It was simply a combination of different deistic arguments against miracles, which Hume compiled into one. Burns and Brown rightly point out that some of those arguments were essentially *a priori*. Others were *a posteriori*. Thus when put together as one single argument we have a combination of both. For example, in part 1 of his essay Hume's definition of miracle and the conclusion that no testimony is sufficient to establish a miracle is essentially *a priori*; for it rules out all possible future establishments of miracles by testimony. The other arguments Hume uses in part 2 of his essay are all *a posteriori*.[129] Knowing these two distinctions will help us to put Hume's argument in its proper context.

Let us now turn to Hume's contention that a firm and unalterable experience has established the laws of nature. This is what I earlier called the uniformity-of-nature argument. Hume argued that a miracle like the resurrection of the dead has never been observed in any age or country. The plain consequence, in Hume's view, is that no testimony is sufficient to establish a miracle; for there is a uniform experience against every miraculous event.

But if we revisit our findings in chapter 3, we will see that Hume's argument fails to undercut the experiences of Pascal and the contentions of Robert Boyle and other evidentialists. Beginning with Pascal, we take note of the fact that his faith was strongly enhanced by what he thought was a miracle. It is recorded, as we saw, that Pascal had a religious experience that profoundly affected his faith, an experience which he recorded as a constant reminder to himself of his devotion to God. More significantly, Pascal kept this personal memoir, not for anyone's benefit but his own.

Hume, of course, would say that a uniform experience refutes the religious experience that Pascal had and that even Pascal's own testimony to himself was not sufficient to establish, for Pascal, the authenticity of his own religious experience. But Pascal, I imagine, would probably be justified to contend, following Swinburne, that he remembers his personal religious experience, and that this experience was not cognitively accessible to Hume. In light of Pascal's ability to remember his personal religious experience, he is perhaps more qualified than Hume to report that what he experienced was authentic.

---

129. Brown, *Miracles*, 79.

Also, I think the evidentialists were correct when they contended that certain types of explanation and methods of discovery must always remain flexible in order to accommodate the diversities of phenomena.[130] Since I dealt with this issue at length in chapter 3, I do not need to repeat it here. It is enough to point out that Hume lays down rigid rules that do not leave open the possibility that testimony can establish the existence of any miracle. According to Boyle and his cohorts, Hume's methodology is not very good science.[131]

In the credibility-of-witness argument Hume seemed to contend that the witnesses of religious miracles have never been of unquestioned good sense, education and learning. According to Hume, they were not of good credit and reputation in the eyes of mankind. Hume's contention here can be easily answered without having to draw from the evidentialists' response. One thing to note is that Hume makes a rather sweeping statement. He does not attempt to locate the factors that would call into question the credibility of witnesses reporting a miraculous event. Sherlock, for example, used pages upon pages to establish the credibility of witnesses to the resurrection of Jesus. It would perhaps have been in Hume's interest to show why evidentialists' like Sherlock were mistaken in their arguments. But this does not feature anywhere in Hume's treatment of miracles.

Next is the credulity-of-witness argument. Here, Hume contends that the many instances of forged miracles and supernatural events prove sufficiently the strong propensity of humankind to the extraordinary and the marvelous. As noted in our treatment of the deists, Warburton and Butler would respond to Hume in much the same way they responded to the deists. They would argue that there is no evidence to support the claim that the New Testament authors were credulous. What they recorded shows that a good number of the miracle stories, which they recorded, were in turn received with skepticism and subjected to scrutiny. But this is a claim that Hume (like the deists) overlooks; for Hume fails to show why the position of the New Testament writers mentioned above fails, if indeed it does, to satisfy the claim to critical examination of the facts.

From the credulity of witness argument, I turn to the *ad hominem* argument. According to Hume, miraculous events are observed chiefly to abound among ignorant and barbarous nations. What we noted with the deists, we also note with Hume. As the name of the argument suggests, to

---

130. Burns, *Great Debate*, 15.
131. Ibid., 15–16.

contend that one is predisposed to argue in a certain way owing to the circumstances in which one was raised is indeed to advance a circumstantial argument against the person. The reason that Hume presents in this argument succeeds only in providing an emotional rather than a logical support for his conclusion.

Finally we turn to Hume's fourth argument. According to Hume, all testimonies of miracles are opposed by an infinite number of witnesses such that the miracle destroys the credit of testimony and the testimony destroys itself. Recall our observation, in chapter 4, that some church fathers did agree that miracles could not be used to establish specific doctrines, or for that matter, a system of religion. In chapter 2, we saw Origen's concession, namely, that counterfeit miracles could be performed by beings other than God. However, as noted in chapter 4, just because miracles happen in different religions does not rule out the possibility that a genuine miracle has happened in a given religion. Rejecting all reports of miracles simply because they cancel each other out runs the risk of rejecting genuine miracles; for it is not too farfetched to imagine that a genuine miracle can cancel out a counterfeit miracle. To reject both on the grounds that one contradicts the other is to run the risk of missing out on truth.

Oddly, Hume never responded to the evidentialists' rebuttal of the deistic arguments against miracles. It is not clear why he did not refer to them in his essay. However, as noted in the first and second sections, various responses were made to Hume's argument. Some rejected it; others tried to improve on it. It is to these arguments that I now turn. What I endeavor to establish is whether there is a sense in which Hume's argument could be restated more forcefully than Hume stated it.

Evaluating Hume's Defenders

Wheeler and Huxley try to come to Hume's rescue. They take Hume's definition of miracle to its logical conclusion by showing that if an event were to really happen miraculously, there will be a law of nature that will accommodate it. Our job is merely to search for the event. Wheeler does not think that the existence of God is a belief that ought to be factored into the whole question of miracles, for two reasons: first, such a belief has its difficulties. Second, the validity of the argument against miracles rests on our experience of the order of nature, whether a cause of that order is assumed or not.

I must make two responses here. First, if we include belief in God's existence as part of the fabric of our belief system, and if part of that belief takes God to be the cause of that order, the argument against miracles turns out to be invalid, specifically because bringing about that state of order is in itself a miracle, by our definition. Second, Wheeler misses the entire point of this discussion in an important way: Hume believed in God's existence. The evidence is compelling. Our earlier contention is that if Hume believes in God, then his rejection of miracles is at serious odds with this belief. The question is not whether or not God exists from Hume's perspective. That has already been established. The argument Wheeler must advance is why belief in the existence of God would not help in establishing the testimony for miracles, in light of Hume's theism. He does not do this.

Let's turn to McKinnon. McKinnon's argument against miracles makes no mention of Hume, but it rules out *a priori* all miracles. But McKinnon's argument is easily refuted, now that we have already refuted Hume's uniformity-of-nature argument. McKinnon's argument seems to make the unwarranted assumption that we know all the laws of nature there are to be known. Therefore no laws can account for miracles. According to McKinnon, I might use "x is a miracle" to mean "x baffles me" or "I know no laws which could account for x."[132] McKinnon thinks *miracle* is being used, in this sense, expressively rather than descriptively. However, people do not use this term in this limited way. In other words, they do not use the term to say they lack a cognitive access to the appropriate law. Rather, they use it to express their belief that such a law does not exist.[133]

In short we know everything that can be known about the laws of nature such that we can rule out *a priori* claims that there are laws to account for the occurrence of x, where x is a miracle. Based on this assumption, McKinnon concludes that all the descriptive senses of miracles, whether expressive or descriptive, are logically improper.[134] As noted, this assumption is unwarranted. How do we know that there are no such laws? For one, we do not know all the laws of nature that can possibly be known in order to make such claims. Hence McKinnon is unjustified in making this assumption.

I will omit any discussion of Anthony Flew since I believe that Richard Swinburne has correctly critiqued Flew. Instead, I will proceed to Mackie.

---

132. McKinnon, "Miracle," 50–51.
133. Ibid., 51.
134. Ibid.

Mackie provided a critique of Hume that was similar to Flew's. And like Flew, Mackie tried to improve Hume's argument. It does not seem to me that the improvement was substantial. Since Mackie was an atheist, it did not seem plausible to him that a miracle could happen in any way, though he maintained that the concept of a miracle was itself coherent. Also, as we noted earlier, he conceded that miracles like successful prophecy are in principle verifiable. Consider his suggestion that the defender of miracles has the double burden of showing that a miracle has occurred and that it violated the laws of nature. There seems, in my opinion, to be no great difficulty here. Mackie himself has accomplished this feat, in principle, when he concedes that a miracle like successful prophecy is verifiable. We noted this in chapter 2 when we considered how prophecy can be verified. Thus Mackie's improvement on Hume's argument does not seem to be forceful.

From Mackie we move to Richard Swinburne. I contend that Swinburne's explication of four kinds of evidence is more comprehensive than Hume's. Hume seems to identify only two kinds of evidence: testimony and our contemporary understanding of what things are physically impossible or improbable. Swinburne adds two more to the list, namely: memory and traces. Hume's two kinds of evidence would rule out, *a priori*, Pascal's testimony alluded to at the beginning of this section. But Swinburne will not; for Pascal remembered his experience, which satisfies one of Swinburne's four kinds of evidence. Swinburne will pay attention to what Pascal remembered when he had his religious experience.

In my view Swinburne also succeeds in showing that Flew's attempt to rescue Hume is a failure. Recall that Flew tried to improve Hume's argument by showing that all historical evidence or information is somewhat inferior to scientific evidence. Thus we must always give greater weight to scientific evidence since scientific evidence is always available to us for our scrutiny. Swinburne tried to show that Flew was mistaken by contending that for historical truths as well as for scientific truths, exactly the same kinds of evidence on particular occasions hold for both. In my opinion, Swinburne succeeded in showing that this is the case. Swinburne's argument is reminiscent of Somerville's view of experience and testimony, and is perhaps a modern version of it. Thus, if Flew was mistaken in his contention, he has not succeeded in supporting Hume's contention that scientific truths ought to be given greater weight over historical (testimonial) truths.

Finally, when we compare Earman and Fogelin, we come face to face with a rather technical dispute over induction. To recall the nature of the dispute, Earman contends that Hume's straight rule of induction reduces the probability of miraculous events to zero. Fogelin thinks Earman is mistaken in attributing the strong rule to Hume.

The dispute between Fogelin and Earman can be settled by considering one important factor: Earman took the historical interpretation of Hume into consideration. That is, he went beyond Hume and considered the deistic arguments against miracles as well as the evidentialists' report. It is this sort of contextual interpretation of the arguments against miracles that led him to conclude that Hume's argument against miracles reduces the probability of miraculous events to zero. When we turn to Fogelin, there is no historical interpretation of Hume. In other words, Fogelin fails completely to put Hume's argument against miracles in its historical context. Indeed, Fogelin makes no statements about deism in his treatment of miracles. He seems completely unaware of the historical context and dynamics behind Hume's argument. Such failure left him open to a misinterpretation of Hume, an openness I think he fell into.

First, Fogelin's interpretation of Hume strikes me as inconsistent in several areas. Consider, for instance two claims that Fogelin makes. He argues that Hume does not attempt to settle the contest between the reverse test and the direct test, though his tone suggests that the reverse test will win. He writes: "Hume does not attempt to settle this contest in part I, though Hume's tone leaves no doubt concerning how he thinks the context will ultimately be settled."[135] Six pages later, Fogelin seems to contradict this very claim. He writes: "it is tempting to think that Hume holds that the proof using the reverse method could win, should such a situation arise. He does not say either of these things."[136] In other words, we should not take Hume to believe that the reverse method will win against the direct method. The contradiction is simply this: On the one hand Fogelin contends that Hume's tone assures us that the reverse method should win against the direct test. On the other hand Fogelin tells us that Hume does not hold that the reverse method will win. These two contentions are at odds with each other.

The second instance of inconsistency appears in Fogelin's interpretation of the law of nature. As we have seen, Fogelin contends that Hume cannot be treating a law of nature as an invariant irregularity in nature. If he did so, the occurrence of a miracle could be ruled out on definitional grounds alone. In Fogelin's view, the expression "law of nature" is used in two ways: as

---

135. Ibid., 9.
136. Ibid., 15.

a label for uniform regularity in nature, and as belief in such regularity.[137] In an explicit contradiction to his contention above, Fogelin claims that Hume speaks in both ways![138] That is, Hume takes the law of nature as a label for uniform regularity in nature, and as a belief in such regularity.

What about Fogelin's attempt to show that Hume's argument cannot be taken as an *a priori* argument against miracles? Do we have reasons for believing that Fogelin has presented a forceful refutation against his opponents? Once again, I do not believe he does, and here's why. First, consider Fogelin's contention that Hume rejects the *a priori* conclusion by acknowledging that under certain circumstances, it could be possible to establish the occurrence of a miracle on the basis of testimony. Fogelin has Hume's eight-days-of-darkness miracle in mind.

Fogelin seems mistaken here. The miracle that Hume admits is really no miracle at all, though Hume calls it a violation of the usual course of nature. The reason Hume should not think that the eight-days-of-darkness is a miracle, strictly speaking, is because Hume himself provides a natural explanation for it. He sees why it is possible for such a miracle to happen. According to Hume, nature's decay and corruption remains quite probable by so many analogies such that any phenomenon with a tendency towards that catastrophe approaches human testimony, assuming the testimony itself is extensive and uniform.[139]

Notice that immediately after allowing that such miracles could be established, he completely rejects, *a priori*, reports of miracles such as the resurrection. He rejects the possibility of such miracles in part 1 of his essay, and he reiterates his rejection of them in the second part of his essay. His rejection of such miracles in part 1 has to be *a priori* for two reasons: similar deistic arguments against miracles were *a priori*. Second, Hume does not believe that resurrection miracles could be established by testimony. That is, irrespective of the impeccability of evidence for a resurrection miracle, the evidence must be rejected, hence the miracle it endeavors to establish must also be rejected.

Hume makes this claim three times, though in different ways: first, he says that no one has ever observed a dead man rising again.[140] Second, he says that no testimony for any kind of miracle has ever amounted to a

---

137. Ibid., 26.
138. Ibid., 27.
139. Hume, *Enquiry*, X.II.36.
140. Ibid., X.I.12.

probability, much less to a proof.[141] Third, he says that we may establish it as a maxim, that no human testimony can have such force as to prove a miracle.[142] The universality of these claims rules out miracles in general, and resurrection miracles in particular.

Whereas the first claim was made in what we have identified as Hume's *a priori* argument against miracles, we would expect its universality to be sustained in Hume's subsequent *a posteriori* arguments. Notice also that even with the miracle related in Cardinal de Retz's story, Hume called it a holy fraud. He made this claim after pointing out that the miracle was witnessed by all the canons of the church and the whole company in town. Also the person who relayed the story to the cardinal was of an incredulous and libertine character as well as a person of great genius. The only explanation for rejecting this story is what C. S. Lewis believed to be a philosophical presupposition that precluded belief in the possibility or actuality of miracles. In short, Hume rejected *a priori* all accounts of miraculous events, events for which there were no naturalistic explanations.

According to Fogelin, Hume's remark on the "cloud of witnesses" in the Abbé Paris case proves that the argument is *a posteriori*. Hume writes the following words in section X.II of his work: "And what have we to oppose such a cloud of witnesses, but the absolute impossibility or miraculous nature of the events, which they relate? And this surely, in the eyes of all reasonable people, will alone be regarded as a sufficient refutation."

Clearly, these words show that Hume's argument against miracles rests on *a priori* footing. Hume rejects the reports of the clouds of witnesses on the grounds that the nature of the events they relate is *impossible*. In other words, he is not ready to accept the reports of such a cloud of witnesses of miraculous events because they are impossible *a priori*.

But my contention is that Fogelin fails to rescue Hume from the observation that Hume's argument against miracles is a combination of both *a priori* and *a posteriori* arguments. But, as we saw, if part of the argument is a rejection of miracles *a priori*, then it must contend that miracles are impossible. This is exactly what C. S. Lewis was contending. In other words, on Hume's view, we know already that they have never occurred. Thus Vince, Huxley, Wheeler and Lewis are right to claim that miracles, that is, violations of the laws of nature, are impossible in Hume's view. And Vince and

---

141. Ibid., X.II.35.
142. Ibid.

Lewis are correct in maintaining that Hume's argument against miracles begs the question.

Let us now form a set of statements that Hume agrees with so far, namely: God exists, God is the cause of the universe, and miracles are impossible. But the second statement leads us to conclude that God's act of causing the universe is a miracle. Therefore, by implication, we must add the following statement into the set of statements forming Hume's belief system, namely: God's act of creating the universe is a miracle. Thus the set should look like this: God exists, God is the cause of the universe, miracles are impossible, and God's act of creating the universe is a miracle. This is an explicit contradiction. Therefore, Hume's argument against miracles is inconsistent with his theism. Thus, Hume's methodological naturalism fails to undermine belief in miracles.

— 6 —
Evolution of Methodological Naturalism

WE HAVE SEEN IN the previous chapter that Hume's argument against miracles is inconsistent with his theism, and that his naturalism fails to undermine belief in miracles. We have noted that it is extremely difficult to rule out the miraculous if one subscribes to belief in the existence of a First Cause, that is, God. Hume's attempt to rule out miracles fails in this regard.

However, a more forceful objection to miracles was raised by the sort of methodological naturalism that tried to explain the origin of the universe through natural, rather than supernatural, means. From Descartes' time to Darwin's time, very few methodological naturalists called into question natural theology's assumption about God's benevolence in creation. To be sure, naturalism during this period was not characterized by the denial of supernatural entities. It seemed to hold that God had a role to play in bringing nature into existence. It was therefore in agreement with natural theology's view of God as a Creator whose benevolence could be inferred by observing the complexity of his creation.

Nevertheless, Hume's methodological naturalism attempted to cast doubt on natural theology's view of God as a benevolent First Cause. For example, in Hume's *Dialogues concerning Natural Religion* Philo, taken by many philosophers to be Hume's mouthpiece, argues by asking his hearers to suppose, for example, the following scenario: An individual with limited intelligence and also completely unfamiliar with our universe was informed that the universe was caused by an all-powerful, all-wise and omnibenevolent being. The intelligence in question would have a preconceived notion of a universe quite different from what it eventually experiences in our world. Such an intelligence would not imagine that the world it countenances would be afflicted with the sort of vice it finds in this world, especially if the intelligence is convinced the universe was caused by the all-powerful and all-wise omnibenevolent being.[1]

In Hume's view, the Design Argument cannot be used to show that the Creator of Nature is benevolent. Hume argues that nature has too many mistakes and errors to warrant such an inference. Despite this contention, however, Hume is quite unwilling to do away or rule out, *a priori* or *a posteriori*, the existence of a designer.

How is it, then, that naturalism became the scientific enterprise that ruled out supernaturalism? Following the findings of Peter Bowler's *Evolution: The History of an Idea*, this chapter will show that the evolution of naturalism from a God-caused view of nature to a naturally-caused view was chiefly motivated by ethical-cum-theological presuppositions and relatively much less by scientific means. The aim is to show that such a move lacked the epistemological warrant commonly assigned to it by Neo-Darwinians. As Bowler will show, the naturalists subscribed to a certain conception of God that enabled them to rule God out of their scientific enterprise. For the most part I agree with Bowler's findings. But I will present my personal findings in places I disagree with him.

On the whole, however, we will see that Charles Darwin used something like the Humean objection to try to rule out the possibility that the universe had a supernatural origin. To see how methodological naturalism evolved, we will begin by examining the views outlined by a select but representative group of methodological naturalists before Darwin.

We will then focus on Darwin's methodological naturalism that dealt with the "mistakes in nature" argument to rule out God's miraculous role in nature. Finally, we will examine the views of Neo-Darwinians that gradually "evolved" into atheism. Let's begin with the forerunners of Darwin.

Methodological Naturalism of Darwin's Forerunners

The first person we will consider here is Rene Descartes. He is important because his philosophy of nature, according to Bowler, sought to explain the origin of all things in physical terms, without reference to supernatural creation. God does not design the individual structures of the universe. He merely established the basic laws of nature and made them responsible for all future developments.[2]

1. Hume, *Dialogues*, XI.
2. Bowler, *Evolution*, 26.

Seemingly, however, Bowler is incorrect about Descartes in this regard. In his *Principles of Philosophy*, Descartes highlights his belief in God as the general cause of motion. For Descartes, God created matter in the beginning, attended with motion and rest. Moreover, God keeps the same motion and rest in the physical universe as he put there at the very beginning. According to Descartes, God imparted various motions into parts of matter when he first brought them into existence, and he currently preserves all this matter in the same way through the same process by which he originally created matter.[3]

Contrary to Bowler's contention, the Cartesian philosophy of nature did explain the origin of all things by making specific reference to supernatural creation. It appears that Bowler makes his conclusions about Descartes in light of Descartes' claims in *Principles of Philosophy III*. There, Descartes postulates certain propositions which he claims are absolutely false, though seemingly valuable. According to him, suppose we wish to comprehend the nature of plants or of humans. We seem better off to consider how they gradually germinate from seeds than to consider how God created them at the very beginning of the world. Hence, we may imagine certain very simple and easily known principles that could serve as seeds—principles from which we can show that everything we observe in this visible world could have sprung. Granted, we may know for sure they never arose in this way. However, we will be able to offer a much better explanation of their nature by this method than if we merely describe them as they now are, that is, as we believe them to have been created by God.[4]

Descartes suggests that this naturalistic method of understanding the universe is a much better way of explaining the nature of things when compared to explaining them as having been supernaturally created. Taken in isolation, Descartes' claim is consistent with Bowler's view. But Descartes is quick to add that things did not arise in this way, a contention that Bowler seems to overlook.

In the course of time the details of Descartes' physics were replaced by those of Newton. The triumph of Newtonian science established a new basis for different hypotheses of the earth's origin, especially in astronomy. For example, in 1755 Immanuel Kant first suggested the "nebular hypothesis" as a theory of the earth's origin. Kant assumed that the whole solar system had begun as a cloud of dust particles that condensed under the

---

3. Descartes, *Principles of Philosophy*, II.37.
4. Ibid., III.45.

force of its own gravity and gradually acquired a tendency to rotate. Small amounts condensed into solid bodies, circling around the main concentration, which ignited to form the sun. But Kant's book was never issued for publication. Hence his idea received little attention.[5]

However, a similar theory was later proposed by astronomer Pierre-Simon Laplace in his *System of the World*, published in 1796. Laplace's nebular hypothesis assumed that all stars condense in the same way and hence the majority of them have planets circling around them. Gradual formation or "evolution" of a planetary system thus became a perfectly natural phenomenon. Such a belief, notes Bowler, did not necessarily remove the possibility that the whole process was designed by God. After all, God could have created the original gas clouds in such a way that they must eventually form planets of a certain kind according to his laws of nature.[6]

But Laplace felt that there was little point in preserving such a vestige of the old way of thinking. If the universe is a physical system that happens to have developed in a certain way over a vast period of time, little is gained, Laplace argued, by assuming that details of the process were worked out in advance by a Creator. The ultimate end of the search for a totally mechanical cosmogony was thus a gradual reduction of the role played by the Deity. Thus in astronomy God's connection with the universe became so indirect that it appeared negligible.[7]

Despite the triumph of Newtonian science in astronomy, the basic Cartesian program was still the source of much Enlightenment materialist speculation in geology.[8] According to Bowler, the Neptunist theory held that all sedimentary rocks were deposited on the floor of a vast ancient ocean that has since disappeared. It acquired its name after the Roman god of the sea. The alternative of invoking the power of earth movements was eventually connected with the belief that the interior of the earth exists in a state of high temperature and pressure, and thus became known as Vulcanism, after the god of fire.[9] Let me begin with Benoit de Maillet, a Neptunist.

In his work *Telliamed*, published in 1748 but probably written between 1692 and 1718, de Maillet depicts a fictional conversation between a French

5. Bowler, 32.
6. Ibid., 32–33.
7. Ibid., 33–35.
8. Ibid., 27.
9. Ibid., 36.

Missionary and an Indian Traveler. De Maillet used this fictional conversation as a way of articulating his geological findings. According to Bowler, *Telliamed* treats the whole history of the earth as a process requiring vast amounts of time before human civilization appeared. De Maillet's views on rock formation seem to have derived from a study of the secondary rocks themselves, and it was this empirical foundation that provided the basis for his bold extension of the timescale beyond traditional limits.[10]

But this conclusion on de Maillet's part seemed different from the biblical doctrine of six days of creation. To reconcile his view with the biblical view, de Maillet suggests a different interpretation of the first few words of the Book of Genesis. According to de Maillet, the sentence, "In the beginning God created the Heavens and the Earth," is a very improper translation of the Hebrew. The words used in that language only imply that God "formed the heavens and earth." Taken in this way, the Bible must have assumed the preexistence of matter when God formed the heavens and the earth.

What de Maillet was trying to show was that irrespective of how the globe was created, it had not remained in the same state in which we see it. If it had been, its solid substance would have been composed of one single matter.[11] According to de Maillet, observations ranging from the shores of the sea to the summits of the surrounding mountains increasingly convinced him that the rocks by the sea were gradually formed in the waters of the sea and emerged through the gradual decrease of the sea. De Maillet believed that this interpretation was not opposed to the Sacred Scriptures.[12]

In de Maillet's views, God could have used the actions of the sea waters for the creation of the earth and the formation of the mountains. De Maillet thought that the separation of the waters from the earth, as mentioned in Genesis, is in favor of such an opinion. He held that the waters of the sea built the mountains and uncovered what they had formed during the first chaos of matter. This emergence, in turn, results in vegetation, which then resulted in the creation of animals. Finally, the animals led to the creation of humans who depends on them as the last handiwork of God.[13]

Despite de Maillet's suggestion that the age of the earth was, in all probability, older than what we get from the biblical account, some naturalists were reluctant to accept de Maillet's thesis. According to Bowler,

10. Ibid., 29–30.
11. Ibid., I.
12. Ibid., III.
13. Ibid.

naturalists-cum-geologists like Nicholas Steno, who wrote before de Maillet, found it impossible to shake off the traditional view that the earth was but a few thousand years old. But Steno's view had to account for the immense geological changes that de Maillet observed in the rock formations. De Maillet maintained that such changes could only be accounted for if the earth was eternal. Steno, however, suggested that such changes were brought about by catastrophic events that the earth experienced, such as the biblical deluge.[14]

Given this vantage point of catastrophism, which was already in place long before de Maillet's time, Steno contended in his *Prodromus*, published in 1669, that there were three ways in which his views could be seen to agree with Scripture. For our purpose, I will focus only on the first way, which contended that Scripture and Nature both agree that all things were covered with water. Nature is silent about how and when this state began, and how long it lasted. But Scripture has the answer. That there was a watery fluid that covered all things is, in Steno's view, a fact proved by the strata of higher mountains, free from all heterogeneous material. Steno argues that the similarity of matter and form in the strata of mountains which are different and distant from each other proves that the fluid was universal. But he adds that these strata, undeniably, are of the sort that could have been directly produced by God, the First Cause. Therefore, according to Steno, we recognize in them the evident agreement of Scripture with nature.[15]

Moreover, Steno adds that the determination of natural motions can be altered by three causes: first, it can be altered by the motion of a fluid permeating all bodies. In such cases we say that things produced in this way are produced naturally. Second, it can be altered by the motion of living beings, namely, by humans. Such things are said to be artificial. Third, it can be altered by the first and unknown cause of motion. In Steno's view, even the pagans believed that there was something divine in motions which originate in this way.[16]

Thus in Steno we find an example of a conservative thinker who could produce works in which the Genesis flood was used to solve all geological problems. However, Bowler observes that those who studied rocks themselves demanded the freedom to follow the logic of their thoughts wherever it might lead. Thus, as the seventeenth century progressed, the spread of

14. Bowler, 31.
15. Steno, *Prodromus*, 263–64.
16. Ibid., 214.

deism and outright atheism encouraged even more naturalists to pay only lip service to the creation and the deluge.[17]

According to Bowler, one such naturalist and geologist was George Louis Leclerc Comte de Buffon. According to Bowler, Buffon was an atheist who wished to dispense with the notion of a Creator who ordered the workings of the universe. He was certainly not a Christian. Neither was he a typical deist.[18] He had no sympathy with those who saw every detail of every species as illustrating the power of the Creator.[19]

Bowler's observations about Buffon seem to be misleading for one major reason. Buffon's writings indicate some kind of commitment to theism. In his work, entitled "Initial Discourse: On the Manner of Studying and Expounding Natural History," published sometime between 1749 and 1767, Buffon clearly shows commitment to belief in the Creator. He notes how the number of productions of nature constitutes the lowest part of the scientist's astonishment. The human mind, he argues, staggers—dwarfed before the immensity of nature and by the number of wonders. According to Buffon, God's hand does not seem opened in order to give existence to a particular limited number of species. Rather, God might have caused, all at once, a world of beings of infinite combinations—a world of perpetual destruction and renewal. This view of the universe inspires in us a sentiment of respect for God.[20]

Once again, Bowler fails to take note of this claim. But he correctly notes that as materialist philosophers of the Enlightenment became bolder in their attacks upon traditional religion, they were encouraged to seek explanations of how life originated on the earth that did not depend upon supernatural intervention. The only plausible concepts available to them were those of spontaneous generation and the transmutation of existing forms in response to environmental pressures.[21]

In spite of this situation, naturalists of the late seventeenth and early eighteenth centuries still hoped that their scientific work could be reconciled with Christianity. For example, the argument from design based on the adaptive purpose of each organic structure was a central feature of the

---

17. Bowler, 32.
18. Ibid., 68.
19. Ibid., 72.
20. Buffon, "Initial Discourse," 101.
21. Ibid.

school of natural theology that flourished in the seventeen hundreds and survived well into the nineteenth century.[22]

A well known example of the design argument is William Paley's *Natural Theology*, which was published in 1802—twenty-three years after Hume's *Dialogues*. We would therefore hope to find, in Paley's work, a response to Hume's "mistakes in nature" argument. As the reality turns out, Paley tries to formulate just such a response. He argues, for example, that when we inquire simply about the existence of an intelligent Creator, imperfect, inaccuracy, disorder and occasional irregularities may show up to a considerable extent without calling his existence to question. This fact happens in much the same way that a watch may, on some infrequent occasions, go wrong and be faulty in some parts. Such inexactitudes do not provide the smallest ground of suspicion against the watch's design.[23] Paley's point is that occasional faults in nature are admissible in our inquiry about the existence of an Intelligent Designer. Just as faults in craftsmanship do not give us reasons to doubt the existence of the craftsman, faults in nature do not give us sufficient reasons to call God's existence into question.

In Bowler's view, natural theology was sophisticated enough to deal with many phenomena that might at first sight seem incompatible with divine benevolence. However, Bowler continues, some new discoveries were creating problems. What about parasites such as intestinal worms—could these be reconciled with the argument?[24]

Bowler thinks that religious naturalists did not provide adequate answers to these questions. Instead, in their attempt to elucidate their scientific position further, the devout naturalists introduced what they called a "chain of being." It was an attempt to see nature as a highly structured system designed overall by God. It began from the naturalist's intuitive sense that living things can be ranked in a hierarchy of complexity from the highest down to the most primitive. The naturalists assumed that a linear plan of creation linked the two extremes.[25]

Besides the "chain of being" theory, the "germ theory" was also formulated by devout naturalists like William Harvey. Harvey held that all animals grow from eggs. The ovum was sometimes seen as the germ or seed containing the complete new organism in miniature. The theory held that

---

22. Bowler, *Evolution*, 48–49.
23. Paley, *Natural Theology*, 44.
24. Bowler, *Evolution*, 50.
25. Ibid., 55.

the whole human race literally was created by God in the beginning, enclosed within a germ, waiting to be unpacked generation after generation. The "germ theory" represented the conservative wing of mechanical philosophy, which attempted to preserve the traditional connection between God and nature. Therefore, it was allied with the "chain of being" theory. In Bowler's view, as ridiculous as it might appear, the fact that the theory was taken seriously is an indication of the influence exerted upon it by the argument from design.[26]

But how did the chain of being and germ theory reconcile divine benevolence with the faults of nature? According to Bowler, they did so through the idea of universal progress, an idea initially advanced by Charles Bonnet. It originated, rather curiously, from Bonnet's interest in the Christian notion of the resurrection of the body. Bonnet speculated that universal progress might be achieved through a second germ supplied to each soul by its Creator. He argued that perhaps animals have souls restricted within their more limited bodies and may themselves be resurrected in the future with a higher form of body. Bonnet speculated that perhaps every soul has been reincarnated in the past through a series of physical bodies, all developed from germs originally provided by God. At each reincarnation the soul would appear in a more perfect body, and thus the history of life would be a gradual ascent up the chain of being from the simplest bodies in distant past to the more perfect form enjoyed by man today. Bonnet concluded that from time to time a geological catastrophe would wipe out existing forms of life, but the germ responsible for future resurrections would survive and would be able to develop into a whole new population when conditions settled down.[27]

According to Bowler, the chain of being theory still did not provide adequate answers to the "faults in nature" argument. This is because the theory was particularly vulnerable to the problem of extinction. Consider, for example, that in its original version, the whole chain had to exist or the pattern of creation would be imperfect. Extinction of a single link would destroy the symmetry of the whole chain.[28]

For this reason, materialists of the eighteenth century replaced the germ concept with the belief that each living body is built up by physical forces. In this way, the materialists removed any guarantee of the fixity of

26. Ibid., 53.
27. Ibid., 57–58.
28. Ibid., 50–51.

species. In their search for a causal explanation of how the world has been shaped into its form, the materialists investigated the possibility that the environment might affect a species over a long period of time. But they could still not explain how matter could organize itself into the complex and purposeful structure of a living body and how it could preserve a similar structure over a long series of generations.[29]

Thus the chain of being view began to break down in the eighteenth century, as exploration revealed more and more species that had to be fitted in. It was becoming clear to most naturalists that nature was too complex to be described in terms of a simple linear pattern.[30] It was inevitable that some more radical thinkers should have the ambition to extend the materialist program to include the generation of life, challenging the theory of preexisting germs created by God. If the living body was formed by natural forces instead of from a preexisting germ, a host of possibilities were opened.[31]

Many of the ideas discussed so far have been based on assumptions quite alien to those of modern evolutionism. At the end of the eighteenth century, however, Erasmus Darwin and Jean Baptiste Lamarck developed ideas that came much closer to the modern concept of organic development. In Bowler's view, both avoided the temptation to see even complex forms of life as derived from spontaneous generation. Hence they were forced to take more seriously the process by which living things can actually change through time. And both have been hailed as the founders of modern evolutionism.[32]

Erasmus Darwin seemed to have assumed that the overall results of this effort to adapt to the environment would be a gradual progress of life toward higher states of organization. According to Bowler, Erasmus Darwin was a deist who believed that God had designed living things to be self-improving through time. In their constant efforts to meet the challenges of the external world, they developed new organs through the "inheritance of acquired characteristics"—a mechanism that Lamarckians would eventually make famous.[33] Interestingly, Erasmus Darwin claimed to have developed his idea of transmutation not from natural history but

29. Ibid., 54.
30. Ibid., 59.
31. Ibid., 54.
32. Ibid., 76.
33. Ibid.

from David Hartley's 1749 account of how the soul is affected by the habits of life.[34]

Let me turn to Lamarck. Bowler holds that Lamarck's real inspiration was Enlightenment materialism, which had also stressed the essentially creative power of nature.[35] A brief examination of Lamarck's views shows that his approach to science did not rule out the supernatural. According to Lamarck, things exist only by the will of the Sublime Author of all things, for there are some aspects in nature that could not be explained in any other way except by recourse to God's wisdom. He argues that the idea of nature's eternality remains an abstract and baseless opinion that failed to satisfy his reason. A lack of positive knowledge on his part on this subject leads him to think that all of nature is only an effect. For this reason, he finds himself believing in a First Cause that brought nature into existence.[36]

Lamarck thus gives God his place as the Creator of nature. But this does not mean that a study of nature is impossible. According to Lamarck, it is possible to respect the decrees of God's infinite wisdom and still carry out a systematic study of nature. Lamarck believes that if he succeeds in unraveling anything in the methods of nature, he shall say without fear of failure that it has pleased God to endow her with that faculty and power.[37]

For this reason, Lamarck's study of nature allows him to see that nature works the following wonders: nature creates organization, life and feeling. Nature has multiplied and diversified within unknown limits the organs and faculties of the organized bodies whose existence she observes or propagates. By the sole instrumentality of needs, establishing and controlling habits, nature has created in animals the fountain of all their acts and all their faculties, from the simplest to instinct, to skill, and finally to reason. Lamarck holds that if he finds all this, he is entitled to recognize this power of nature. In other words, he is allowed to say that in the order of existing things, he recognizes in nature the execution of the will of her Sublime Author, with all the mutations that take place at large among existing things.[38]

One such mutation, for Lamarck, could be seen through the environment's impact on an animal's body. Lamarck believed that the needs of an

---

34. Ibid.
35. Ibid., 78.
36. Lamarck, *Zoological Philosophy*, 187–88.
37. Ibid.
38. Ibid., 41.

animal determine the organs that its body will develop. That is, the environment creates the animal's needs, which in turn determine how it will use its body. According to Lamarck, the resultant characteristics acquired through such use would be transmitted to the offspring. For example, the short-necked ancestors of the modern giraffe were at some point in their history forced to begin feeding from trees. All the individuals stretched their necks upwards. As a result, this part of the body grew in size. The next generation inherited the extra neck-length and stretched it even further. Thus, over a long period of time the giraffe gradually acquired the long neck we see today.[39]

Lamarck attracted no immediate followers, and died in relative obscurity. To a large extent, his eclipse was engineered by his greatest rival, George Cuvier, who also rose to political power in France. This eminence enabled Cuvier to ensure that Lamarck's views were dismissed as outdated speculations. Cuvier developed techniques of comparative anatomy that even Lamarck adopted. According to Bowler, Cuvier astounded the world by applying his techniques to the reconstruction of extinct species from their fossil remains. But Lamarck failed even to see the possibility of using the new paleontology to support the idea of an evolutionary progression.[40]

Along with their attempts to discover the natural history of animals, Lamarck, Cuvier and other naturalists also turned to the natural history of humans. This was inevitable for one major reason: as travelers went around the world, they encountered new races of human beings, some of whom "lived under conditions so primitive that there was a temptation to question their true humanity. Specimens of the great apes were collected, confirming that such creatures represented man's closest relative in the animal kingdom."[41]

Yet Lamarck was the only naturalist in his time who suggested a genuine connection between man and the apes. Lamarck's theory of development naturally implied that man was evolved from a lower form.[42] Cuvier, however, divided humans from the apes as follows: the apes are four-handed in the sense that the structure of their feet hardly differs from that of their hands. Only humans have truly distinct feet adapted to their upright gait. This complete distinction between man and his closest animal relatives

39. Bowler, *Evolution*, 81.
40. Ibid., 83.
41. Ibid., 86.
42. Ibid., 87.

was still being used as an argument against human evolution in Darwin's time.[43] Cuvier's unwillingness to rank humans with apes stemmed from his overall reluctance to rank any classes one above the other. In Cuvier's view, a vertebrate is not necessarily superior to a mollusk; it is merely different. Cuvier regarded fishes and mammals as simply different kinds of vertebrate adapted to different habitats.[44]

According to Bowler, the implications of this view for the rise of the theory of evolution were enormous. This is because it no longer would be possible to think in terms of a linear progress through the animal kingdom. Each group would have to be pictured as a separate branch in a treelike process of development.[45]

Cuvier believed that the fossils of animals now extinct showed that they could not have evolved into their modern counterparts. For Cuvier, ancient species proved to be just as complex and well-balanced in their structure as living forms, confirming Cuvier in his belief that each species is a functional whole that cannot be disturbed by significant variation.[46]

Why then did each of the ancient populations die out, and how were new forms introduced to replace them? Cuvier argued that geological revolutions caused the extinction of the populations in question. For example, an invasion of Europe by the sea would dispose of all the animals living there, if they could not migrate elsewhere. Thus "new" animals that could have been living in a part of the world unaffected by the revolution would then migrate from that part of the world to take the place of those now extinct. Hence, Cuvier insisted that a new creation was not necessary to explain the repopulation of a particular area. The only case in which Cuvier left room for supernatural creation was at the beginning of the Tertiary, when he supposed that all mammals were introduced simultaneously.[47]

By the 1820s, other geologists were beginning to realize how much evidence there was to suggest that movements of the earth's crust played a role in shaping the surface of the earth today. In London, the Geological Society was founded in 1807 with the aim of encouraging a spirit of empirical enquiry that would be free from the acrimony of Neptunist-Vulcanist debate. Under its auspices a new breed of geologists emerged,

43. Ibid.
44. Ibid., 107.
45. Ibid.
46. Ibid., 109.
47. Ibid., 110–11.

committed to a philosophy of the earth's history that would eventually be called "catastrophism."[48]

The catastrophists postulated massive earth movements in the past, far beyond the scale of anything known today. These upheavals would raise mountain ranges in a short period of time and would cause gigantic tidal waves capable of large-scale erosion. There was hard evidence to suggest that a great deluge indeed had swept across the whole of Britain. Great boulders occurred in certain areas, formed of rock quite unlike that on which they rested. Only in the 1840s did an alternative explanation based on the greater extent of glaciers in a recently ended ice age begin to emerge. In the meantime, "diluvialism," the postulation of an extensive flood in the recent past, seemed a reasonable explanation of evidence such as the erratic boulders.[49]

Within the context of Paley's natural theology, catastrophists formulated a rational explanation of the historical development of life. According to Bowler, their accounts left one question open: exactly how did the Creator accomplish the introduction of new forms at appropriate times in the earth's history? Their most obvious answer was by miracles, although their creationism was not necessarily of the most simpleminded variety. But the catastrophists did not think that new species appeared through the operation of everyday laws of nature. The acts of creation were discontinuous, occurring only at the beginning of each geological period. Moreover, creation was a systematic process, revealed by the gradual progress of life. It might be legitimate even to talk of "laws of creation." But because these laws must involve the Designer's intelligence, they were not a fitting subject for scientific investigation.[50] This contention by the catastrophists, it seems, was motivated by the fact that some species appeared much later in the natural history of the world. For example, it seemed significant that the absence of human fossils suggested a very recent origin for humans, the highest purpose of creation.[51]

The theories hitherto examined were built around the general theme of development through time, irrespective of whether this development was caused by a progressive plan of creation or whether it merely followed from changing conditions in the earth's physical history. There was still direction

48. Ibid., 112.
49. Ibid., 114.
50. Ibid., 119.
51. Ibid., 116.

in the process. It was defined most clearly by sequential introduction of the vertebrate classes.[52]

To challenge this view, Charles Lyell, another geologist, found it necessary to revive the steady state world view. According to Bowler, Lyell's emphasis on gradual change brought about by observable causes eliminated the need for catastrophes. It has been hailed by geologists as the foundation stone of modern geology. Lyell's method of using observable causes wherever possible was a great step forward. This is because the catastrophists all too often had been tempted to invoke mysterious past causes instead of trying to work out a natural explanation. But the steady-state world-view gained few converts, and remains unacceptable to modern geologists.[53]

Lyell's own opinions on the origin of new species made use of the "deliberate vagueness" of the idea of creation typical of the pre-Darwinian period. He certainly introduced an element of continuity in the process by suggesting that new forms appear from time to time in the regular course of nature.[54] For example, in one of his journals, Lyell believes species must die out and new ones must come in. Otherwise, the earth would be uninhabited.[55] Later, in the same journal entry, Lyell adds that of the many ways God might fit a new species to all present and future conditions of its existence, only one preferable way to all the others may exist. Suppose this would cause the new species to be allied to preexisting and extinct or with numerous coexisting species of the same genus, then what we understand as necessity may merely imply that God finds pleasure not to ordain mere fitness, but the greatest fitness.[56]

Thus Lyell had decided that species could not be modified by natural causes, and was convinced that adaptation of every species to its environment reflects the Creator's wisdom and benevolence. As Bowler notes, Lyell seems to have been implying that the Creator could build powers into nature that would fulfill his wishes without his direct intervention, although these powers would manifest themselves in a series of discrete events not linked by ordinary laws of nature.[57]

---

52. Ibid., 126.
53. Ibid., 127.
54. Ibid., 133.
55. Lyell, "Journal," I.
56. Ibid.
57. Bowler, Evolution, 133.

According to Bowler, Lyell's religious convictions gave him profound aversion to the belief that our spiritual character might have been derived from the merely physical world of the brutes. Hence Lyell found it necessary to treat the appearance of man as a recent event of a unique character. The last thing Lyell wanted was that the introduction of man be downgraded to merely the last step in a progression through the animal kingdom.[58]

Lyell argued that physically, humans were not necessarily the highest form of life. Their superiority lies in their mental and moral powers, not in bodily structure. By rejecting the normal idea of progression Lyell was able to reinforce the gulf between man and the animals, for one reason: if there was no real progress in earlier periods, it would not be possible to connect the eventual appearance of man with earlier stages in the history of life.[59]

However, in his *Vestiges of the Natural History of Creation*, published in 1844, naturalist Robert Chambers seemed to believe that the superiority of humans over other forms of creation could still be seen in a way that not only maintains the dignity of humans, but also gives dignity to the so-called lower forms of life. According to Bowler, although Chambers promoted the basic idea of evolution, his conception of how the process occurred was in no way an anticipation of Darwinism. Darwin provided a mechanism based on natural causes to explain how a species can adapt to a changing environment. Chambers tried to link the whole of natural philosophy under the all-embracing conception of progression. His biology fell back on what Bowler calls "the vague notion of the law of creation."[60]

Chambers begins his explanation by noting that everything we see is brought about by certain laws of matter. We see these laws to be at work as follows: certain natural events proceed in an invariable order under certain conditions. We thus infer the existence of an essential arrangement which, for the origination of these events, retains a force and certainty of action similar to, but more precise and unfailing than those arrangements which human society makes for its own benefit and calls laws.[61] According to Chambers, it should not escape our careful notice that the regulations on which all the laws of matter operate are established on a rigidly accurate mathematical basis.[62]

58. Ibid., 132.
59. Ibid.
60. Ibid., 134.
61. Chambers, *Vestiges of the Natural History of Creation*, 24.
62. Ibid., 25.

For Chambers, this allows us to advance from the law itself in order to determine the cause of that law. In Chambers' view, science leaves us with no option but only to infer, from some other basis, that a First Cause exists, to which all others are secondary and ministrative."[63] What these other basis is, Chambers does not say. The immediate context suggests that he has philosophical grounds in mind, since he elsewhere states that we infer God's existence by observing the laws of nature and conclude that only a being like God could bring about such laws.[64]

In Chambers' view, God created animated beings, as well as the "terraqueous theatre of their being." Chambers holds that this is a fact so powerfully evidenced and so universally received that he at once takes it for granted. He thus concludes that the Almighty Author produced the progenitors of existing species by some sort of personal or immediate exertion.[65]

But this leaves Chambers with a concern: how can one imagine an immediate exertion of this creative power at one time to produce zoophytes, to produce crustaceous fishes, again perfect fishes, and so on all the way to the end? In other words, how does this view of God's immediate exertion of his power comport with what we have seen of the gradual advance of species, from the humblest to the highest?[66]

Chambers tries to solve the concern as follows: there is powerful evidence that the design of the universe was the result, not of any immediate or personal exertion on the part of Deity, but of natural laws which are expressions of his will. Therefore, nothing keeps us from supposing that the organic creation is also a result of natural laws, which are in like manner an expression of his will.[67]

It is not clear what Chambers' position is here. On the one hand he contends that God produced the progenitors of existing species by some sort of personal or immediate exertion. On the other, he holds that the design of the universe was not the result of God's immediate or personal exertion. Rather, it was the result of natural laws which are expressions of his will. It may appear that Chambers is inconsistent. A better way out, perhaps, is to argue as follows: Chambers thinks that Creation by personal

63. Ibid.
64. Ibid.
65. Ibid., 152–53.
66. Ibid., 153.
67. Ibid., 153–54.

exertion, though powerfully evidenced as the means by which God could have created progenitors of existing species, is not sufficient to account for the existing species themselves. A more realistic understanding is needed, which, in Chambers view, is creation as a result of natural law. This not only accounts for the creation of progenitors of existing species, it sufficiently accounts for the existing species themselves. In other words, it seems to eliminate the concern that Chambers has about zoophytes, crustaceous fishes, and so on.

At any rate, Chambers believes that his position can be reconciled with Scripture. He holds that when we carefully read the first chapter of the book of Genesis, we find that the procedure in that chapter is represented primarily and preeminently as flowing from commands and expressions of God's will, and not from direct acts. For example, to create the natural order, God uses expressions like, "Let there be light," or "Let there be a firmament," or "Let the dry land appear." In Chambers' view, these are terms in which the principle acts are described.[68]

Chambers thinks that the Divine attributes are not diminished or reduced in any way by supposing that God created by law; rather, the attributes are infinitely exalted. He argues that it is the narrowest of all views of the Deity to suppose him acting constantly in particular ways for particular occasions. For one thing, according to Chambers, it greatly detracts from God's foresight, which is the most undeniable of all the attributes of omnipotence.[69] Chambers contends that when all is seen to be the result of law, the idea of an Almighty becomes irresistible. This is because the creation of a law for an endless series of phenomena, which is an act of intelligence above all else that we can conceive, could have no other imaginable source.[70]

In Chambers' view, it pleased Providence to arrange that one species should give birth to another, until the second highest gave birth to man, who is the very highest.[71] According to Chambers, the gradual progression of life is revealed by the fossil record. He argues that each genus began with its lowest forms and gradually rose to the highest. For example, the first fishes were only primitive vertebrates, with armored skin and vertebral column of cartilage rather than true bone. This shows their relationship to the invertebrates from which they had evolved. The geological history

68. Ibid., 155.
69. Ibid., 156.
70. Ibid., 157.
71. Ibid., 234–35.

of the reptiles is unclear and does not fit the pattern very clearly. But the mammals began with the primate marsupials of the Mesozoic and rose at last to the highest form—human beings. Assuming a certain amount of imperfection in the record, Chambers argued that the history of life showed a gradual progression in which each new form could have evolved by a small chance from the one immediately below.[72]

Thus in Chambers' view there is evolution only within a genus but not from one genus to another. For Chambers, a species does not change by gradual accumulation of minute variations; rather, it breeds true despite such variations, until something sparks off the extension of growth that will allow members of the new generation to appear as the next highest form.[73]

Chambers saw evolution as a designed process with the nature of the guiding powers that God has built into the universe. Sometimes Chambers implied that these powers can be seen operating in the normal course of nature. But his more detailed discussions imply that the constructive forces are not observable. During the acts of transmutation, a higher force steps in and produces a change which could not have been predicted on the basis of regular observation. But this change, in Chambers' view, follows the will of the Creator. The changes were higher manifestations of a "higher law" built into nature and capable of interfering from time to time with the laws we observe normally. Thus it seems that the first members of a genus were created directly by this "higher" law.[74]

Chambers' view allowed him to maintain the superiority of humans as the highest developed of creatures in creation, while at the same time upholding the dignity of other animals in creation. Chambers argued that other creatures are also products of the Almighty Conception. They all display wondrous evidences of God's wisdom and benevolence. God has assigned to all of them, as well as to ourselves, a part in the drama of the organic world. We therefore have no reason to hold them in contempt.[75]

Bowler notes that the naturalists we have encountered so far shared a common belief that the law of creation represented the unfolding of the Creator's purpose. This law was suited exactly to this continued acceptance

---

72. Bowler, *Evolution*, 135.
73. Ibid., 136.
74. Ibid., 137–38.
75. Chambers, *Vestiges*, 236.

of the argument from design and no one was worried that it did not specify the details of how life evolved.[76]

Therefore, what we find, in this section, is the frequent acceptance of God's role in creating nature. If this role is accepted, it becomes extremely difficult to rule out the doctrine of God's miraculous creation of nature. But this was the attitude that Charles Darwin challenged. He started off in a totally new direction, attempting to explain the process of adaptation through blind operation of everyday laws of nature. According to Bowler, the mechanism of natural selection refuted the claim that the final product of universal development was of personal concern to any superintending Power such as God.[77] Or did it? The answer remains to be seen.

Methodological Naturalism of Darwin

Since most of Darwin's findings are well known and readily available, this section will focus only on the aspect of Darwin's naturalism relevant to this project, namely, the reasons for his rejection of natural theology as a way of explaining the natural history of the world and the origin of the universe.

According to Bowler, Charles Darwin's real intellectual origins can be traced to his Cambridge years: his reading of Paley's *Natural Theology* and his contact with the botanist, John Henslow, and Adam Sedgwick, the geologist. Darwin's decision to train for the ministry was not based on wild enthusiasm. Neither was it hypocritical. He still accepted the literal truth of the Bible and was quite prepared to follow Paley's reasoning. He read with delight the examples of adaptation used by Paley to demonstrate the Creator's wisdom and benevolence. His attention was fixed on the significance of adaptation in nature.[78] However, Darwin later turned the logic of Paley's argument on its head. For Paley, adaptation was a fixed state in which the connection between structure and function was explained by supernatural design. For Darwin, adaptation became a process by which species adjust to changes in their environment by purely natural means.[79]

In *The Origin of Species* Darwin distinguished between natural selection and artificial selection. The former involved the preservation of

---

76. Bowler, *Evolution*, 140–41.
77. Ibid., 141.
78. Ibid., 147.
79. Ibid.

favorable variations and the rejection of injurious variations by natural means.[80] The latter, also called "variation under domestication," involved the preservation of favorable variations and rejection of injurious variations by artificial means. It involved the steps by which domestic races have been produced, either from one or from several allied species.[81]

The first chapter of *The Origin of Species* focuses on variation under domestication. In this chapter, Darwin explains the process of artificial selection from the data he collected from artificial breeders. He believed that studying some special group is always best. For this reason, he took up some domestic pigeons, and kept every breed he could obtain. He was also favored with skins from several quarters of the world. He found the diversity of species somewhat astonishing. In comparing the English carrier, for example, with the short-faced tumbler, he was able to see the wonderful difference in their skulls.[82]

In light of Darwin's examples, artificial selection involves the element of choice, exercised by the will of intelligent humans. But how is it that natural selection rules out this element of choice? Darwin contends that on this view we find several reasons for holding that varieties of species have been produced by secondary laws rather than by special acts of creation. According to Darwin, natural selection explains how it is that in each region where many species of a genus have been produced, we find those same species representing many varieties. Dominant species belonging to the larger groups tend to give birth to new and dominant forms. In this way, each large group tends to become still larger, and at the same time more divergent in character. But all groups cannot succeed in increasing in population; for the world would not hold them. Thus, the more dominant groups beat the less dominant in this struggle for existence.[83]

Darwin inferred the selective power of struggle from Thomas Malthus' principle of population, coupled with the observed fact that the population of any species must remain more or less constant. Malthus' principle showed that numbers of any species potentially can increase at an exponential rate. But observation and common sense tell us that the population of a wild species cannot increase significantly from year to year, because of the limited nature of the food supply. Many individuals born in each

80. Darwin, *Origin of Species*, 64.
81. Ibid., 29.
82. Ibid., 23–24.
83. Ibid., 360–61.

generation must die before their time, because available resources simply cannot support the potential increase in population. From this Darwin deduced that there must be a constant struggle for existence in nature, as individuals compete to see who will get enough of the limited food supply to stay alive and breed.[84]

In Darwin's view, this tendency in the large groups to continue increasing population and diverging in character, together with the inevitability of much extinction, explains the arrangement of all the forms of life, in groups subordinate to groups, all within a few great classes.[85] According to Darwin, this grand fact of the grouping of all organic beings seems to be "utterly inexplicable" on the theory of creation.[86]

Darwin also believes that natural selection is better equipped to explain many other facts in nature; for example, Darwin found no reason to marvel at the sting of a bee which, after it gets used against an enemy, causes the bee's death. For Darwin, the wonder remains on the theory of natural selection that more cases of the lack of absolute perfection have not been detected.[87]

Darwin believes that these cases are completely inexplicable on the theory of creation. He cites many more instances he thinks are best explained by the theory of natural selection, and completely inexplicable by the doctrine of creation. For example, he believes that the doctrine of creation cannot explain the occasional appearance of stripes on the shoulder and legs of the several species of the horse-genus and in their hybrids. Darwin also believes that the doctrine of creation cannot explain why a part developed in a very unusual manner in any one species of a genus should be eminently liable to variation.[88]

Quite significantly, however, Darwin seemed to make room for the Creator in *The Origin of Species*. There, he observed that all living things have much in common in their chemical composition, their germinal vesicles, their cellular structure and their laws of growth and reproduction. According to Darwin, we see this even in trifling circumstances. For example, the same poison often similarly affects plants and animals. This leads him to infer, by analogy, that probably all the organic beings which have ever

---

84. Bowler, *Evolution*, 156–57.
85. Darwin, *Origin of Species*, 360.
86. Ibid.
87. Ibid., 362.
88. Ibid., 362–63.

lived on this earth have descended from some one primordial form, into which life was first breathed by the Creator.[89] However, Darwin dropped this passage in the sixth edition of *The Origin of Species*. All that remained to indicate belief in God was a reference in the last paragraph of the work when he seemed to suggest that we can find grandeur in his proposed view of life, with its several powers, having been originally brought into being by God into a few forms or into one.[90]

According to Bowler, given Darwin's original faith in Paley's argument from design, Darwin originally must have believed that by miracles the Creator was directly responsible for the appearance of new species. But his *Beagle* experiences turned him away from miracles; the Galapagos discoveries provided a kind of *reductio ad absurdum* of simple creationism.[91] The *reductio* amounted to something like this: Assume a benevolent and wise Designer exists. If he exists, his benevolence and wisdom would be evident in nature. But the harsh realities of nature seem inconsistent with such benevolence and wisdom. Hence the original assumption must be false.

But it is still not clear how this logic applies to the Galapagos. This is because such "harsh realities" are apparent everywhere. If this was Darwin's argument, it does not seem to be much of a *reductio ad absurdum*. At best it is an inductive argument that still leaves room for the existence of a designer. Thus the *reductio* does not imply that Darwin necessarily became an atheist or that he rejected any concept of design. The key step seems to have been when Darwin began to believe that transmutation comes about through the differential survival of essentially random variants struggling to cope with the environment. This forced Darwin to question whether a benevolent God would rely on what seemed to be such a harsh and uncoordinated process. Individual competition did not benefit the whole population, because the fruits of progress could be enjoyed only by those lucky enough to survive. For Darwin, this ruthless selection constituted a new kind of determinism that did not seem reconcilable with design. And from this point onward, Bowler observes, it can be argued that Darwin became an agnostic, if not an outright atheist.[92]

Although the *Origin of* Species is inconclusive on this point, a more solid conclusion can be established by examining Darwin's autobiography.

89. Ibid., 391.
90. Darwin, *Origin of Species*, 396.
91. Bowler, *Evolution*, 158.
92. Ibid.

He begins by stating his beliefs about revealed religion, and then proceeds to his beliefs about natural religion. According to Darwin, the more one knew about the fixed laws of nature, the more incredible the idea of miracles became, and that believers in miracles were incomprehensible, ignorant and credulous. Moreover, Darwin believes the gospels could not have been written in tandem with the events they report. To be sure, Darwin argues, they differed in numerous significant details, and those details rarely get admitted as inaccuracies of eyewitnesses. Upon reflecting on these problems, Darwin eventually disbelieved in the authenticity of Christianity's claim to divine revelation.[93]

Not only do we see Darwin rejecting the postulates of Christianity as a revealed religion. He also registers his rejection of natural theology. He reports how he reflected on the existence of a personal God much later in his life. Earlier in life, he had found Paley's teleological argument for the existence of God quite conclusive. However, after discovering the law of natural selection, Darwin found Paley's design argument flawed. For Darwin, both organic beings and the blowing of the wind obeyed the fixed laws of nature and, for that reason, had no elements of design in them.[94]

Thus in both instances Darwin not only rejects divine revelation as proof of Christianity; he also rejects natural theology as proof for God's existence. But one of the chief reasons for Darwin's rejection of Paley's arguments was ethical-cum-theological. According to Darwin, if God is as omniscient and omnipotent as traditionally depicted, the idea that his benevolence remains unlimited should be revolting to us specifically because we find no advantage in the sufferings of millions of lower animals almost through endless time. Darwin believes that this argument against God's existence from the reality of suffering remains quite strong. However, natural selection best explains the presence of suffering we find among organic beings, for it explains how organic beings have developed through variation.[95]

In short since there are too many faults in nature, it could not have been created by a wise and benevolent God. The faults seem to militate against his benevolence. By implication, a benevolent God would have to create a faultless and perfect universe, without the sort of suffering we see around us. Thus, the existence of suffering on the one hand, and God on the other, are mutually exclusive. This observation forced Darwin to rule

---

93. Darwin, *Autobiography*, 86.
94. Ibid., 87.
95. Ibid., 90.

God out as the Creator of species. Once God was "out of the way" Darwin would then look for the origin of species from other quarters, namely, natural selection.

This ruling out of God as the Creator of species is a claim that Darwin makes in the *Origin of Species*. However, we find a slight change in this respect between the third edition and the sixth edition of the same work. In the third edition Darwin draws our attention to the following strange realities if God designed the universe. Why, for example, would God create a woodpecker to prey on insects on the ground? Why would God create upland geese, which rarely swim, with webbed feet? Why would God create a thrush to dive and feed on sub-aquatic insects? These facts remain inexplicable if we posit God as the Creator of these species. However, on the view that species survive and constantly try to increase in number through the help of natural selection, the facts he lists find a proper explanation.[96] Darwin wanted to show that a wise and benevolent God would not have created the animals in question with the apparent "faults." Thus for Darwin, his understanding of God would not allow him to invoke God as a Creator playing an active role in Creation.

In order to be sure that he was right in eliminating God from the processes of nature, Darwin explored other arguments given for God's existence and found them inadequate. For example, he noted that arguments for God's existence, drawn from a person's deep inward conviction and feelings, were unsuccessful since adherents of rival faiths, some of them quite polytheistic and others atheistic, had similar convictions in the same manner and with equal force. Darwin believed that this argument would be a valid one if all humans of all races had the same inward conviction of the existence of one God. But Darwin thought that this possibility was very far from being the case.[97]

However, Darwin draws our attention to an argument for God's existence, which he believed had more weight than the inner conviction argument. According to Darwin, the existence of God seemed to follow from the impossibility of seeing how our immense and wonderful universe could have been caused by blind chance and necessity. Upon reflection, Darwin feels compelled to posit a First Cause as having an intelligent mind

---

96. Darwin, *Origin of Species*, 381.
97. Darwin, *Autobiography*, 90–91.

somewhat analogous to the human mind. For that reason, Darwin says he deserved to be called a theist.[98]

Despite his initial attraction to this argument, Darwin admits that his convictions about theism gradually became weaker. Just the same, He would find himself wondering whether the human mind, which, as he believed, developed from minds as low as that possessed by the lowest animals, could be trusted to draw such grand conclusions. The reason for this stems from the fact that these conclusions could be the result of a necessary cause and effect connection. Moreover, he wonders whether we should overlook the probability that a constant inculcation in a belief in God exists in the mind of children such that it produces a strong inherited effect on their developing brains. For that reason, throwing off their belief in God would be as difficult as having a monkey abandoning its fear of a snake. Darwin admits he has no way of shedding light on these problems. He finds the mystery of the origin of all things completely insoluble, and for that reason he considered himself an agnostic.[99]

How should we understand Darwin's use of the term "agnostic"? According to Bowler, Thomas Huxley coined the term "agnosticism" to describe a state of active doubt on the religious question. Huxley argued that science is neutral concerning the existence of a Creator; it could neither prove nor disprove it.[100] Darwin used the term in this sense, for he contends that the beginning of all things remains insoluble to us. Agnosticism so understood contends that we cannot know, at least through science, whether God exists or not. Quite possibly, however, Darwin might have been a theist with respect to belief in the existence of God, but an agnostic with respect to how God caused the universe to exist.

But did this species of agnosticism, on the one hand, and confidence in natural selection, on the other, dominate nineteenth-century scientific thinking? Daniel Dennett reports that there were large gaps in Darwin's theory, despite the fact that the articulation of his theory was monumental and its powers were immediately recognized by many of the scientists and other thinkers of his day. According to Dennett, in all his brilliant musings, Darwin never hit upon the central concept of a *gene*, without which the theory of evolution is hopeless. Darwin had no proper *unit* of heredity.

---

98. Ibid., 92–93.
99. Ibid., 93–94.
100. Bowler, *Evolution*, 230.

Hence his account of the process of natural selection was plagued with entirely reasonable doubts about whether it would work.[101]

Bowler adds that the complexity of the situation was increased by the sheer number of alternatives to Darwinism suggested at the time. For example, in the late nineteenth century, the most important alternatives were neo-Lamarckism and orthogenesis. By 1900 the more "scientific" work of the laboratory was beginning to displace the old natural history approach in areas such as the study of heredity.[102]

From these experimental studies came the rediscovery of Mendel's work and the origins of modern genetics. Bowler observes that although genetics ultimately would solve many of the problems facing the selection theory, the new science was at first presented as yet another alternative to Darwinism. Genetic mutations were seen not as the raw material of selection, but as an autonomous driving force of evolution. But Mendelism was incompatible with Lamarckism, and instead of combining to destroy Darwinism, the opponents fought among themselves. Lamarckism was eliminated from orthodox biology, and eventually it was realized that genetics was by no means as incompatible with Darwinism as its early overenthusiastic supporters had believed.[103]

Thus, genetics was eventually and triumphantly established at the heart of what Dennett calls the "Modern Synthesis" of Mendel and Darwin. This synthesis was eventually made secure in the 1940s. It anticipated and opened the door for Neo-Darwinism.[104] A brief outline of how this happened is given in the next section.

Highs and Lows of Darwinian Methodological Naturalism

Exactly when and how did Darwinian methodological naturalism become the ruling view in biology? It had its highs and lows in terms of popularity. According to Bowler, when the theory of natural selection was originally outlined by Darwin, there was little opposition to it on the grounds that it challenged the literal word of the Genesis creation story. The great controversies over geology and paleontology earlier in the nineteenth century had

101. Dennett, *Darwin's Dangerous Idea*, 19–20.
102. Bowler, *Evolution*, 234.
103. Ibid.
104. Dennett, *Darwin's Dangerous Idea*, 20.

convinced almost everyone that the text of Genesis must be understood in a less rigorous way that would allow the earth and its inhabitants to change over a vast period of time.[105]

However, in its most extreme form, Darwinism's challenge to traditional thought manifested itself not in the details of Darwin's theory, but in the more comprehensive world view into which evolution was incorporated by more radical thinkers. Darwinism came to symbolize a new system of values, derived more from the evolutionary philosophy of Hebert Spencer. Universal progress was seen as a necessary outcome of the mechanical operations of the laws of nature. Moreover, human beings were seen as a product of the evolutionary process, and, in the absence of any transcendental source of moral values, humans would have to create a new ethics based on the guidance of nature itself. An increasing confidence in the power of science to generate a complete explanation of the universe was an important part of this new materialism.[106]

Darwinian evolution played its role in promoting this confidence. But a number of Darwin's immediate followers were unwilling to accept the materialist program. Some scientists like Alfred Russell Wallace and Huxley found the complete extension of evolutionary naturalism into a way of life distasteful. Wallace believed that the last stages of human evolution were supernaturally guided, while Huxley eventually became a severe critic of so-called evolutionary ethics.[107]

Just as biologists differed in their willingness to accept a naturalistic world view, the theologians showed varying degrees of willingness to accommodate evolution into their thinking. Some resisted any compromise with the new theory. But some strict Calvinists (Bowler leaves them unnamed) expressed a willingness to adopt the complete Darwinian scheme. They noticed the compatibility of a theory in which the rigid operations of law do not guarantee progress with the Christian view that human beings are fallen creatures whose salvation must come from a source external to this world. In the early debates over the *Origin of Species*, many scientists and theologians opted for a compromise position in which evolution is guided toward adaptation and progress by some kind of supernatural power. According to Bowler, this concept of theistic evolution proved unsatisfactory

---

105. Bowler, *Evolution*, 206.
106. Ibid., 207.
107. Ibid.

in science, however, because it still prevented the biologist from providing a completely natural explanation of the phenomena.[108]

Interestingly, from the high point of the 1870s and 1880s, when "Darwinism" had become virtually synonymous with evolution itself, the selection theory had by 1900 slipped in popularity to such an extent that its opponents were convinced it would never recover. Evolution itself remained unquestioned. But an increasing number of biologists preferred mechanisms other than selection to explain how it occurred.[109] Field naturalists preserved the original Darwinian emphasis on the role of geographical factors in evolution. But they were strongly tempted by alternative mechanism of adaptation, such as Lamarckism. Paleontologists were convinced that evolution is directed along linear paths by either Lamarckism or orthogenesis.[110]

In the 1920s the first moves were made toward a reconciliation between the divided branches of biology, and Darwinism emerged from its eclipse to provide the key to a new approach that would solve many outstanding problems. It was realized that the more sophisticated understanding of heredity provided by Mendelism would have to be applied to populations containing a wide range of individual variation and that selection might affect the relative frequencies of the genes. By 1940 many naturalists had come to recognize that their own work could be reconciled with this new form of selectionism, eliminating the need for unsubstantiated alternatives, such as Lamarckism. The resulting "evolutionary synthesis" or "modern synthesis" allowed Darwinism to reemerge as a driving force in biology.[111]

According to Bowler, there has been some debate over how the evolutionary synthesis was put together. But it seems the decisive breakthrough came with the creation of population genetics as a new foundation for natural selection. This was a revived form of Darwinism, which was exploited by field naturalists and paleontologists who had been looking for a way out of the confused state of their thinking on the evolutionary mechanism. Population genetics was important because it destroyed the legacy of anti-Darwinian feeling and focused attention on

---

108. Ibid., 207–8.
109. Ibid., 233.
110. Ibid., 289.
111. Ibid.

new research opportunities. It enabled natural selection to reemerge as a viable mechanism of adaptive evolution.[112]

A parallel development that helped to boost the revival of Darwinism was the appearance of the first modern theory of the origin of life on earth. In 1936 the Russian biologist Alexander Oparin introduced a new approach to the question in which the notion of a single act of spontaneous generation was replaced by a process of chemical evolution through levels of increasing complex organization.[113] Oparin believed that the earth originally had been enveloped in a reducing atmosphere containing hydrocarbons and ammonia. Chemical reactions among these gases produced complex organic molecules that dissolved in the oceans to form a rich "primordial soup." At this stage, the chemicals combined again to form poly-molecular open systems, minute droplets with a definite structure, capable of absorbing materials from their surroundings. Natural selection came into play, allowing those minute droplets with more stable structures to survive at the expense of the less stable. The more successful structures became the prebionts, the intermediate stages before the appearance of true life in the form of first cells.[114] Admittedly, now that the chemical structure of the DNA in the genes is understood, we have a better idea of the level of complexity that must be achieved. But the idea that a self-replicating system must have been built up gradually has remained popular if only because, according to Bowler, the alternative "one step" process returns us to a situation in which complex structure must arise suddenly out of chance collisions of much smaller molecules.[115]

In this way, Darwinism came of age under the name Neo-Darwinism. It became the dominant view in biology, outdoing Lamarckism and incorporating Mendelism as its ally.

Methodological Naturalism of Neo-Darwinists

In this section I will focus on two prominent Neo-Darwinists: Stephen J. Gould and Richard Dawkins. They represent two different camps of Darwinists: those open to the possibility of God's existence and those who reject it completely. Dawkins is clearly an avowed atheist. But Gould seems open,

112. Ibid., 289–90.
113. Ibid., 300.
114. Ibid., 302.
115. Ibid., 302–3.

though extremely skeptical, to the possibility that God could have played a role in bringing about the processes of nature. For Gould, the universe should no longer be viewed as designed to serve a particular human purpose. A more mechanical view of nature has replaced this idea of design. In Gould's view, God may have played a part in designing the universe, but only as a clockmaker who winds the clock and leaves it to run on its own. Clearly, he does not create each blade of grass or grain of sand as his way of instructing or sustaining some favored earthly species.[116]

These words suggest that Gould may have been open to the possibility of a deistic view of nature. In *Hen's Teeth and Horses' Toes* published in 1983, Gould reports that all evolutionary biologists had concluded, by 1959, that natural selection provided the creative mechanism necessary for evolutionary change. In Gould's words, Darwin had finally triumphed at age 150. By the time Gould wrote his book he observed that Darwinian theory was in a vibrantly healthy state.[117]

Gould's confidence in the occurrence of evolution is based on three general arguments. First, he argues that abundant, direct, and observational evidence of evolution in action is available in the field and in the laboratory. The evidence ranges from countless experiments on change in nearly everything about fruit flies subjected to artificial selection in the laboratory to the famous populations of British moths that became black when industrial soot darkened the trees upon which the moths rest.[118] This is similar to Darwin's argument in the first chapter of the *Origin of Species*.

Second, Gould argues that the imperfection of nature reveals evolution. Evolution lies exposed in the *imperfections* that record a history of descent. For example, the only reason a rat should run, or a bat should fly, or a porpoise should swim, or why he should type essays with structures built of the same bones is if we all inherited these structures from a common ancestor. In Gould's view, an engineer, starting from scratch, could design better limbs in each case.[119]

Third, Gould argues that transitions found in the fossil record support the theory of evolution. Preserved transitions are not common. But they are not entirely wanting. The lower jaw of reptiles contains several bones, that of mammals only one. The non-mammalian jawbones are reduced, step

---

116. Gould, *Hen's Teeth and Horse's Toes*, 81.
117. Ibid., 12–14.
118. Ibid., 257.
119. Ibid., 258.

by step, in mammalian ancestors until they become tiny nubbins located at the back of the jaw.[120] Turning to humans, Gould draws our attention to a transitional form in human ancestry called *Australopithecus Afarensis*, the oldest human with apelike palate and upright stance, though smaller than humans by 1000 cubic centimeters. According to Gould, if God created each of the six human species discovered in ancient rocks, we find no explanation why he created a larger size in an unbroken temporal sequence of progressively more modern features. Could God have done this act of creation to test human faith by mimicking evolution?[121] Gould, of course, is using this example to demonstrate the veracity of evolution and the implausibility of positing God as an explanation for the variations in species.

For Gould, whereas the first argument for evolution is based on observation and lab experiments, the second and third arguments rest upon inference, though, as he hastens to add, this does not mean that they are less secure. He observes that major evolutionary change requires too much time for direct observation on the scale of recorded human history. Hence, all historical science rest upon inference and evolution is no different from geology, cosmology, or human history in this respect. In principle, Gould adds, we cannot observe the processes that operate in the past. We must infer them from results that still surround us: living and fossil organisms for evolution, documents and artifacts for human history, strata and topography for geology.[122]

One of the more fierce contemporary supporters of Darwinism is Richard Dawkins. In *The Blind Watchmaker* published in 1986 Dawkins famously remarked that Darwin made it possible to be an intellectually fulfilled atheist.[123] Arguing against Paley, Dawkins thinks that nature was designed, not by an intelligent mind, but by the blind forces of physics, namely, natural selection. Moreover, Dawkins adds that natural selection can account for the complexity we find in nature.[124]

To show just how this happens, Dawkins draws distinctions between what he calls single-step selection and cumulative selection. In order to understand single-step selection, Dawkins uses the analogy of the sieve. Consider, for example, the wave action of pebbles on the beach. These are

---

120. Ibid., 259.
121. Ibid., 258–59.
122. Ibid., 257–58.
123. Dawkins, *Blind Watchmaker*, 6.
124. Ibid., 5.

sorted, arranged and selected, with the heavier pebbles accumulating in one area of the beach and the lighter ones gathering in another area. The blind forces of physics, namely, wave action, perform this selection.[125]

Or take the example of a hole. According to Dawkins, only objects smaller than the hole can pass through it. Thus if we begin with a random collection above the hole, and imagine some forces shaking the objects at random, we see that the objects above and below will be non-randomly selected.[126]

Single step selection helps to explain the arrangement of the solar system. It is a stable arrangement of plants, comets, and debris orbiting the sun. The nearer a satellite is to the sun, the faster it has to travel. It does so in order to counter the sun's gravity and remain in a stable orbit. Every single planet of our solar system, Dawkins argues, moves at exactly the right velocity. This keeps it stable in its orbit around the sun. According to Dawkins, this is not a blessed miracle of provident design. It is just another kind of sieve.[127]

The problem with single step selection, Dawkins concedes, is that it is not sufficient to account for nonrandom order in living things. It is equivalent to a combination lock with only one dial. Hence, once entities are selected, the result does not change. Single step selection is an essential ingredient in the generation of living order. But it is very far from being the whole story.[128]

For this reason, Dawkins argues that something more, like cumulative selection, is needed to explain the non-randomness found in living systems. Cumulative selection is like a gigantic lock of an uncountable number of dials. Here, the results of one sieving process are fed into a subsequent sieving. This is then fed into another subsequent sieving. The process continues until we have many generations of sorting and sieving.[129]

To illustrate how single-step selection might take a long time to work, think of a monkey trying to type out the phrase METHINKS IT IS LIKE A WEASEL on a typewriter. Suppose the monkey is given a restricted keyboard

---

125. Ibid., 43.
126. Ibid., 44.
127. Ibid.
128. Ibid., 45.
129. Ibid.

typewriter with 26 capital letters. If the monkey types the sentence correctly, the experiment ends. If not, we allow him another try of 28 characters.[130]

To calculate the possibility of this phrase, consider that the monkey will use 27 possible keys (which include the spacebar). The monkey has a 1 in 27 chance of getting the first letter correctly. Assume it gets the first letter right. The chance of getting both the first and the second letter right is 1 in 729. But this means that the chance of getting the whole phrase right is extremely small. Thus, in a single step selection, the target phrase will be a long time coming.[131]

However, the effectiveness of cumulative selection can be seen by the following illustration. Think of a computer that chooses a random sequence of 28 letters. It duplicates the phrase repeatedly. But it has a certain chance of random error (analogous to mutation) in the copying. The computer then examines the mutant nonsense of phrases, which Dawkins calls "the 'progeny' of the original phrase."[132] Exactly how this happens Dawkins does not say. However, we can fairly assume, perhaps, that Dawkins thinks this process of examining and selecting is somehow built into the computer program that performs this very sort of thing.

Dawkins imagines the following phrase as the winning phrase of the next generation: WDLTMNLT DTJBSWIRZREZLMQCO P. Although an improvement from the previous one, the resultant phrase is, perhaps, not an obvious one. Still, the procedure gets repeated and mutant progeny gets bred from the winning phrase, which yields a new winner. After repeatedly producing mutant progenies and newer breeds, we find the following 10th generational phrase: MDLDMNLS ITJISWHRZREZ MECS P. Moreover, after 20 generations, the new winner is: MELDINLS IT ISWPRKE Z WECSEL. One immediately sees that the 20th generational phrase bears some resemblance to the target phrase, which, after 30 generations comes out as follows: METHINGS IT ISWLIKE B WECSEL. The 40th generation brings us to within a letter of the target phrase as follows: METHINKS IT IS LIKE I WEASEL. Generation 43 then yields the final target.[133]

Dawkins' point is that there is a big difference between cumulative selection and single-step selection. In the former, each improvement, however slight, is used as a basis for future building. But in the latter, each new

130. Ibid., 46.
131. Ibid., 46–47.
132. Ibid., 47.
133. Ibid., 48.

"try" is a fresh one.[134] Dawkins warns that the evolutionary process would never achieve much if it were to rely solely on single step selection. However, suppose a way existed in which the necessary conditions could have, in some way, been put in place by nature's blind forces, the consequences would be both strange and wonderful.[135] As a matter of fact, Dawkins concludes, that is exactly what happened on this planet, and we ourselves are among the most recent, if not the strangest and most wonderful, of those consequences.[136]

This observation allows Dawkins further to contend that the events we commonly call miracles are not supernatural. Rather, they are part of a spectrum of more-or-less improbable natural events. Thus, if a miracle occurs at all, it is a tremendous stroke of luck. According to Dawkins, events do not fall neatly into natural events versus miracles. He believes that there are some would-be events that are too improbable to be contemplated, but we cannot know this until we have done some calculation. But to do the calculation, we must know how much time was available—more generally how many opportunities were available—for the event to occur. Given infinite time, or infinite opportunities, Dawkins contends, anything is possible.[137]

This sums up the Neo-Darwinists relevant to the purpose of this chapter. I now turn to a critique of the views of methodological naturalism. I will show that none of them provide any serious challenge to the kind of supernaturalism already outlined in the second and third chapters of this project.

Pitfalls of Methodological Naturalism

Evaluating Pre-Darwinian Methodological Naturalism

What should we make of pre-Darwinian methodological naturalism? It grew out of the attempt to understand the universe mechanistically. Mechanistic explanation involved attempting to understand the universe by appealing only to material events and causes. It gradually replaced teleological explanation, which, until the dawn of methodological naturalism

---

134. Ibid., 49.
135. Ibid.
136. Ibid.
137. Ibid., 139.

had been the dominant view, carried over from the ancient and medieval philosophers and theologians.

Mechanistic explanation went hand-in-hand with rationalist explanation, which attempted to elevate reason over faith. As we have noted, it not only rejected the possibility of miracles; it also tried to demonstrate that the existence of evil was intensely problematic given a theistic view of the universe. For example, if God is both rational and good, why would he allow any more evil than absolutely necessary? According to Leibniz, God permits evil only when it is necessary for the greater good of the whole.

Thus both the mechanistic and the rationalist understanding led to a new conception of God. Whereas both understandings retained God in their epistemology, they saw him as an ideal engineer who designed the world to be as good as possible. Perhaps, they argued, he occasionally intervenes in nature; or perhaps he designed the laws of nature to eventually produce the best possible result. Otherwise, he leaves the world alone. Either way, God was seen as one who was good, but not the Ultimate Good in the Platonic sense, or in the sense adumbrated by Christian theology.

And yet Laplace, De Maillet, Steno, Buffon, Erasmus Darwin, Lamarck, Cuvier, Chambers and Lyell did not provide any reasons that decisively eliminated belief in a First Cause. Except perhaps for Laplace, for the most part they all tried to modify their understanding of God in a way that allowed that understanding to fit in their materialistic-cum-rationalist understanding. But despite the fact that this view of God began to change in this way, there is little (if any) reason to believe that God was decisively eliminated from the scientific enterprise by pre-Darwinian methodological naturalism. A number of them went as far as reconciling their mechanistic and rationalist views with Scripture.

The overall implication, from our findings in pre-Darwinian methodological naturalism, is this: if God was still retained in their scientific enterprise, then the concept of miracles as explicated in the first four chapters remains firmly in place. And we do find that the idea of God was retained. Hence it would be difficult for them to do away with a miraculous creation of the universe, whether we understand such creation (in de Maillet's sense) as happening through the laying down of certain laws that bring about specific results, or as due to God's direct action on matter. But as we shall see, the rational conception of God that allowed for the actuality of miracles was called into question by Darwinian evolution. It is to this view that I now turn.

Evaluating Darwin and Huxley

Two things need to be said about Darwin's view of God. First, recall his contention that there were many things in nature that God, being perfectly good, omniscient and omnipotent, would not have created. In other words, Darwin made certain assumptions about what God would do and what he would not do in creating life. He made these assumptions because previous thinkers had been doing so since Descartes and Locke. They espoused a rationalist view of God in which God was seen as an ideal engineer. This meant that God must have a reason for doing everything he did, and that he must also maximize good and minimize evil. The implication is that God would do nothing arbitrary or pointless; He would not permit suffering that could be avoided.

In the *Origin of Species* there seem to be signs that God, if he exists at all, must fit the rationalist model. For example, Darwin wonders whether believers in special creation embrace the view that God commanded certain elemental atoms suddenly to become living tissues at innumerable epochs in the history of the earth. He wonders whether, in each act of creation, one individual or many were brought into existence. He finds no explanation from believers in special creation whether the numerous kinds of animals and plants were created as seeds, or eggs or as full-grown entities.[138]

Darwin's example illustrates that science is not independent of philosophy: philosophical assumptions can be found throughout science. This becomes quite clear when science deals with things that happened long ago or far away. At the end of the *Origin of Species,* Darwin views all beings as the lineal descendants of a few beings that evolved over time rather than as created beings. If so, they become ennobled. All the living forms of life are lineal descendants of their progenitors living long before the Silurian epoch. For this reason, Darwin remains certain that the ordinary succession by generation has always been intact and never been broken and that no kind of cataclysmic event desolated the planet. This observation allows Darwin to have confidence in the fact that a future of equally inappreciable length will be secured. Natural selection works for the good of each being. Therefore, Darwin believes all corporeal and mental endowments will progress towards perfection.[139]

---

138. Darwin, *Origin of Species*, 369.
139. Ibid., 373.

What should we make of this claim? This passage assigns to natural selection a role much like that of God. As already noted, Darwin holds that from the war of nature, famine and death, natural selection brings "the most exalted object which we are capable of conceiving," the production of higher animals. In other words, natural selection, like God, brings good out of evil and ensures that ultimately history will come to a good end by progressing towards perfection. Thus it is much like God being perfectly beneficent.

But this sort of confidence on Darwin's part does not appear to be scientifically verifiable. It seems only to be a hopeful expression of future security. It may be said that Darwin draws this hope from observing that natural selection works solely for the good of each being, and that on the basis of this we can hope for progress towards perfection. But still this does not escape the fact that progress expressed in this way (that is, through natural selection) is at best, a pious hope.

Interestingly, Darwin's hope brings him dangerously close to a teleological explanation of nature, the very idea he has taken pains to avoid throughout his work. If it really is reasonable to suppose that natural selection heads toward perfection and the good of each being, then he seems to be conceding that natural selection is leading to a predetermined goal. But if natural selection is as blind as Darwin would have us to believe, it would be inconsistent to maintain that natural selection works toward such a goal.

The second thing to note about Darwin's view of God concerns his belief in God's existence. We have already noted that Darwin was initially open to the possibility that a First Cause could have brought nature into existence. But we also noted that this was not his final view. He chose to remain agnostic, for he noted that if natural selection unguided by the hand of God is true, the human mind developed from minds as low as that possessed by the lowest animals. But he wondered whether the human mind could be trusted to draw such grand conclusions. To push the argument further, if the human mind evolved from nonrational entities, to what extent should Darwin trust that he has arrived at reliable conclusions about the doctrine of natural selection?

Darwin's doubts are quite devastating to his own theory. We rightly believe that we perceive a necessary relationship between reasons and the conclusions they imply. If we go by the doctrine of natural selection, we are merely responding according to how we have been programmed by our evolutionary past. If that is true, then we do not really reason at all; we are merely responding to stimuli. This leads to the obvious question: if our reasoning cannot be trusted, why should we trust the reasoning that led us to believe in evolution? Any theory that ends up undermining the power of reason itself is self-refuting. Darwin leaves us to wonder whether evolution is such a theory.

Thomas Huxley, Darwin's contemporary, tried to show that the doctrine of natural selection was overwhelmingly supported by scientific evidence; hence the doctrine was correct. According to Huxley, to say that one is certain of the objective truth of any proposition seems wrong unless one can produce evidence which logically justifies that claim.[140]

What should we make of Huxley's test? We could take the uncharitable route of logic chopping and argue as follows. Huxley's claim is itself unsupported by evidence. Hence it would be wrong for us to believe it. Whereas this could be a forceful objection, I think it fails to deal with Huxley's worry of doing one's best to distinguish the certain from the uncertain.

Hence we need a more charitable way of evaluating Huxley's argument. It is important to note that Huxley is no longer making a scientific claim. He seems to be making an ethical claim. On what basis, we might ask, is it wrong to believe a proposition unsupported by sufficient evidence? The wrongness cannot be derived from natural selection. First, it would be question-begging to appeal to natural selection as the process from which and by which we derive our values, since natural selection is what Huxley was trying to prove in the first place. Second, natural selection unguided by an intelligent First Cause is itself a blind process. That is to say, it has no value, meaning or purpose. Hence, to say that natural selection enables us to make valid value judgments is to accept a vantage point that is at odds with itself. It involves admitting that blind valueless processes somehow create value.

As it turns out, Huxley saw this difficulty but still believed, as Bowler points out, that the highest qualities of the human mind are intrinsically valuable, even though they are produced neither by nature nor by God. Huxley believed that by a cosmic accident, man has been given faculties that allow him to recognize the meaningless character of the system that give him birth.[141] Huxley admits that cosmic evolution may instruct us about the origins of the good and evil tendencies of humans. However, evolution, in itself, remains incompetent to explain why what we call good

---

140. Huxley, *Agnosticism and Christianity*, 193.
141. Bowler, *Evolution*, 231.

is preferable to what we call evil. To be sure, it gives us no better explanation than what we had before. Huxley registers his confidence in the possibility that some day we will have an understanding of the evolution of the aesthetic faculty. Still, he thinks no understanding will increase or diminish the force of the intuition that one thing is good and the other ugly.[142]

Huxley also suggests that we must cherish our moral feelings precisely because they go beyond nature to establish a sphere of activity that has become an integral part of our humanity.[143] For Huxley, what we call goodness or virtue involves a course of behavior which remains opposed to what leads to success in the struggle for survival. Rather than demanding ruthless self-assertion, it opts for self-restraint. Rather than thrusting aside or trampling on all competitors, it demands that the individual should not only respect his fellows, but should also help them. The influence of this goodness is directed to the fitting of as many people as possible to survive rather than to the survival for the fittest.[144] According to Huxley, the mind may be a cosmic accident, but its value to human beings is crucial because it is the only thing that makes them human, the only thing that can give meaning to an otherwise meaningless universe.[145]

Unjustifiably, Huxley seems to want it both ways. He wants to maintain the supremacy and value of the human mind as an entity uncaused by nature, but at the same time contend that Darwinian evolution is true. But why exempt the human mind from natural processes if everything is the product of blind chance? There seems to be no basis for this unique exception. But then again, Huxley also maintains that the mind is the product of a cosmic accident. Huxley provides no basis for his belief in these claims. Hence, it seems to me that Huxley fails his own test. The standard he sets is too high for him to meet.

But perhaps the Neo-Darwinists have formulated a more adequate defense of Darwin. It is to them I now turn.

Evaluating Neo-Darwinian Methodological Naturalism

Before providing a critique of the Neo-Darwinists, several things should be pointed out. First, Neo-Darwinists sometimes claim that "evolution" means

142. Huxley, *Evolution and Ethics*, 138.
143. Ibid.
144. Ibid., 139–40.
145. Bowler, *Evolution*, 231.

simply change over time. No rational person denies the reality of change. According to molecular and cell biologist Jonathan Wells, if evolution meant only "change over time," the doctrine would be utterly uncontroversial. But biological evolution as articulated by Neo-Darwinists is simply not change over time. It is something more, as will be shown below.[146]

Also, no one doubts that descent with modification occurs in the course of ordinary biological reproduction. The question is whether descent with modification accounts for the origin of every species. Like change over time, descent with modification within a species is utterly uncontroversial. But Darwinian evolution claims much more. In particular it claims that descent with modification explains the origin and diversification of all living things.[147]

Let us now turn to Gould. As already noted, Gould argues that the theory of natural selection is supported by three arguments. Several things can be said about the first argument. First, it assumes that some form of analogy can be drawn between natural selection and lab experiments. Yet natural selection is a process that takes millions of years. Strictly speaking, it cannot be observed. Gould himself admits that it cannot be observed. At best, it can only be inferred.

Moreover, natural selection, unguided by an intelligent First Cause, is supposed to be just that—natural. Neo-Darwinians would like to think of it as involving no superintending Intelligent First Cause. But lab experiments are controlled by the choice of the artificial breeders, and fundamentally involve intelligence and purpose. It is extremely difficult to find a process that can illustrate blind natural selection unguided by intelligence. Thus the analogy seems to break down. In *Darwin on Trial*, Phillip E. Johnson puts his finger on this problem. Johnson finds the analogy of artificial selection quite misleading. He notes how plant and animal breeders employ intelligence and specialized knowledge to select the stock for breeding and to protect their charges from natural dangers. However, Darwin was trying to establish the idea that purposeless natural processes can take the place of intelligent design. Darwin made this point, but in receiving his theory, his audience remained highly uncritical.[148]

Johnson argues that artificial selection is not the same sort of thing as natural selection. Rather, it is something fundamentally different. Human

---

146. Wells, *Icons of Evolution*, 5.
147. Ibid.
148. Johnson, *Darwin on Trial*, 17–18.

breeders produce variations among sheep and pigeons for purposes absent in nature. This includes, for example, sheer delight in seeing how much variation can be achieved. Johnson goes on to argue that what artificial selection shows is that there are definite limits to the amount of variation that even the most skilled breeders can achieve. Breeding domestic animals has produced no new species, in the commonly accepted sense of new breeding communities that are infertile when crossed with the parent group.[149] Admittedly, this does not mean that natural selection is a false theory. It simply means, as Johnson observes, that we will have to look for more direct evidence to see if natural selection really has a creative effect.[150]

In his first argument for natural selection, Gould also cites the famous peppered moth (*Biston betularia*) experiments as evidence for evolution. But what should we make of this example? Following Jonathan Wells, we note the following: in 1950 biologist Bernard Kettlewell[151] conducted observations which suggested that predatory birds ate light-colored moths when they became more conspicuous on pollution-darkened tree trunks, leaving the dark-colored variety to survive and reproduce. Industrial melanism in peppered moths thus appeared to be a case of natural selection.[152]

To determine whether birds preyed on peppered moths at all, Kettlewell released some moths into an aviary containing a pair of nesting birds and their young. Then he watched through his binoculars as the moths settled onto various resting sites and were eaten by the birds. This established that birds actually preyed on peppered moths. Kettlewell then released some moths onto tree trunks in a polluted woodland area near Birmingham, England. He watched through binoculars as the moths settled on nearby tree trunks, and noted that melanics were much less conspicuous than typicals, as judged by the human eye. He also noticed that birds took the conspicuous moths more readily than inconspicuous ones.[153]

Since 1980, however, evidence has accumulated showing that peppered moths do not normally rest on tree trunks. Finnish zoologist Kauri Mikkola reported an experiment in 1984 in which he used caged moths to assess normal resting places. Mikkola observed that the normal resting place of the peppered moth is beneath small, more or less horizontal

---

149. Ibid., 18.
150. Ibid., 20.
151. Kettlewell, "Selection," 323–42.
152. Wells, *Icons of Evolution*, 138.
153. Ibid., 140–41.

branches (but not on narrow twigs), probably high up in the canopies. The species probably only exceptionally rests on tree trunks.[154] Although Mikkola used caged moths, data on wild moths supported his conclusion. In twenty-five years of field work, Cyril Clarke and his colleagues found only one peppered moth naturally perched on a tree trunk; they concluded that they know primarily where the moths do not spend the day.[155]

When Rory Howlett and Michael Majerus studied the natural resting sites of peppered moths in various parts of England, they found that Mikkola's observations on caged moths were valid for wild moths as well. Their conclusions were as follows: Quite certainly, most *B. betularia* rest where they are hidden, and exposed areas of tree trunks are not an important resting site for any form of *B. betularia*.[156] In a separate study reported in 1987, British biologists Tony Liebert and Paul Brakefield confirmed Mikkola's observations that the species rests predominantly on branches. And many moths will rest underneath, or on the side of, narrow branches in the canopy.[157] Gould does not account for this disparity; he does not even seem to be aware of it.

Gould also cites the fruit fly example as evidence for natural selection. In a normal fruit fly, the second thoracic segment bears a pair of wings, and the third bears a pair of "halteres," or balancers. These are tiny appendages that enable the insect to maintain its balance in flight. In 1915 geneticist Calvin Bridges, working in Thomas Hunt Morgan's laboratory, discovered a mutant fruit fly in which the third thoracic segment looked a bit like the second, and the halteres were slightly enlarged and looked like miniature winglets. This spontaneously occurring "bithorax" mutant has been maintained as a laboratory stock ever since.[158]

In 1978 California Institute of Technology geneticist Ed Lewis reported that by breeding flies possessing the bithorax mutation with flies possessing another mutation, "postbithorax," he was able to produce a fruit fly in which the halteres were even more enlarged, and looked almost like a second pair of wings. He subsequently discovered that if flies combining these two mutations were bred with flies possessing a third, "antebithorax,"

---

154. Mikkola, "Selective Forces," 409–21.
155. Clarke and Sheppard, "Evolution," 189–99.
156. Howlett and Majerus, "Understanding," 31–44.
157. Liebert and Brakefield, "Behavioral Studies," 129–50.
158. Morgan et al., *Genetics of Drosophila*, 79.

the triple-mutant offspring had an extra pair of wings that looked like the fly's normal wings.[159]

But biologists have known since the 1950s that the extra wings on bithorax mutants lack flight muscles. The hapless insect is therefore disabled, and the disability increases with the size of the mutant appendages. In aerodynamic terms, a triple-mutant four-winged fruit fly is like an airplane with an extra pair of full-sized wings dangling loosely from its fuselage. It may be able to get off the ground, but its flying ability is seriously impaired. Because of this, four-winged males have difficulty mating. Unless the line is carefully maintained in a laboratory, it quickly dies out.[160] Hence, four-winged fruit flies are not evidence for evolution. Neo-Darwinists like Ernst Mayr also acknowledge this. Mayr wrote in 1963 that major mutations such as bithorax remain such evident freaks that they can be designated only as "hopeless." They are so utterly unbalanced that they would not have the smallest chance of avoiding extinction through natural selection. In addition, finding a suitable mate for the "hopeless monster" seemed to Mayr to be an insurmountable difficulty.[161]

Moreover, textbook accounts typically leave the reader with the impression that the extra wings represent a gain of structures. But four-winged fruit flies have actually lost structures that they need for flying. Their balances are gone, and instead of being replaced with something new, these have been replaced with copies of structures already present in another segment.[162] Thus Gould's use of the example of fruit flies is wholly inadequate as a support for the theory of natural selection.

Turning to Gould's second and third arguments for evolution we find at once that they presuppose the sort of rationalistic conception of God typical of Darwin. Gould assumes that he knows what God would do or would not do if he exists. But as noted in my evaluation of Darwin, this assumption is based on highly debatable theological assumptions. As Cornelius Hunter notes,[163] the argument seems to be as follows: God could not have created the universe in a way that includes x. Natural selection best accounts for properties x that we find in the universe. Hence, the doctrine of natural selection is true. Notice the metaphysical, or for that

---

159. Lewis, "Gene Complex," 565–70.
160. Wells, *Icons of Evolution*, 186.
161. Mayr, *Population, Species and Evolution*, 251–53.
162. Wells, *Icons of Evolution*, 186–87.
163. Hunter, *Darwin's God*, 10.

matter, theological premise that finally leads to the supposedly scientific conclusion that natural selection is true. The point of this consideration is to show that the foundations of Darwinian methodological naturalism are not strictly scientific. Some are fundamentally metaphysical.

What we find from Gould, then, is a lack of epistemic warrant to rule God out as a First Cause that miraculously interacted with nature. However, Richard Dawkins seems to believe he has just this epistemic warrant for his atheistic stance. He does not think that positing God as a First Cause explains much. If anything, it explains nothing specifically because it leaves the origin of the Designer unexplained. One will just have to say God was always there. Dawkins then wonders why one would not merely say DNA always existed or that life always existed and be done with the task of explaining.[164]

Dawkins makes several mistakes in this argument. First, he holds that we explain "precisely nothing" by invoking a supernatural designer. We must note, however, that any explanation leaves the explanans unexplained. That does not mean that "it explains nothing," but only that it is partial. The second mistake Dawkins makes is that he believes it is lazy talk to simply say God is always there. But this objection can be easily answered. Those who contend that God is always there do not arrive at this conclusion out of laziness. They do so out of serious philosophical reflection. We see this in Thomas Aquinas' five ways, in Descartes' meditations and in Copleston's debate with Bertrand Russell. This is certainly not lazy talk. To deem it so is to commit the *ad hominem* fallacy.

Prior to rejecting belief in the existence of the first cause, Dawkins suggested that single step selection (which he also called the sieve illustration) can help us understand just how the universe arrived at the complex state in which we find it today. Dawkins' sieve illustration fails to provide the theory of evolution with the grounds it needs to take off. As Dawkins himself admits, if natural selection depended on single-step selection, then we would probably not get where we are today in terms of complexity. But Dawkins believes that cumulative selection can account for the complexity we see in nature. To illustrate this, Dawkins uses the illustration of a monkey typing out a given phrase.

Dawkins' monkey illustration makes a mistake somewhat similar to the one made by the analogy between artificial and natural selection. The analogy is a false one for two reasons. First, Dawkins' constant reference to "METHINKS IT IS LIKE A WEASEL" as a target phrase is teleological.

---

164. Dawkins, *Blind Watchmaker*, 141.

Dawkins' use of this target phrase to illustrate what in principle is understood as the blind force of nature, is a disanalogy. The doctrine of natural selection tells us that the blind forces of nature have no purpose, hence no target. It is misleading to use something like the target phrase above to argue for what essentially has no target.

The second reason Dawkins' monkey illustration fails is that the framework for intelligence has already been built into the computer in question. In other words, the computer has been intelligently designed for the purpose of conveying or storing information. Moreover, the monkey also possesses some degree of intelligence, though quite limited compared to human beings. But natural forces are supposed to be blind, unintelligent, and without any predetermined goals. Suppose what the monkey *is* to the computer, natural forces *are* to nature. According to Dawkins, it follows that the computer has been intelligently designed, but nature has not. Clearly we find a disanalogy here. Why should we accept that one has been intelligently designed, and the other, which is more complex, has not? To say that the blind forces of nature have been responsible for the latter is to beg the question, since the notion of the blind forces of nature is what Dawkins is trying to justify.

Notice the change that methodological naturalism undergoes. Before the advent of Darwinian methodological naturalism, belief in God was seen as a rational postulate that could quite consistently be combined with the scientific enterprise. However, when Darwin developed his theory, naturalists who despised the theistic postulates of natural theology found an alternative in Darwinism.

What reasons could be advanced for this change? If the reasons were scientific, they were not decisive; for this research has shown that nothing in science eliminates belief in a First Cause. It seems, however, that the reasons were theological. God had to be understood in a certain way in order for him to be ruled out as a possible cause for the existence of nature. But as we have seen, God did not have to be understood in the rationalistic sense. There was nothing philosophically decimating about understanding God in the way the church fathers understood him. Hence the theological reasons for adopting Darwinism are not, in themselves, warranted. The upshot of this consideration is this: pre-Darwinian, Darwinian and Neo-Darwinian methodological naturalism fail to undercut belief in a Creator of the universe, and belief in a Creator provides strong support for belief in the possibility of miracles. Hence, pre-Darwinian, Darwinian and Neo-Darwinian methodological naturalism fail to undercut belief in miracles.

— 7 —

Conclusion

WE HAVE SEEN, FROM the second chapter, that supernaturalism, the view that supernatural entities can figure in a legitimate explanation of natural phenomena, was seen as an acceptable epistemological enterprise. It was acceptable because it seemed rational to think of the supernatural in this way. In the view of the supernaturalists, some events in nature could only be explained by appealing to supernatural agency. This was not a leap of faith on their part. They accepted this vantage point because it seemed to be the best explanation of how the universe came to be the way it is.

However, I hasten to point out Plantinga's claim that the very thought that there is such a person as God is not, according to supernaturalism, a hypothesis postulated to explain something or other.[1] Christian theism, for example, does not say that the fact that there are phenomena that elude the best efforts of current science is a major reason for believing that there is such a person as God. Rather, as we have already noted in chapter 2, our knowledge of God comes by way of general revelation (which involves something like Aquinas' general knowledge of God) and more importantly, by way of God's special revelation. The former involves perceiving marks of design in nature, and is perhaps less controversial to people inclined to deistic thinking (owing to its apparent non-miraculous nature). The latter is more controversial because it assumes that God has revealed himself miraculously to a select group of people.

I believe the supernaturalists were essentially correct in maintaining this vantage point. They were correct in the sense that their view was not contrary to reason; rather it was consistent with the way natural features seemed to present themselves to their cognitive faculties. They perceived

---

1. Plantinga, "Should Methodological Naturalism," 122.

marks of design, and from that perception, envisioned or inferred the existence of a designer as the best explanation for the origin of the universe. The supernaturalist sees any attempt to understand the nature and origin of the universe without appeal to the supernatural as fundamentally incomplete. Nor is this merely what a methodological naturalist would deem "wishful thinking" on the part of the supernaturalist; it is an admission that some contemporary Darwinian naturalists make.

For example, methodological naturalist Francisco J. Ayala believes that there is an important missing link in the scientific account of natural phenomena—namely, the origin of the universe. According to Ayala, the creation or origin of the universe involves a transition from nothing into being. But a transition can only be scientifically investigated if we have some knowledge about the states or entities on both sides of the boundary. Nothingness, however, is not a subject for scientific investigation or understanding. This leads Ayala to conclude that as far as science is concerned, the origin of the universe will remain forever a mystery.[2]

Ayala seems to be admitting that science, as a way of knowing, is not as comprehensive as we would like it to be. Ayala argues that a scientific view of the world is "hopelessly incomplete." There are matters of value and meaning that are outside science's scope. Even when we have a satisfying scientific understanding of the natural object or process, we are still missing knowledge concerning matters that may well be thought by many to be of equal or greater import. Although scientific knowledge may enrich aesthetic and moral perceptions, and illuminate the significance of life and the world, these remain matters fundamentally outside science's realm.[3]

The supernaturalist will say that only when coupled with the supernaturalistic world-view of nature can our epistemological system pride itself in being comprehensive. For the supernaturalist, supernatural agency can accomplish much more than what nature is capable of doing. Thus, for example, when the incompleteness of science leads us to believe that the origin of the universe will forever remain a mystery, the supernaturalist attributes just this origin to the Creator. And when the naturalist, in the spirit of Ayala, admits that matters of value are outside the scope of science,[4] the supernaturalist believes that value is derived from a Creator who endows his creation with moral and aesthetic qualities.

2. Ayala, "Design," 67–68.
3. Ibid., 72.
4. Ibid.

CONCLUSION

For the supernaturalist God created the universe and continues to sustain it by his power. This is a vantage point the supernaturalist maintains without being vulnerable to the flaws of the God-of-the-gaps theology. A God-of-the-gaps theology holds that the world is a vast machine that is almost entirely self-sufficient, and that divine activity in nature is limited to those phenomena for which there is no naturalistic explanation. Hence the existence of God is a kind of large-scale hypothesis postulated to explain what cannot be explained naturalistically.[5]

The supernaturalism of the sort articulated in the first two chapters maintains, however, that God is constantly, immediately, intimately and directly active in his creation. He constantly upholds it in existence and providentially governs it. Natural laws are not in any way independent of God, and are perhaps best thought of as regularities in the ways in which he treats the stuff that he has made, or perhaps as counterfactuals of divine freedom.[6] This form of supernaturalism was shown, in the third chapter, to be consistent with the scientific world view of the early modern era. Science and religion were not seen to be mutually exclusive. Both were widely accepted as legitimate aspects of explanation. Admittedly, the New Pyrrhonists and the evidentialists did not think that science was unproblematic; but the postulates of their faith remained relatively intact. For scientists like Descartes, God was the foundation of all knowledge. Put differently, Descartes believed that knowledge would be incomplete without God. Wilkins, Boyle and Newton also spoke in a similar vein.

Ayala sparingly alludes to this mode of thinking when he observes that knowledge also derives from other sources such as common sense, artistic and religious experience, and philosophical reflection. Ayala further suggests that the existence of such knowledge acquired by nonscientific modes of inquiry can be established simply by pointing out that science, in the modern sense of empirically tested laws and theories, dawned in the sixteenth century, but that mankind had for centuries built cities and roads, brought forth political institutions and sophisticated codes of law, advanced profound philosophies and value systems, and created magnificent plastic art as well as music and literature.[7] But if Ayala is willing to admit that religious experience is a legitimate source of knowledge we begin to wonder whether he is conceding that the supernatural is, after all, a possible

5. Plantinga, "Should Methodological Naturalism," 121.
6. Ibid.
7. Ibid.

candidate for explaining certain phenomena. He seems to be tripping over a mistake similar to that of the deists already outlined in the fourth chapter. On the one hand, Ayala seems to rule out the supernatural by adopting methodological naturalism; but on the other, he admits the supernatural. David Hume, in the fifth chapter, also made a similar mistake.

Howard Van Till, Diogenes Allen and John Stek, although they are theologians, have made similar mistakes as well. For example, Van Till contends that a scientific hypothesis cannot properly claim that God does something immediately or directly. Van Till's position is not that such a hypothesis would not be scientific, but that it would be false. But Van Till is also a theist. He would agree that if God does anything in the world indirectly, he also does something directly: presumably God cannot cause an effect indirectly without also, at some point, acting directly. Hence there seems to be no warrant for Van Till's supposition that God no longer acts directly in the world.[8]

Diogenes Allen has also implied that Christians cannot propose, as part of science, that God has done something directly. Moreover, he implies that it would be out of order to appeal, in science, to such ideas as that human beings have been created in God's image. Allen's main point is that a scientific account cannot properly be formulated in terms of the relationship of anything to God.[9]

Allen gives no reason for this claim. Allen's position here seems rather arbitrary. If the supernaturalist believes that human beings have been created in the image of God, but have also fallen into sin, this dual truth might turn out to be very useful in giving psychological explanations of various phenomena. If it is, the Christian psychologist has no reason not to employ it, and there is no reason why the result would not be scientific.[10] Plantinga points this out quite correctly. He wonders why the result would not count as science. Perhaps, he argues, the inquiry would suggest that God created life directly, and that it was not caused by other created things. If things turn out in this way, or if this is how things appear at a given time, nothing should keep the scientist from saying so.[11]

In the view of the supernaturalist, God made the world and could have done so in many different ways. There is no reason for the supernaturalist

---

8. Van Till, "Faith and Reason," 42.
9. Allen, *Christian Belief*, 45.
10. Ibid.
11. Ibid.

to fail to employ this knowledge in evaluating the probability of various hypotheses.

Let me now turn to John Stek. Stek insists that we must exclude all notions of immediate divine causality in our understanding of the created realm. His reason for this contention is that appeal to a notion of immediate divine causality would introduce a God-of-the-gaps theology, and to do that would presume to exercise power over God. In Stek's view, God is not an internal component within the created realm.[12] However, it hardly follows that God does not act immediately or indirectly in the created realm. Stek is a theist, and he too would agree that God directly and immediately conserves his creation in existence. And if God creates anything indirectly, then he creates some things directly. We do not seem to have arguments from any other source to suggest that God does not create anything directly or indirectly. Hence, it is not clear why Stek thinks that we must observe his version of methodological naturalism.[13]

At any rate, if Van Till, Allen and Stek are theists on the one hand and methodological naturalists on the other, they make the same mistake that Hume and the deists made; for they rule out the supernatural as a legitimate way of explaining natural phenomena on the one hand, while on the other, they subscribe to belief in the supernatural. In short, Van Till's, Allen's and Stek's belief systems are internally inconsistent.

The sixth chapter has shown that the ideological shift from supernaturalism to methodological naturalism was not scientific; it was theological and ethical. This shift can be traced back to Darwin's difficulty in reconciling the existence of a benevolent Designer with what he thought were the faulty aspects of nature. This can be plausibly viewed as the Darwinian version of the problem of evil. But if it can be viewed in this way then it is not scientific. This is because the notion of evil is itself a value judgment. Hence to find an inconsistency between God's existence and the existence of faults in nature is not a scientific discovery. It is a theological inference drawn from value judgments about the observed phenomena in nature. But if it is based on a theological inference, the ruling out of the supernatural is based on theology rather than science.

Do these considerations mean that we should abandon methodological naturalism altogether? There is a sense in which a moderate version of methodological naturalism might be acceptable. The believer in miracles

---

12. Stek, "What Says," 261.
13. Ibid.

does not wish to endorse gullible superstition. He may agree that miracles are strange and surprising things and he will agree that some degree of initial skepticism is reasonable when faced with miracle claims. Thus the believer in miracles does not deny that there is some presumption in favor of natural explanations. He merely denies that this presumption is so strong that it will always outweigh the evidence in favor of a miracle.

According to Evans, the amount of evidence that would be required will vary depending on the intrinsic plausibility and apparent religious significance of the miracle.[14] Plantinga takes this idea further. According to Plantinga, there are two strong commonsense arguments for methodological naturalism[15]—arguments that, on the one hand, give methodological naturalism its place in epistemology, but on the other, do not necessarily rule out the supernatural as originally defined.

I will slightly modify both arguments for my purposes.[16] First, according to Plantinga, there will be little advancement in science if, in answer to the question, "Why does so and so work the way it does?" or, "What is the explanation of so and so?" we often reply, "Because God did it that way" or, "Because it pleased God that it should be like that." Whereas this could be true, Plantinga thinks that it is not the sort of answer we want at that juncture. What we want to know in science are the answers to questions like, "What is this made out of? What is its structure? How does it work? How is it connected with other parts of nature?"[17] A claim to the effect that God has done this or that directly is a science stopper. If such a claim is true, then presumably we cannot go on to learn something further about how the effect came about or how the phenomenon in question works; if God did it directly, there will be nothing further to find out. For example, how does it happen that there is such a thing as light? If we answer by saying that God said, "Let there be Light," and there was light, the answer is of enormous importance. But if taken as science, it is not helpful. It does not help us to find out more about light, what its physical character is, how it is related to other things, and the light. Thus, ascribing something to the direct action of God tends to cut off further inquiry.[18]

---

14. Evans, *Historical Christ*, 159.
15. Plantinga, "Should Methodological Naturalism," 124.
16. What I state as the first reason is really Plantinga's second reason, and vice versa.
17. Plantinga, "Should Methodological Naturalism," 128.
18. Ibid.

Second, it is important that all people of different ideological and religious backgrounds be able to work at science cooperatively. Therefore we should not employ in science views, commitments, and assumptions that would make the science unacceptable to someone who does not share those commitments or assumptions. This means we cannot employ such ideas as that the world and things therein have been designed and created by God. In Plantinga's view, proper science, if it is to be common to all of us, will have to eschew any dependence upon metaphysical and religious views held by only some of us and to that extent (and for that limited purpose) will presuppose methodological naturalism.[19]

This is what Plantinga calls Duhemian science, after the Catholic scientist Pierre Duhem. Duhemian science is maximally inclusive; we can all do it together. But each of the groups involved—naturalists and theists, for example—could then go on to incorporate Duhemian science into a fuller context that includes the metaphysical or religious principles specific to that group. This then becomes a broader form of science that Plantinga calls Augustinian science.[20] Thus in Plantinga's view, the Christian scientific community should observe the constraints of methodological naturalism in those areas where Duhemian science is possible and valuable. However, the Christian scientific community should also engage in non-Duhemian, Augustinian science where that is relevant; for in Plantinga's view, nothing suggests that, if the enterprise is not Duhemian it fails to count as scientific.[21]

Thus, there are several ways in which the supernaturalism of Christianity, for instance, might enter into the texture of science: First, it must specify and use the hypothesis according to which God does things in a direct fashion. Second, it should specify and employ hypotheses according to which God does things in an indirect fashion. Third, it should appraise theories with respect to background data that includes Christian theism. Fourth, either directly or indirectly as background, it should employ propositions such as humans being created in God's image. Fifth, it should do the same things for other theological doctrines such as original sin—doctrines that do not mention God directly. Finally, it should decide what needs explanation by referring to the same background.[22]

19. Ibid., 126
20. Ibid
21. Ibid., 127.
22. Ibid., 129.

In Plantinga's view, the claim that God has directly created life may be a science stopper; but it does not follow that God did not directly create life. The fact that claims of this sort are science stoppers means that, as a general rule, they will not be helpful; it does not mean that they are never true, and it does not mean that they cannot be part of a proper scientific theory. Moreover, it is a giant and unwarranted step from the recognition that claims of direct divine activity are "science stoppers" to the insistence that science must pretend the created universe is just there, refusing to recognize that it is indeed created.[23]

What are the implications of these findings? First, supernaturalism can reasonably be factored in a legitimate explanation of natural phenomena. Second, methodological naturalism insofar as it attempts to eliminate the supernatural from scientific and historical explanation, is ungrounded. But third, a more modest form of methodological naturalism, of the sort which Plantinga ascribes to "Duhemian science," is legitimate and appropriate.

23. Ibid.

Bibliography

Adams, William. "Extract from an Essay on Mr. Hume's Essay on Miracles." In Tweyman, *Hume on Miracles.*
Allen, Diogenes. *Christian Belief in a Postmodern World.* Louisville: Westminster John Knox, 1989.
Ambrose. *The Six Days of Creation.* In *The Fathers of the Church: A New Translation.* Translated by John J. Savage. Washington, DC: Catholic University of America Press, 2003.
Annet, Peter. *Supernaturals Examined.* London, Forgotten, 2015.
Aquinas, Thomas. *Summa Contra Gentiles.* Vol. 3. Translated by Vernon J. Bourke. New York: Hanover, 1957.
———. *Summa Theologica.* Vols. 1–3. Translated by Fathers of the English Dominican Province. New York: Benziger, 1947–1948.
Aristotle. *De Anima.* In McKeon, *Basic Works of Aristotle.* New York: The Modern Library, 2001.
———. *De Caelo.* In McKeon, *Basic Works of Aristotle.*
———. *De Divinatione Per Somnum.* In McKeon, *Basic Works of Aristotle.*
———. *De Generatione Animalium.* Translated by A. L. Peck. Cambridge: Harvard University Press, 1942.
———. *De Partibus Animalium.* In McKeon, *Basic Works of Aristotle.*
———. *Metaphysics.* In McKeon, *Basic Works of Aristotle.*
———. *Physics.* In McKeon, *Basic Works of Aristotle.*
Athenagoras. *On the Resurrection of the Dead.* In Schaff, *Nicene and Post-Nicene Fathers,* 2:237–58.
Augustine. *City of God.* Translated by Marcus Dodds. New York: Modern Library, 1993.
———. *De Trinitate.* In *The Works of Saint Augustine: A Translation for the 21st Century,* edited by John E. Rotelle. New York: New City, 1997.
———. *The Letters of St. Augustine.* In *The Fathers of the Church: A New Translation,* translated by Sister Wilfrid Parsons. New York: Fathers of the Church, 1953.
———. *On the Profit of Believing.* In Schaff, *Nicene and Post-Nicene Fathers,* vol. 3.
———. *Literal Meaning of Genesis.* Translated by John Hammond Taylor. New York: Newman, 1982.
Ayala, Francisco J. "Design without a Designer." In *Debating Design,* edited by William Dembski and Michael Ruse, 67–72. Cambridge: Cambridge University Press, 2004.

BIBLIOGRAPHY

Bayle, Pierre. "Historical and Critical Dictionary." In Popkin, *Philosophy of the 16th and 17th Centuries*, 340–57.
Blount, Charles. *The Oracles of Reason*. London: Kessinger, 1963.
Bowler, Peter. *Evolution: The History of an Idea*. Berkeley: University of California Press, 1984.
Boyle, Robert. *The Works of Robert Boyle*. Edited by Michael Hunter and Edward B. Davis. 14 vols. London: Pickering & Chatto, 2000.
Brakefield, Paul, and Tony G. Liebert. "Behavioral Studies on the Peppered Moth *Biston betularia* and a Discussion of the Role of Pollution and Lichens in Industrial Melanism." *Biological Journal of the Linnean Society* 31 (1987) 129–50.
Brown, Collin. *Miracles and the Critical Mind*. Grand Rapids. Eerdmans, 1984.
Browne, Peter. *A Letter*. Chapter 2 in Waring, *Deism and Natural Religion*.
Buffon, Georges Louis Leclerc, comte de. "The History and Theory of Earth." In Lyon and Sloan, *From Natural History to the History of Nature*.
———. "Initial Discourse: On the Manner of Studying and Expounding Natural History." In Lyon and Sloan, *From Natural History to the History of Nature*.
Burns, R. M. *The Great Debate on Miracles: From Joseph Glanvill to David Hume*. Lewisburg, PA: Bucknell University Press, 1981.
Burtt, Edwin Arthur. *Metaphysical Foundations of Modern Physical Science: A Historical and Critical Essay*. London: Routledge & Paul, 1950.
Butler, Joseph. *The Analogy of Religions*. London, 1736.
Calvin, John. *Institutes of the Christian Religion*. Edited by John T. McNeill. Philadelphia: Westminster, 1992.
Chambers, Robert. *Vestiges of the Natural History of Creation and Other Evolutionary Writings*. Edited by James A. Secord. Chicago: University of Chicago Press, 1994.
Chandler, Samuel. *A Vindication of the Christian Religion*. London, 1725.
Chapman, John. *Eusebius*. Cambridge, 1739.
Chubb, Thomas. *Discourse on Miracles*. London, 1741.
———. *Posthumous Works*. Vol. 2. London, 1748.
Chrysostom. *The Gospel of St. Matthew*. In *Nicene and Post-Nicene Fathers*, series 1, edited by Philip Schaff, 10:51–68. Grand Rapids: Christian Classics Ethereal Library, 1893.
Cicero. *The Nature of the Gods*. Translated by P. G. Walsh. New York: Oxford University Press, 1998.
Clarke, Cyril, and P. M. Shepard. "Evolution in Reverse: Clean Air and the Peppered Moth." *Biological Journal of Linnean Society* 26 (1985) 189–99.
Coady, C. A. J. *Testimony*. New York: Oxford University Press, 1992.
Cohen, S. Mark, et al. *Readings in Ancient Greek Philosophy from Thales to Aristotle*. 2nd ed. Indianapolis: Hackett, 2000.
Collins, Anthony. "A Discourse on Free-Thinking." In Waring, *Deism and Natural Religion*, 87–104.
Conybeare, John. *Defense of Revealed Religion*. London, 1732.
———. *Discourse on Miracles*. London, 1727–1729.
Copleston, Frederick. *A History of Philosophy*. Vol. 1. New York: Doubleday, 1993.
Coulston, Charles, ed. *Dictionary of Scientific Biography*. New York: Scribner, 1970–1990.
Craig, Edward, ed. *Routledge Encyclopedia of Philosophy*. New York: Routledge, 1998.
Crick, Francis. *What Mad Pursuit*. London: Penguin, 1988.

BIBLIOGRAPHY

Darwin, Charles. *The Autobiography of Charles Darwin 1809–1882, with Original Omissions Restored and Edited with Appendix and Notes by His Grand-daughter Norah Barlow*. New York: Norton, 1958.

———. *Origin of Species*. 3rd ed. Edited by Gillian Beer. New York: Oxford University Press, 1996.

———. *Origin of Species by Means of Natural Selection; or, The Preservation of Favored Races in the Struggle for Life 6th Ed and The Descent of Man and Selection in Relation to Sex*. New York: Random House, 1936.

Dawkins, Richard. *The Blind Watchmaker: Why the Evidence for Evolution Reveals a Universe Without Design*. New York: Norton, 1987.

Deferrari, Roy Joseph. *The Fathers of the Church: A New Translation*. New York: Fathers of the Church, 1954.

De Maillet, Benoit. *Telliamed; or, Discourses between an Indian Philosopher and a French Missionary on the Diminution of the Sea*. Edited by Albert V. Carozzi. Urbana: University of Illinois Press, 1968.

Dennet, Daniel. *Darwin's Dangerous Idea: The Evolution and Meanings of Life*. New York: Simon & Schuster, 1995.

Descartes, Rene. *Meditations*. In Popkin, *Philosophy of the 16th and 17th Centuries*, 121–88.

———. *Philosophical Writings of Descartes*. Translated by John Cottingham et al. New York: Cambridge University Press, 1991.

Donaldson, James, and Alexander Roberts, eds. *The Ante-Nicene Fathers: Translations of the Writings of the Fathers Down to A.D. 325*. Grand Rapids: Eerdmans, 1979.

Dupre, John. "The Miracle of Monism." In *Naturalism in Question*, edited by Mario De Caro and David Macarthur, 42–65. Cambridge: Harvard University Press, 2004.

Earman, John. *Hume's Abject Failure: The Argument Against Miracles*. New York: Oxford University Press, 2000.

Edwards, Paul, ed. *The Encyclopedia of Philosophy*. New York: MacMillan & Free, 1967.

Eusebius. *The Church History of Eusebius*. In Schaff, *Nicene and Post-Nicene Fathers*, 382–494.

Evans, C. Stephen. *The Historical Christ and the Jesus of Faith: The Incarnational Narrative as History*. New York: Cambridge University Press, 1995.

Flew, Anthony. "Scientific versus Historical Evidence." In Swinburne, *Miracles*, 97–102.

Fogelin, Michael. *A Defense of Hume on Miracles*. Princeton: Princeton University Press, 2003.

Furley, David J. "Zeno of Citium." In Coulston, *Dictionary of Scientific Biography*, vol. 14.

Galilei, Galileo. *The Assayer*. In Popkin, *Philosophy of the 16th and 17th Centuries*, 58–64.

———. *Letters on Sunspots*. In Popkin, *Philosophy of the 16th and 17th Centuries*, 65–68.

Gilkey, Langdon. "Cosmology, Ontology and the Travail of Biblical Language." In *God's Activity in the World: The Contemporary Problem*, edited by Thomas C. Owen, 23–41. Chico, CA: Scholars, 1983.

Gould, Stephen. *Hen's Teeth and Horse's Toes*. New York: Norton, 1983.

Grant, Robert. *Miracle and Natural Law in Graeco-Roman and Early Christian Thought*. Amsterdam: North-Holland, 1952.

Hankinson, R. J. "Pyrrhonism." In *Routledge Encyclopedia of Philosophy*, edited by Edward Craig, 7:850. New York: Routledge, 1998.

Harvey, Van. *The Historian and the Believer*. New York: MacMillan, 1966.

Hastings, James, ed. *Encyclopedia of Religion and Ethics*. New York: Scribner, 1922.

BIBLIOGRAPHY

Hilary of Poitiers. *The Trinity*. http://www.newadvent.org/fathers/330202.htm.

Houston, J. *Reported Miracles: A Critique of Hume*. Cambridge: Cambridge University Press, 1998.

Howlett, Rory, and Michael E. N. Majerus. "The Understanding of Industrial Melanism in the Peppered Moth (*Biston betularia*) (Lepidoptera: Geometridae)." *Biological Journal of the Linnean Society* 30 (1987) 31–44.

Hume, David. *Dialogues concerning Natural Religion*. Reprinted in *Classics of Western Philosophy*, edited by Stephen M. Kahn, 677–94. 5th ed. Indianapolis: Hackett, 1999.

———. *Enquiry concerning Human Understanding*. Reprinted in *Classics of Western Philosophy*, edited by Stephen M. Kahn, 633–56. 5th ed. Indianapolis: Hackett, 1999.

———. *David Hume: Principle Writings on Religion including Dialogues concerning Natural Religion and the Natural History of Religion*. Edited by G. C. A Gaskin. New York: Oxford University Press, 1993.

Hunter, Cornelius. *Darwin's God*. Grand Rapids: Brazos, 2001.

Hurley, Patrick. *A Concise Introduction to Logic*. 8th ed. Belmont, CA: Wadsworth, 2003.

Huxley, Thomas H. *Agnosticism and Christianity and Other Essays*. Buffalo: Prometheus, 1992.

———. *Evolution and Ethics: T. H. Huxley's Evolution and Ethics with New Essays on Its Victorian and Sociobiological Context*. Edited by James Paradis and George C. Williams. Princeton: Princeton University Press, 1989.

———. "The Order of Nature: Miracles." In Tweyman, *Hume on Miracles*, 34–40.

Johnson, Phillip E. *Darwin on Trial*. 2nd ed. Downers Grove: InterVarsity, 1993.

Kettlewell, H. B. D. "Further Selection Experiments on Industrial Melanism in the Lepidoptera." *Heredity* 10 (1956) 287–301.

———. "Selection Experiments on Industrial Melanism in the Lepidoptera." *Heredity* 9 (1955) 323–42.

Lactantius. *The Divine Institutes*. In Roberts and Donaldson, *Ante-Nicene Fathers*, vol. 7.

Lamarck, Jean Baptiste. *Zoological Philosophy: An Exposition with Regard to the Natural History of Animals*. Translated by Hugh Elliot. Chicago: University of Chicago Press, 1984.

Larmore, Charles. "Pierre Bayle." In *Routledge Encyclopedia of Philosophy*, edited by Edward Craig, 7:673. New York: Routledge, 1998.

Leland, John. *Defence of Christianity (Against Tindal)*. London, 1733.

Lenoir, Timothy. *The Strategy of Life*. Chicago: University of Chicago Press, 1992.

Lewis, C. S. *Miracles*. New York: Simon & Schuster, 1996.

Lewis, E. B. "A Gene Complex Controlling Segmentation in *Drosophila*." *Nature* 276 (1978) 565–70.

Locke, John. *Essay concerning Human Understanding: Collected and Annotated, with Prolegomena, Biographical, Critical and Historical*. Edited by Alexander Campbell Fraser. New York: Dover, 1959.

———. *The Reasonableness of Christianity: With a Discourse on Miracles and Part of a Third Letter concerning Toleration*. Edited by I. T. Ramsey. Stanford: Stanford University Press, 1958.

Lyell, Charles. *Sir Charles Lyell's Scientific Journals on the Species Question*. Edited by Leonard G. Wilson. New Haven: Yale University Press, 1970.

Lyon, John, and Philip R. Sloan. *From Natural History to the History of Nature: Readings from Buffon and His Critics*. Notre Dame: University of Notre Dame Press, 1981.

BIBLIOGRAPHY

Mackie, J. L. *The Miracle of Theism: Arguments For and Against the Existence of God.* Oxford: Oxford University Press, 1982.

MacLean, Ian. "Pascal, Blaise." In *Routledge Encyclopedia of Philosophy*, edited by Edward Craig, 7:243. New York: Routledge, 1998.

Macquarrie, John. *Principles of Christian Theology.* 2nd ed. New York: Scribner, 1977.

Marthaler, Berard L., ed. *The New Catholic Encyclopedia.* Palatine, IL: Heraty, Catholic University of America, 1988.

Martin, Clancy, and Robert C. Solomon. *Since Socrates: A Concise Sourcebook of Classic Readings.* Belmont, CA: Thomson Wadsworth, 2005.

Martin, Michael. "Critique of Religion Experience." In *Philosophy of Religion: Selected Readings*, edited by Michael Peterson et al. 2nd ed. New York: Oxford University Press, 2001.

Martyr, Justin. *Dialogue with Trypho.* Edited by Arthur Lukyn Williams. New York: McMillan, 1930.

Mayr, Ernst. *Population, Species and Evolution.* Cambridge: Harvard University Press, 1970.

McKenna, Stephen, ed. *The Fathers of the Church: A New Translation.* New York: Fathers of the Church, 1954.

McKeon, Richard. *The Basic Works of Aristotle.* New York: Random House, 1941.

McKinnon, Alastair. "Miracle." In Swinburne, *Miracles*, 49–52.

McMullin, Ernan. "Plantinga's Defense of Special Creation." *Christian Scholar's Review* 21 (1991) 55–79.

Methodius. *The Discourse on the Resurrection.* In Roberts and Donaldson, *Ante-Nicene Fathers*, 6:139–52.

Mikkola, Kauri. "On the Selective Forces Acting in Industrial Melanism of Biston and Oligia Moths (Lepidoptera: Geometridae and Noctuidae)." *Biological Journal of the Linnean Society* 21 (1984) 409–21.

Montaigne, Michel de. *Apology for Raimond Sebond.* In Popkin, *Philosophy of the 16th and 17th Centuries*, 69–81.

Morgan, Thomas. *Letter to Eusebius.* London, 1739.

Morgan, Thomas, et al. *The Genetics of Drosophila.* New York: Garland, 1988.

Newton, Isaac. *Newton's Philosophy of Nature: Selections from His Writings.* Edited by H. S. Thayer. New York: Hafner, 1953.

Novatian. *A Treatise of Novatian concerning the Trinity.* In Roberts and Donaldson, *Ante-Nicene Fathers*, 5:611–52.

Origen. *Origen: Contra Celsum.* Translated by Henry Chadwick. Cambridge: Cambridge University Press, 1953.

Paley, William. *Natural Theology; or, Evidences of the Existence and Attributes of Deity, Collected from the Appearances of Nature.* In *The Works of William Paley*, 25–197. London: Smith, 1830.

Pascal, Blaise. "Pensées." In Popkin, *Philosophy of the 16th and 17th Centuries*, 218–30.

Patterheads, T. G. "Miracles (Theology of)." In *New Catholic Encyclopedia*, edited by Thomas Carson. Farmington Hills, MI: Gale, 2003.

Pease, Arthur Stanley. "Ceali Enarrant." *Harvard Theological Review* 34 (1941) 163–200.

Plantinga, Alvin. "Should Methodological Naturalism Constrain Science?" In *Science: Christian Perspectives for the New Millennium*, edited by Scott B. Luley et al., 107–34. Addison: CLM/RZIM, 2003.

Plato. *Apology.* In Jowett, trans., *Dialogues of Plato.*

BIBLIOGRAPHY

Plato. *The Dialogues of Plato*. Translated by B. Jowett. New York: Random, 1937.

———. *Philebus*. Translated by Dorothea Frede. Indiana: Hackett, 1993.

———. *Timaeus*. Translated by Donald Zeyl. Indiana: Hackett, 2000.

Plutarch. "Pericles." In *Plutarch's Lives III*, edited by T. E. Page. London: Heinemann, 1916.

Popkin, Richard, ed. "Montaigne, Michel Eyquem De." In *Routledge Encyclopedia of Philosophy*, edited by Edward Craig, 6:488. New York: Routledge, 1998.

———. *The Philosophy of the 16th and 17th Centuries*. New York: Free Press, 1966.

———. "The Religious Background of Seventeenth Century Philosophy." *Journal of the History of Philosophy* 25 (1987) 35–50.

———. "Skepticism, Theology and the Scientific Revolution in the Seventeenth Century." In *Problems in the Philosophy of Science*, edited by Imre Lakatos and Alan Musgrave, 1–39. Amsterdam: North-Holland, 1968.

Ratzsch, Del. "Perceiving Design." In *God and Design: The Teleological Argument and Modern Science*, edited by Neil Manson, 125–45. New York: Routledge, 2003.

Ruse, Michael. *Darwinism Defended: A Guide to the Evolution Controversies*. Reading, MA: Addison-Wesley, 1982.

Russell, Bertrand. *A History of Western Philosophy and Its Connection with Political and Social Circumstances from the Earliest Times to the Present Day*. London: Allen & Unwin, 1946.

Rutherford, Thomas. "The Credibility of Miracles Defended against the Author of Philosophical Essays." In Tweyman, *Hume on Miracles*, 22–31.

Schaff, Philip, ed. *A Select Library of the Nicene and Post-Nicene Fathers of the Christian Church*. Grand Rapids: Eerdmans, 1978.

Sherlock, Thomas. *The Trial of the Witnesses of Jesus Christ*. London, 1729.

Simplicius. *Commentary on Aristotle: Physics 1.3–4*. Translated by Pamela Huby and C. C. W. Taylor. New York: Bloomsbury, 2011.

Somerville, James. "Remarks on an Article in the Edinburgh Review, in Which the Doctrine of Hume on Miracles Is Maintained." In Tweyman, *Hume on Miracles*, 118–21.

Stek, John H. "What Says the Scripture?" In *Portraits of Creation: Biblical and Scientific Perspectives on the World's Formation*, edited by Howard J. Van Till et al., 203–65. Grand Rapids: Eerdmans, 1990.

Steno, Nicholas. *The Prodromus of Nicholas Steno's Dissertation concerning a Solid Body Enclosed by Process of Nature within a Solid*. New York: MacMillan, 1916.

Swinburne, Richard, ed. "Historical Evidence." In *Miracles*, 133–51.

———. *Miracles*. London: Collier Macmillan, 1989.

Tertullian. *Tertullian Against Marcion*. Edited by Peter Holmes. Edinburgh: T. & T. Clark, 1868.

Tindal, Matthew. *Christianity as Old as the Creation*. In Waring, *Deism and Natural Religion*, 108–27.

Toland, John. *Christianity Not Mysterious*. In Waring, *Deism and Natural Religion*, 1–22.

Tweyman, Stanley, ed. *Hume on Miracles*. Bristol, UK: Thoemmes, 1996.

Van Till, Howard. "When Faith and Reason Cooperate." *Christian Scholar's Review* 21 (1991) 33–45.

Vince, Samuel. "Extract from 'Remarks on Mr. Hume's Principles and Reasoning,' in His 'Essay on Miracles.'" In Tweyman, *Hume on Miracles*, 99–101.

Warburton, William. *A Critical and Philosophical Enquiry into the Causes of Prodigies and Miracles as Related by Historians*. London, 1727.

Ward, Benedicta. *Miracles and the Medieval Mind*. Philadelphia: University of Pennsylvania Press, 1982.
Waring, E. Graham, ed. *Deism and Natural Religion: A Sourcebook*. New York: Ungar, 1967.
Wells, Jonathan. *Icons of Evolution: Science or Myth? Why Much of What We Teach about Evolution Is Wrong*. Washington, DC: Regnery, 2000.
Weston, W. *An Enquiry into the Rejection of the Christian Miracles by the Heathens*. London, 1746.
Wheeler, Joseph Mazzini. "Introduction to Hume's Essay on Miracles." In Tweyman, *Hume on Miracles*, 156–58.
Wilkins, John. *Of the Principles and Duties of Natural Religion*. London: Johnson Reprint, 1969.
Wojcik, Jan. "This Due Degree of Blindness." In *Everything Connects: In Conference with Richard Popkin; Essays in His Honor*, edited by James E. Force and David S. Katz, 292–362. Leiden: Brill, 1999.
Wolterstorf, Nicholas. *Divine Discourse: Philosophical Reflections on the Claim That God Speaks*. Cambridge: Cambridge University Press, 1995.
Woolston, Thomas. *Six Discourses on the Miracles of Our Savior*. London, 1727–28.
Xenophon. *Memorabilia, Oeconomicus, Symposium, Apology*. Translated by E. C. Marchant and C. J. Tood. Cambridge: Harvard University Press, 1997.
Zeno. *Stoicorum Veterum Fragmenta*. Edited by Hans Von Anim. Toronto: Saur, 1979.

Index

acquired characteristics, inheritance of, 168, 170
actions, free versus necessary, 69
ad hominem argument (against miracles), 103–4, 111–12, 114, 151–52
Adams, William, 120–21
adaptation, Paley versus Darwin on, 178
adequate ideas, 96
admiration, 103
adventitious ideas, 60
agnosticism, 149, 184, 196
Allen, Diogenes, 208, 209
Alston, William, 3–4
Ambrose, 21
analogy, principle of, 7, 10–11
The Analogy of Religion (Butler), 107
Anaxagoras, 15–16, 17, 22
ancient period, view of miracles, 30–39
 See also supernaturalism, in ancient and medieval periods
animals, 53, 167, 169–70, 177
Annet, Peter, 100, 106, 109
anti-supernaturalism. *See* deism and supernaturalism
apes, differences from humans, 170–71
Apollonius Tyanaeus, 112
Apology (Socrates), 30
Apostles, 35, 110
appearances, beliefs versus, 69
Aquinas, Thomas, 21, 203
Aristodemus (*Memorabilia* character), 16–17
Aristotle, 17–18, 25–26, 27, 28, 31–32

artificial selection, 178–79, 199–200
astronomy, God's role in, 161–62
atheism, Hume and, 149
Athenagoras, on miracles, 32–33
Augustine, Saint, 25, 27, 38, 39–44, 112
Augustinian science, 211
Australopithecus Afarensis, 190
authority, for critical historians, 7, 8–9
Autobiography of Charles Darwin (Darwin), 181–82
Ayala, Francisco J., 206–8

Balbus, on miracles, 32
Balme, D. M., 17–18
Bayle, Pierre, 57–59
being. *See* existence
beliefs, 69, 96
 See also skepticism
"beyond reasonable doubt," first use of phrase, 63
Bible
 design perception in, 19–20
 Exodus, 41
 Genesis, 163, 176, 186
 historicity of miracles in, 6
 liberties, on scriptural interpretation, 90
 Psalms, 19–20
 See also New Testament
big bang, repeatability of, 5
Blair, Hugh, 141
The Blind Watchmaker (Dawkins), 190

INDEX

Blount, Charles, 89–92, 99
bodies
    of animals, 169–70
    question of substance of, 78
    resurrection of, 167
    sensory experiences and, 57
    suspension of judgment and, 58
Bonnet, Charles, 167
Bowler, Peter
    on agnosticism, 184
    on biology, evolutionary synthesis in, 187
    on Buffon, 165
    on catastrophists, 172
    on Chambers, 174
    on Cuvier, 170–71
    on Darwin (Charles), 178, 181
    on Darwin (Erasmus), 168
    on Darwinism, acceptance of, 185
    on Descartes, 160–61
    on faults of nature, chain of being theory and, 167
    on geological theories, 162, 164
    on Lamarck, 169
    on Lyell, 173–74
    on natural selection, 178, 185
    on natural theology, 166
    on naturalists' belief in law of creation, 177–78
    on *Telliamed*, 163
    on theistic evolution, 186–87
Boyle, Robert, 65, 66, 71–77, 86, 207
Brakefield, Paul, 201
Bridges, Calvin, 201
Brown, Colin
    on Augustine, 41, 43
    on Blount, 89
    deists, definition of, 88
    on evidentialists, 48
    on Hume, sources of arguments of, 150
    on new Pyrrhonism, 49
    on Pyrrhonistic skepticism, interest in, 50
Browne, Peter, 95–96
Buffon, George Louis Leclerc, Comte de, 165, 194

Burns, R. M.
    on Boyle, 65–66
    on Catholic apologists, 50
    on deism, 89, 99–102
    on English scientists, 64–65
    on evidentialists, 48, 65, 107, 111
    on Hume, sources of arguments of, 100, 101–6, 150
    on Liberal Anglicans, 62–64
    on miracles, deists' attack on, 99
    on new Pyrrhonism, 49
Burtt, Edwin Arthur, 77
Butler, Joseph, 107, 110–11, 112–13, 151

Calvin, John, 49–50
Calvinists, adoption of Darwinism, 186
Cartesian rationalists, 63
catastrophism (in geology), 164, 171–73
Catholic Church. *See* Roman Catholic Church
causation, 6, 7, 42
celestial bodies (heavens), 17, 18–19
Celsus, 34–35
certitude (certainty), 63, 68, 70
chain of being theory, 166–68
Chambers, Robert, 174–77, 194
Chandler, Samuel, 111–12
Chapman, John, 112
Christ. *See* Jesus
Christianity. *See* Bible; church fathers; the gospel; Protestantism; Roman Catholic Church
Christianity as Old as the Creation (Tindal), 96–97
Christianity not Mysterious (Toland), 92
Chrysippus, 19
Chrysostom, John, 37
Chubb, Thomas, 102, 103, 105, 110, 114
church fathers, 21, 34
Cicero, on Zeno, 18
Clarke, Cyril, 201
Cleanthes, 18–19, 32
clear and distinct ideas, 92, 93, 94, 96
clouds, nature of, 51
Coady, C. A. J., 8–9
coercive proof, 64

INDEX

Collins, Anthony, 90–92
Concise Introduction to Logic (Hurley), 114
contemporary theology, supernaturalism in, 6
contexts
    for historical events, 7
    for miracles, 14, 29, 38, 115, 147
continuity, in miracles, 37
"contrary to nature," 24–25, 26, 27, 29, 40, 44–45
Conybeare, John, 110, 111, 113
Copernican Revolution, 66
Copleston, Frederick, 15–16, 203
correlation, 7, 11, 138–39
cosmogony, mechanical, 162
creation (the created world)
    discontinuities in, 172
    as evidence of God's existence, 18–19, 21–22
    explanations of, 193–94
    God as cause of, 71
    as miracle, 40, 46, 112, 149
    origin of, 2–3, 206
    See also nature
creation, doctrine of, 180
creationism, Darwin's views on, 181
Creator. *See* First Cause; God; Mind
credibility, of matters of faith and religion, 69–70
The Credibility of Miracles Defended against the Author of Philosophical Essays (Rutherford), 117–20
credibility-of-witness argument (against miracles), 101–2, 110, 113, 121, 126, 151
credulity-of-witness argument (against miracles), 102–3, 110, 113, 151
Crick, Francis, 23
A Critical and Philosophical Enquiry into the Causes of Prodigies and Miracles as Related by Historians (Warburton), 102–3
critical historical investigation, principles of, 7–10
criticism, principle of, 7
cumulative selection, 190–92, 203

custom, evidence from, 68–69
Cuvier, George, 170–71, 194

Darwin, Charles, methodological naturalism of
    description of, 178–85
    establishment of, as ruling view in biology, 185–88
    evaluation of, 195–97, 204
    See also Neo-Darwinism
Darwin, Charles, methodological naturalism of forerunners of, 160–78
    Buffon, 165
    catastrophist geologists, 171–73
    Chambers, 174–77
    Cuvier, 170–71
    Darwin (Erasmus), 168–69
    de Maillet, 162–64
    Descartes, 160–62
    Harvey, 166–67
    Lamarck, 169–70
    Laplace, 162
    Lyell, 173–74
    Paley, 166
    Steno, 164–65
Darwin, Erasmus, 168–69, 194
Darwin on Trial (Johnson), 199–200
Dawkins, Richard, 188, 190–93, 203–4
De Caelo (Aristotle), 17
De Divinatione (Aristotle), 18
De Genesi ad Litteram (Augustine), 42
de Maillet, Benoit, 162–64, 194
De Philosophia (Aristotle), 18
De Trinitate (Augustine), 39
dead, raising of
    Augustine on, 42
    by God, 9, 29, 32
    by humans, 121
    Hume on, 150
    as impossibility, 75
    by Jesus, 104, 108
    by magic, 36
    as miracle, 116, 125
    testimony on, 109
death, as awakening, 56

INDEX

definitional methodological naturalism, 1–5
deism and reason, 89–99
    Blount on, 89–92
    Browne on, 95–96
    Collins on, 90–92
    conclusions on, 99
    Tindal on, 96–98
    Toland on, 92–95
deism and supernaturalism, 88–115
    miracles, deist-evidentialist debate on, 112–15
    miracles, evidentialists' defense of, 106–12
    miracles and, 99–106
    overview, 88–89
    reason and, 89–99
demarcation problem, 4
Dennett, Daniel, 184
Descartes, Rene
    on belief in God, 59–62
    Copernican Revolution, embrace of, 66
    epistemological methods of, 84
    God, considerations about, 203, 207
    methodological naturalism of, 160–62
    supernatural, commitment to, 48
    Toland and, 93
descent with modification, 199
design
    design recognition, nature of, 22
    marks of, in nature, 28
    See also intelligent design and designer
design perception, as support for supernaturalism, 15–24
    Anaxagoras and, 15–16, 17, 22
    Aquinas and, 21
    Aristotle and, 17–18
    in book of Psalms, 19–20
    Chrysippus and, 19
    conclusions on, 23–24
    designer, belief in existence of, 21–22
    early church fathers and, 21
    Plato and, 16, 17
    Ratzsch and, 22–23

    of St. Paul, 20
    Stoics and, 18–19
    Xenophon and, 16–17
Dialogue with Trypho (Justin Martyr), 33
Dialogues concerning Natural Religion (Hume), 148–49, 159–60
Dictionary of the English Language (Johnson), 88
diluvialism, 172
Diogenes Laertius, 27
direct test, for evaluating testimony, 143–45, 155
A Discourse of Free-Thinking (Collins), 90
Discourse on Miracles (Chubb), 102
Discourse on the Resurrection (Methodius), 32
divination, Stoics' belief in, 32
divine intervention, 3, 4
    See also design perception, as support for supernaturalism
divine revelation, 74, 182
doubt, 60, 61, 84
dreams, Aristotle on, 18, 25
dualism, 15–16, 57
Duhemian science, 211, 212
Dupre, John, 5

early church fathers, design perception of, 21
early modern era. See supernaturalism and epistemology, in early modern era
early Roman Empire, on nature, 27
Earman, John, 141–43, 154–55
earth
    age of, 163–64
    theories of origins of, 161–62
eggs, in germ theory, 166–67
Egypt (ancient), Pharaoh's magicians, 41, 83
eight days of darkness (miracle), 145, 156
Elijah (prophet), 29
Elizabeth, Queen, 142
empiricism. See evidentialism
English scientists (evidentialists, empiricists), 64–66

INDEX

Enlightenment, understanding of causation, 6
Enquiry concerning Human Understanding (Hume), 141, 148
An Enquiry into the Rejection of the Christian Miracles by the Heathens (Weston), 111
enthusiasm, effects on testimony, 110–11
environment, influence on animal bodies, 169–70
    See also natural selection
epistemology. See supernaturalism and epistemology, in early modern era
Essay concerning Human Understanding (Locke), 80–82, 94–95
essences, 51–52, 53, 94
eternity, Blount on, 90
ethics, world knowledge and, 20
Eusebius (Chapman), 112
Evans, C. Stephen, 8–9, 210
evidence
    from custom, 68–69
    of miracles, types of, 154
    of past events, 135–39
    of the probable and possible, 108
    publicly assessable, 8, 9
    reason and, 92
    See also testimony
evidentialism and evidentialists, 62–87
    Boyle and, 71–77
    English scientists, 64–66
    epistemological methods of, 85
    flexibility of arguments of, 151
    implications for supernaturalism, 84–87
    Liberal Anglicans and, 62–64
    Locke and, 80–84
    miracles, deist-evidentialist debate on, 112–15
    miracles, evidentialists' defense of, 106–12
    Newton and, 78–80
    overview of, 48
    science, views on, 207
    Wilkins and, 66–71
evil, 24, 194, 209

evolution
    Chambers on, 175–77
    Cuvier on, 170–71
    Darwin versus Chambers on, 174
    evolutionary ethics, 186
    evolutionism, founders of modern, 168
    Gould's confidence in, 189
    Neo-Darwinists on, 198–99
    theistic, 186–87
    See also natural selection; Neo-Darwinism
Evolution: The History of an Idea (Bowler), 160
evolution of methodological naturalism, 159–204
    Darwinian methodological naturalism, 178–85
    Darwinian methodological naturalism, as ruling view in biology, 185–88
    Darwin's forerunners, methodological naturalism of, 160–78
    methodological naturalism, pitfalls of, 193–204
    Neo-Darwinists, methodological naturalism of, 188–93
    overview, 159–60
existence, 58–59, 60, 62, 118
    See also God, existence of
Exodus (Bible), 41
expectations, of extraordinary facts, 121–22
experience, 117–18, 122–23, 127
    See also uniform experiences
extinction, problem of, 167
Extract from an Essay on Mr. Hume's Essay on Miracles (Adams), 120–21
Extract from "Remarks on Mr. Hume's Principles and Reasoning, in His 'Essay on Miracles'" (Vince), 121–22

factitious ideas, 60

INDEX

faith
    bodily existence and, 58–59
    certitude as basis for, 63
    knowledge of God and, 59
    miracles and, 45
    reason and, 73–77, 80
    revelation and, 82
    rule of faith, debate over nature of, 49
faults (mistakes) in nature, 166, 167, 182–83
fideism, 54, 59, 63, 65
fifth way (of proving God's existence, Aquinas), 21
finitude, 74–75
first cause
    nature as, 26
    world order and, 44
First Cause
    Chambers on, 175
    Darwin on, 183–84
    Dawkins on, 203
    God as, 87, 159, 164
    Lamarck's belief in, 169
    Neo-Darwinists on, 199
    pre-Darwinists on, 194
    See also God
first principles, 55–56, 61–62
fish, progression of, 176
Flew, Anthony, 130–32, 154
Fogelin, Michael, 143–46, 154–57
fossils, transitions in, 189–90
free actions, 69
freethinking, 90–91
fruit flies, 201–2
Furley, David J., 32
future events, foreknowledge of, 18

Galapagos Islands, Darwin and, 181
Galilei, Galileo, 51–52, 54, 66, 74
Gassendi, 51, 66
Genesis (Bible), 163, 176, 186
genetics, Darwinism and, 184–85
Geological Society (London), 171–72
geology
    Cartesianism in, 162–63
    catastrophism, 164, 171–73
geologists, steady state world view, 173
geometry, divisibility of lines, 72
germ theory (of animal origins), 166–67
Gildon, Charles, 106
Gilkey, Langdon, 6
God
    as causal power, 11, 149
    as creator, 19, 207
    Darwin on, 180–81, 195–97
    Descartes on, 61, 161
    direct acts versus will of, 175–76
    essence of, 94
    faith and knowledge of, 59
    Gould's assumptions on, 202
    human understanding of nature of, 96
    as ideal engineer, 194, 195
    laws of, 20
    laws of nature and, 100
    miracles, control of, 41
    nature and, 24, 30, 90
    power of, 28–29, 36–37
    as source of miracles, 36, 44, 46–47
    as source of prophecy, 30–31
    as source of reason, 97
    as warrant for historical testimony, 10
    See also supernaturalism
God, existence of
    creation as evidence of, 18–19, 21–22
    Darwin on, 183, 196
    evil as evidence against, 24
    Gould on, 188–89
    Hume's belief in, 148–49, 153
    Lamarck's belief in, 169
    miracles and, 152–53
    planetary systems and, 78–80
    reason and, 93
    theology and, 74
    Tindal on, 97–98
    Wilkins on, 71
    See also deism and reason; fideism; intelligent design and designer; miracles; theism
God-of-the-gaps theology, 207, 209
goodness (virtue), Huxley on, 198
the gospel

INDEX

Browne on, 95
divine revelation of, 83
figurative rules in, 98
law of nature and, 97
mystery of, 59
problem of traditional Christian approaches to, 7
Toland on, 92, 93
Gould, Stephen J., 188–90, 199–203
Grant, Robert, 25, 26, 27, 33, 41–42, 43
growing things, definition of nature and, 25

Hankinson, R. J., 50–51
Hartley, David, 168
Harvey, Van, 6–8
Harvey, William, 166–67
heart
knowledge of truth "by the heart," 55
as site of intuition and faith, 56–57
heavens (celestial bodies), 17, 18–19
Hen's Teeth and Horses' Toes (Gould), 189
Henslow, John, 178
Hilary of Poitiers, 36–37
Hippocratic writers, on nature, 27
"Historical Evidence" (Swinburne), 135–39
history
historians, appropriate methodology for, 7–10
historical knowledge, 57
science versus, 131–32
Hooke, Robert, 66
Houston, J., 41–44, 45–46, 139–41
Howlett, Rory, 201
humans
human mind, value of, 197–98
human nature, 56–57, 80, 97, 148
immorality of, 97
Lyell on, 174
natural history of, 170–71
Hume, David, 13, 66, 99–100, 115, 208
Hume, David, arguments against miracles, 116–58
contemporary responses to, 127–46

eighteenth- and nineteenth-century responses to, 117–27
evaluation of, 147–52
evaluation of defenders of, 152–58
overview, 116–17
sources of, 101–6
Hume, David, contemporary responses to, 127–46
Earman, 141–43
Flew, 130–32
Fogelin, 143–46
Houston, 139–41
Lewis, 127–28
Mackie, 132–35
McKinnon, 128–30
Swinburne, 135–39
Hume, David, eighteenth- and nineteenth-century responses to, 117–27
Adams, 120–21
Huxley, 124–26
Rutherford, 117–20
Somerville, 122–24
Vince, 121–22
Wheeler, 126–27
Hume's Abject Failure (Earman), 141
Hunter, Cornelius, 202
Hurley, Patrick, 114
Huxley, Thomas, 124–26, 152, 157, 184, 186, 197–98

ice, 108, 126, 143
ice ages, 172
ideas
adequate ideas, 96
categories of, 60
clear and distinct ideas, 92, 93, 94, 96
proper (immediate) ideas, 96
immediate divine causality, 208, 209
immediate (proper) ideas, 96
imperfection in nature, evolution and, 189
improbability and the improbable, 108–9, 121–22, 133, 134–35, 140–41
incomprehensible things, 72
Indian Prince (disbeliever in ice), 143

227

INDEX

indubitable certainty, 68
induction, straight rule of, 141–42, 145–46, 155
inexplicability, 3, 72
infallible certainty, 68
inference, 22–23, 190
infinitude, 73, 74–75
inheritance of acquired characteristics, 168, 170
"Initial Discourse: On the Manner of Studying and Expounding Natural History" (Buffon), 165
innate ideas, 60
intelligent design and designer
   acceptability of belief in, 24, 28
   in ancient and medieval periods, 14
   Dawkins's rejection of, 190
   Hume's belief in, 148–49
   mistakes in nature and, 166, 167
   nature as source of testimony for, 15, 28
   Newton on, 78–80
Introduction to Hume's Essay on Miracles (Wheeler), 126–27

jawbones, of reptiles versus mammals, 189–90
Jesus
   credibility of witnesses to resurrection of, 151
   as messenger of God, 83
   miracles of, 33–36, 40, 101–2, 104
John, Saint, 113
John Chrysostom, 37
Johnson, Phillip E., 199–200
Johnson, Samuel, 88
judgment
   balanced, of historians, 8
   suspension of, 58
Julius Caesar, 118
Justin Martyr, 33

Kant, Immanuel, 7, 161–62
Kettlewell, Bernard, 200
knowledge
   "by the heart," 55
   ethics and world knowledge, 20
   of first principles, skepticism of, 62
   of future events, 18
   of God, 59, 205
   historical knowledge, 57
   Montaigne on, 52
   principles of morality of, 7–10
   scientific, as evidence of past events, 136, 139
   See also fideism; reason

Lactantius, 36
laity, scriptural interpretation by, 91–92
Lamarck, Jean Baptiste, and Lamarckism, 168, 185, 187, 188, 194
Laplace, Pierre-Simon, 13, 162, 194
Larmore, Charles, 57, 58, 59
late antiquity, study of nature in, 27
law of nature
   Chambers on, 175
   evidence contradicting, 109
   Flew's critique of Hume on, 130
   Fogelin on, 155–56
   God as author of, 100
   miracles and, 116, 129, 132–34
   nomological aspect of, 131–32
   Tindal on, 97, 98
laws
   of creation, 172, 177–78
   of God, 20
   of motion, 75
   scientific laws, 4
   universal, nature of, 138
Le Maistre de Saci, Isaac, 55
leg, recovery of (miracle), 105–6, 142
Leibniz, Gottfried Wilhelm, 194
Leland, John, 112
Lenoir, Timothy, 23
A Letter (Browne), 95
Lewis, C. S., 22, 127–28, 157–58
Lewis, Ed, 201–2
Liberal Anglicans, evidentialism and, 62–66
liberties, on scriptural interpretation, 90
Liebert, Tony, 201
life on earth, theories of origins of, 188

INDEX

lines, divisibility of, 72
living objects, creator of, 17
Locke, John, 65, 66, 80–84, 90, 92, 94–95
Lucilius, 24
Luke, Saint, 113
Lyell, Charles, 173–74, 194

Mackie, J. L., 132–35, 154
MacLean, Ian, 54, 56
Macquarrie, John, 1–3, 6, 11
magic, 34–36, 39–41, 49
Majerus, Michael, 201
Malthus, Thomas, 179
mammals, geological history of, 177
Martin, Michael, 85
materialism, 167–68, 169
mathematics, uncertainty in, 63
Mayr, Ernst, 202
McKinnon, Alastair, 128–30, 153
McMullin, Ernan, 1, 2
mechanical philosophy, 167
mechanistic explanation (of the universe), 193–94
medical research, base assumption of, 3
medieval period
    miracles, view of, 39–46
    theologians, on nature, 27
    See also supernaturalism, in ancient and medieval periods
Meditations (Descartes), 59–60, 61
Memorabilia (Xenophon), 16
memory, as evidence of past events, 135, 139
Mendel, Gregor, and Mendelism, 185, 187, 188
The Metaphysical Foundations of Modern Science (Burtt), 77
Metaphysics (Aristotle), 17, 18, 25
Methodius, 32–33
methodological naturalism
    conclusions on, 205–12
    Darwinian, as ruling view in biology, 185–88
    deism and supernaturalism, 88–115
    evolution of, 159–204

miracles, Hume's arguments against, 116–58
    overview, 1–13
    supernaturalism, in ancient and medieval periods, 14–47
    supernaturalism and epistemology, in early modern era, 48–87
    See also definitional methodological naturalism; substantive methodological naturalism; *detailed entries for each chapter*
Mikkola, Kauri, 200–201
Mind (intelligent creator), 15–16, 19, 22
mind-matter dualism, 15–16
"Miracle and Paradox" (McKinnon), 128–30
The Miracle of Theism (Mackie), 132–35
miracles
    analogy principle and, 10–11
    ancient view of, 30–39
    belief in, in early modern period, 87
    Boyle on, 74
    Calvin's belief in, 50
    Catholic Church on, 49
    Darwin on, 182
    Dawkins on, 192
    definitions of, 29, 147
    deism and, 99–106
    deist-evidentialist debate on, 112–15
    deistic arguments against, types of, 116
    end of, 38
    evidentialists' defense of, 106–12
    God as creator of the universe and, 149
    God's power and, 28–29
    historical explanations for, 10
    intelligent designer and, 14
    Locke on, 82
    Macquarrie on science and, 6
    medieval view of, 39–46
    mystical miracles, 101–2
    natural versus religious, 145
    nature and, 24–30, 46, 124–25, 147, 149
    purposes of, 147–48
    religious beliefs in, 1

229

INDEX

miracles *(continued)*
    testimony on, 104, 116–24, 143–45, 151, 155–57
    Toland on, 93
    See also *ad hominem* argument; credibility-of-witness argument; credulity-of-witness argument; dead, raising of; Hume, David, arguments against miracles; law of nature; testimony; uniformity-of-nature argument; witnesses
miracles (specific)
    eight days of darkness, 145, 156
    leg, recovery of, 105–6, 142
    Red Sea, parting of, 28, 45, 123
    walking on water, 36, 136, 139–40
    water into wine, 29, 37, 104
Miracles (Lewis), 127–28
Miracles (Swinburne), 129
mistakes (faults) in nature, 166, 167, 182–83
modern evolutionism, founders of, 168
modes (contexts), 50–51
Mohammed (prophet), 83
monstrosities, in nature, 25–26
Montaigne, Michel de, 52–55, 61–62
morality
    moral issues, proofs of, 67
    moral (practical) certainty, 63
    moral tests, for miracles, 36, 38
Morgan, Thomas, 99, 104–5, 110
Moses (biblical), 49–50, 83
motions, natural, causes of alteration of, 164
mountains, strata in, 164
mysteries, Toland on, 93–94

Natural History of Religion (Hume), 148
natural law. *See* law of nature
natural miracles, 145
natural motions, causes of alteration of, 164
natural selection, 173, 178–79, 185, 195–98, 199–203
    See also Darwin, Charles, methodological naturalism of; evolution
natural theology, 74, 166, 178–85
Natural Theology (Paley), 166, 178
Nature (as creator), 17–18
nature (*phusis*)
    Aristotle on, 18
    Augustine on, 43
    common understanding of, 28
    design in, 23
    God, relationship to, 24, 90
    history of concept of, 25–27
    imperfection in, evolution and, 189
    intervention in, 133
    lack of uniform definition of, 27–28
    miracles and, 24–30, 39
    possibility of study of, 169
    regularity of, 128
    religion of, 98
    as source of testimony for intelligent designer, 15
    uniform regularity in, 155–56
    usual course of, question of objectivity of, 109
    See also "contrary to nature"; creation
nebular hypothesis, 161–62
necessary actions, 69
Neo-Darwinism, 13, 188–93, 198–204
Neptunist theory (geology), 162
New Pyrrhonists, 49–59
    Bayle, 57–59
    Calvin, 49–50
    Galileo, 51–52
    Liberal Anglicans versus, 63
    Montaigne, 52–55
    overview, 48, 49
    Pascal, 54–57
    Pyrrhonistic skepticism, 50–51
    science, views on, 207
New Science, 66
New Testament
    clarity of doctrines of, 93
    credulity of miracle stories in, 151
    deists' criticisms of, 101
    See also Apostles; the gospel
Newton, Isaac, 65, 66, 78–80, 207

INDEX

Newtonian science, triumph of, 161–62
nominal essences, 94
nomological universal propositions, 130–31
Novatian, 21

objects. *See* things
Of the Principles and Duties of Natural Religion (Wilkins), 66
Oparin, Alexander, 188
The Oracles of Reason (Blount), 89
order, 16, 26
The Order of Nature: Miracles (Huxley), 124–26
Origen (early theologian), 34–36, 115, 152
The Origin of Species (Darwin), 178–79, 183, 186, 195

paganism, 83
paleontology, 170
Paley, William, 166, 178, 181, 182
parasites, natural theology and question of, 166
Paris, Abbé, 144–45, 157
parting of the Red Sea (miracle), 28, 45, 123
Pascal, Blaise, 54–57, 66, 86, 150, 154
Pascal, Jacqueline, 54
Patterheads, T. G., 28–29
Paul, Saint, 20
Pease, Arthur Stanley, 15, 17, 18
peppered moth (*Biston betularia*) experiments, 200–201
perception, inference versus, 22–23
perfection, as object of natural selection, 195–96
Pericles (Plutarch), 15
Peter, Saint, 113
Philo, 42
philosophy
    difficulties of, 16
    science, relationship with, 195
phusis (φύσις). *See* nature
physical traces, as evidence of past events, 136, 139

Physics (Aristotle), 18, 25
pigeons, Darwin's study of, 179
pitfalls of methodological naturalism, evaluation of, 193–204
    Darwin and Huxley, 195–98
    Neo-Darwinian methodological naturalism, 198–204
    pre-Darwinian methodological naturalism, 193–94
planetary systems, 78–80, 162
Plantinga, Alvin, 2–5, 22, 205, 208, 210–12
Plato, 16, 17, 27
Plutarch, 15
Popkin, Richard, 54, 66, 86
population genetics, 187–88
Port-Royal-des-Champs, Pascal at, 55
power
    of God, 28–29, 36–37
    of miracles, 83
    in perceptions of design, 28
practical (moral) certainty, 63
pre-Darwinian methodological naturalism, evaluation of, 193–94, 204
prebionts, 188
priests, freethinking and conduct of, 91
primordial soup, 188
principles
    of analogy, 7, 10–11
    of correlation, 7, 11
    of criticism, 7
    first principles, 55–56, 61–62
    Wilkins's foundational, 66–67
Principles of Philosophy (Descartes), 161
privileged things, 72–77, 95
probability, 70, 128, 146
prodigies, unnatural, 32
Prodromus (Steno), 164
progression (in natural philosophy), 174, 176–77
proofs, 67, 141–42, 146
proper (immediate) ideas, 96
prophecy, 26, 31–33, 46–47, 134
propositions
    evidence for, 197
    nature of, 80–82

INDEX

Protestantism, 49, 91–92
protons, decay of, 142
Prudence (Providence), 18
Psalms (Bible), design perception in, 19–20
publicly assessable evidence, 8, 9
Pyrrhonistic skepticism, 50–51

Quadratus, 33
qualities, as marks of design, 22–23

rationalist explanation (of the universe), 193–94, 195
rationality. *See* reason
Ratzsch, Del, 22–23, 24, 149
real essences, 94
reason (rationality)
    belief in God and, 59–60
    Boyle on, 73
    Cartesian rationalists, attitude toward Liberal Anglicans, 63
    faith and, 73–77, 80
    foundation of religion in, 148
    God as source of, 97
    of historical assessments, 8, 9
    knowledge of truth "by the heart" and, 55
    Montaigne on, 54
    rationalism, English scientists versus, 65
    in religion, 92
    revelation and, 81–84
    Rutherford on, 119
    self-destructiveness of, 58–59
    of substantive methodological naturalism, 5
    See also deism and reason; Descartes, Rene; evidentialism
Reichenbach, Hans, 141
religion
    beliefs as foundation of, 96
    Blount on, 90
    Hume on, 148
    miracles as support for, 104–5
    miracles of rival, 104, 111, 114–15, 152
    Montaigne on religious beliefs, 54
    of nature, 98
    religious miracles, 145
    See also Bible; church fathers; deism and reason; fideism; the gospel; Protestantism; Roman Catholic Church; supernaturalism; theism
Remarks on an Article in the Edinburgh Review, in which the Doctrine of Hume on Miracles Is Maintained (Somerville), 122–24
reptiles, geological history of, 177
resurrection, 108, 167
    See also dead, raising of
Retz, Cardinal de, 105–6, 142, 146, 157
revelation, 74, 81–82, 89, 93, 182, 205
reverse test, for evaluating testimony, 144–45, 155
rock formation, de Maillet on, 163
Roman Catholic Church
    Calvin versus, 49–50
    miracles reported by, 105
    on scriptural interpretation, 91
Roman Empire, on nature, 27
rotation (activity of Mind), 15
rule of faith, debate over nature of, 49
rules, question of universal applicability of, 74–75
    See also laws
Ruse, Michael, 1, 2–5, 11
Russell, Bertrand, 15–16, 203
Rutherford, Thomas, 117–20

Saul, King, 36
science
    Alston on, 3–4
    characteristics of, 5
    creationism versus, 2–3
    demarcation problem of, 4
    Descartes on, 61–62
    English scientists, 64–66
    existence of God and, 210–11
    history versus, 131–32
    incompleteness of, 206
    non-naturalism, exclusion of, 1
    philosophy, relationship with, 195

INDEX

science stoppers, 210, 212
scientific knowledge, as evidence of past events, 136, 139
scientific laws, as approximations, 4
scientific method, evidentialists on, 65
scientific nature, master conception of, 5
  See also Boyle, Robert; definitional methodological naturalism; Locke, John; Newton, Isaac; Wilkins, John
Scientific Creationism, 2
"Scientific versus Historical Evidence" (Flew), 130–32
Scripture, Protestants' belief in primacy of, 49
  See also Bible
Sedgwick, Adam, 178
seeds, 25, 40–43
selection, single-step versus cumulative, 190–92
  See also natural selection
self-evidence, as mark of truth, 57–58
senses, 52–53, 57, 127
Sextus Empiricus, 50
Sherlock, Thomas, 107, 108–9, 112–13, 151
Siam, King of, 126
Simon Magus, 112
single-step selection (sieve illustration), 190–92, 203
Six Discourses on the Miracles of our Savior (Woolston), 101–2
skepticism
  Bayle's, 57
  doubts of, 68–69
  English scientists versus, 65
  epistemological methods of, 84
  on knowledge of first principles, 62
  roots of, 50–51
sleep, wakefulness in, 56
social status, prophecy and, 31–32
Socrates, 16–17, 30–31
Somerville, James, 122–24, 154
sorcerers, 35–36
souls, of animals, 167

space, nature of, 58
special creation, 195
Spencer, Hebert, 186
Spinoza, Baruch, 90
spontaneity, in nature, 26
statistical correlation, 138–39
Stek, John, 208, 209
Steno, Nicholas, 164–65, 194
Stoics, 18–19, 24, 26–27, 32
straight rule of induction, 141–42, 145–46, 155
substantive methodological naturalism, 5–11
succession of causes, nature as, 27
suffering, Darwin on, 182
supernaturalism
  acceptability of, 205–6, 208–9
  in Locke's philosophy, 80–84
  methodological naturalism and, 1–2
  in Montaigne's philosophy, 54
  in Newton's philosophy, 78–80
  as not problematic, 12
  political correctness and, 85–86
  power of, 28
  Troeltsch's and Harvey's critique of, 6–7
  See also deism and supernaturalism
supernaturalism, in ancient and medieval periods, 14–47
  conclusions on, 46–47
  design perception, as support for supernaturalism, 15–24
  miracles, ancient view of, 30–39
  miracles, medieval view of, 39–46
  miracles, nature and, 24–30
  overview, 14
supernaturalism and epistemology, in early modern era, 48–87
  conclusions on, 84–87
  Descartes, 59–62
  evidentialism, 62–84
  New Pyrrhonists, 49–59
  overview, 48
  See also evidentialism
Supernaturals Examined (Annet), 100
Swinburne, Richard, 129, 135–39, 154
sympathy, unnatural prodigies and, 32

INDEX

System of the World (Laplace), 162

teleology
    ancient and medieval embrace of, 24
    resistance to, in biology, 23
    teleological explanation (of the universe), 193–94, 196
Telliamed (de Maillet), 162–63
terror, source of, 18
Tertullian, 34
testimony
    enthusiasm's effect on, 110–11
    as evidence of past events, 135–36, 139
    on miracles, 104, 116–24, 143–45, 151, 155–57
    nature of, 8–9
    See also evidence
theism, 86, 165, 184, 205
theology
    contemporary, supernaturalism in, 6
    natural theology, 74, 166, 178–85
    theologians, theory of evolution and, 186–87
things
    above reason, 71–77, 85, 95
    changing nature of, miracles and, 42–43
    coming into being of, 25
    corporeal, origins of, 60
    knowledge of properties of, 52
    nominal versus real essences of, 94
    Plato's classes of, 16
thinking, doubt as evidence of, 60, 84
Thomas Aquinas, Saint, 21, 44–46
Timaeus (Plato), 16, 17
Tindal, Matthew, 96–98, 99
Toland, John, 92–95, 99, 103, 114
traces, as evidence of past events, 136, 139
Tractatus Theologico Politicus (Spinoza), 90
Treatise concerning the Trinity (Novatian), 21
Trial of the Witnesses of Jesus (Sherlock), 108

The Trinity (Hilary of Poitiers), 36–37
Troeltsch, Ernst, 6–7
truth
    experience and discovery of, 117–18
    of extraordinary facts, improbability and, 121–22, 140–41
    Pascal on, 55
    revelation and, 82
    self-evidence as mark of, 57–58

uniform experiences
    miracles and, 100, 116, 124, 128, 141, 150
    as not proof against miracles, 142–43
uniformity, assumption of, 7
uniformity-of-nature argument (against miracles), 100, 107, 112–13, 120, 122–24, 150
universality
    universal correlation, 138–39
    universal laws, nature of, 138
    universal progress, 167, 186
universe, origin of. *See* creation
unnatural prodigies, 32
unsociable things, 72

Van Till, Howard, 208, 209
variation under domestication, 179
Vestiges of the Natural History of Creation (Chambers), 174
Vince, Samuel, 121–22, 157–58
A Vindication of the Christian Religion (Chandler), 111–12
virtue (goodness), Huxley on, 198
Vulcanism, 162

walking on water (miracle), 36, 136, 139–40
Wallace, Alfred Russell, 186
Warburton, William, 102–3, 110, 113, 151
Ward, Benedicta, 41, 43
Waring, E. Graham, 90
warrants, for historical testimony, 8–10
water into wine (miracle), 29, 37, 104

INDEX

Wells, Jonathan, 199, 200
Weston, W., 111
Wheeler, Joseph Mazzini, 126–27, 152–53, 157
Wilkins, John, 65, 66–71, 86, 207
Wisdom (intelligent creator), 16
witnesses, 7–8, 101, 135, 140
Wollaston, William, 109
wonder(s), 39–40, 44, 169

Woolston, Thomas, 101–2, 104, 113
world knowledge, ethics and, 20

Xenophon, 16–17

Zeno, 18, 26–27

www.ingramcontent.com/pod-product-compliance
Lightning Source LLC
Chambersburg PA
CBHW051637230426
43669CB00013B/2336